Study Guide to Accompany Bob Garrett's

BRAIN & Behavior

An Introduction to Biological Psychology

3
EDITION

Prepared by Beth Powell

Smith College

Los Angeles | London | New Delhi
Singapore | Washington DC

For information:

SAGE Publications, Inc.
2455 Teller Road
Thousand Oaks, California 91320
E-mail: order@sagepub.com

SAGE Publications India Pvt. Ltd.
B 1/I 1 Mohan Cooperative
   Industrial Area
Mathura Road, New Delhi 110 044
India

SAGE Publications Ltd.
1 Oliver's Yard
55 City Road
London EC1Y 1SP
United Kingdom

SAGE Publications Asia-Pacific
   Pte. Ltd.
33 Pekin Street #02-01
Far East Square
Singapore 048763

Printed in the United States of America

Paperback ISBN 9781412994323

This book is printed on acid-free paper.

13 14 15 16 17 10 9 8 7 6 5 4 3

Acquisitions Editor:	Vicki Knight
Associate Editor:	Lauren Habib
Editorial Assistant:	Kalie Koscielak

1

What Is Biopsychology?

Chapter Outline

The Origins of Biopsychology

Prescientific Psychology and the Mind-Brain Problem

Descartes and the Physical Model of Behavior

Helmholtz and the Electrical Brain

The Localization Issue

IN THE NEWS: THE MIND BRAIN DEBATE ISN'T OVER

Nature and Nurture

The Genetic Code

APPLICATION: A COMPUTER MADE OF DNA

Genes and Behavior

The Human Genome Project

Heredity: Destiny or Predisposition?

Learning Objectives

After reading this chapter, you should be able to answer the following questions.

1. How did biological psychology develop from its roots in philosophy and physiology? Be sure to address the contributions of Descartes, Frisch and Hitzig, Helmholtz, Broca, Gall, and Lashley.

2. What is the mind-brain problem? How do most brain scientists currently think about this problem?

3. What are genes, and how do they work?

4. How are heredity and environment interrelated in the development of behavioral characteristics?

The Origins of Biopsychology

Summary and Guided Review

After studying this section in the text, fill in the blanks of the following summary.

_____ (1) is the multidisciplinary study of the nervous system and its role in behavior. During the 1990s, also known as the Decade of the _____ (2), intensive research into the role of biology in behavioral problems led to new treatments for depression, addiction, and age-related memory impairment. Advances were also made in the area of genetics, including a _____ (3) of all human genes and a greater understanding of the genes involved in diseases such as _____ (4).

_____ (5) is the branch of psychology that studies the relationships between behavior and the body, and it attempts to answer questions about the biological basis of diverse phenomena such as mental illness, emotions, perception, cognition, and consciousness. Psychology emerged as a separate discipline in 1879 when _____ (6) established the first psychology laboratory, and biopsychology arose as a distinct subfield of psychology some time after this.

Biopsychology addresses the _____ (7) problem, which concerns the nature of the relationship between the physical brain and the mind. Most modern neuroscientists believe that the _____ (8) is not a real thing, but rather is a concept we use to explain our awareness of experience. This position is known as material _____ (9) and assumes that everything is physical. The position that the mind is nonmaterial and separate from the physical brain is called _____ (10). This issue of lack of consensus on the mind-brain problem is not a new one: Among the ancient Greek philosophers, Democritus and _____ (11) were monists, whereas _____ (12) was a dualist.

Scientists often use _____ (13) to help them explain how things work. The hydraulic model of behavior was developed by the 17th-century French philosopher _____ (14) to explain the physical basis of behavior. According to this model, when the mind willed the body to action, the _____ (15) gland pumped animal spirits through the nerves (believed to be hollow tubes) to the muscles, resulting in movement. The pineal gland, therefore, was considered the seat of the _____ (16). This model was ultimately shown to be wrong based on the approach of _____ (17), which involves use of the methods of observation and experimentation.

Important principles of nervous system anatomy and physiology were discovered during the 1700s and 1800s. Work by several physiologists showed that nerves operated via _____ (18), not "animal spirits." However, the German physiologist _____ (19) performed experiments which indicated that nerve conduction was not as fast as electricity conducted through wires, which suggested that something more than just electricity was operating in the nervous system.

In the 1800s, well-documented cases of brain injury suggested that specific parts of the brain have specific functions, a concept known as _____ (20). For example, railroad worker _____ _____ (21) underwent extreme changes in personality following an accident in which an iron rod was driven through his skull and _____ (22) lobes. Another case was reported by the French physician _____ (23); his patient was unable to speak, and after the patient died, it was discovered that he had damage in the _____ (24) hemisphere of his brain. Gall took the localization concept to an extreme in his theory of _____ (25), which stated that several emotional and intellectual faculties were located in specific areas of the brain based on bumps on the skull. On the other extreme, Lashley's theory of _____ (26) argued that brain functions are evenly distributed across the brain. Currently, brain researchers know that brain functions are both localized and _____ (27), which means that several brain areas interact to produce specific experiences such as learning or emotion.

Evidence that the mind-brain problem is not resolved comes from researchers allied with the Discovery Institute, the headquarters for _____ _____ (28). This group studies non-material neuroscience and point to studies in which _____ (29) altered brain function in obsessive-compulsive patients as evidence for their position. Material neuroscientists interpret these findings as the _____ (30) changing the brain. Non-material neuroscientists are now focusing on _____ (31), which they believe cannot be explained by materialism.

Short Answer and Essay Questions

Answer the following questions.

1. Give two examples of the types of research questions that biological psychologists might ask.

2. Regarding the mind-brain question, compare monism and dualism. What are (or were) the problems with each position? How do most modern neuroscientists explain the relationship between the brain and mind? What is the opinion of neuroscientists associated with the Discovery Institute?

3. Why was the case of Phineas Gage important for brain science? What did it reveal about the localization of function issue?

4. Compare the theories of localization and equipotentiality. What is the current position of brain researchers on this issue?

Nature and Nurture

Summary and Guided Review

After studying this section in the text, fill in the blanks of the following summary.

The question of _____ versus _____ (32) asks how important genes and environment are in influencing behavior. Evidence is accumulating that many behaviors have a genetic or _____ (33) component.

_____ (34), which direct cellular processes and transmit inherited characteristics, are located mostly on _____ (35), which are paired in all cells, with the exception of some in the sex cells. The sex of an individual is determined by the sex chromosomes: Females are _____ (36), and males are _____ (37). Most body cells have _____ (38) chromosomes, but _____ (39) and egg cells have 23. When conception occurs, the fertilized egg, or _____ (40), contains half of each parent's genetic material. For the first 8 weeks following conception, the developing baby is considered a(an) _____ (41), and then it is called a _____ (42) until it is born.

Genes are composed of a double strand of molecules known as _____ (43), or

deoxyribonucleic acid. The strands are connected by pairs of nucleotides (adenine, _____

(44), guanine, and _____ (45)) that carry instructions for producing

_____ (46), which are used in the construction of the body or act as

_____ (47). Researchers at the Weizmann Institute are building computers out of

_____ (48); in test tubes, these can identify and kill _____ cells (49).

Different versions of a gene are called _____ (50). In some cases the effects of the

two genes blend to produce a result; one example of this would be _____ (51). A

_____ (52) gene will produce its effects regardless of which gene it is paired with. In order

for a _____ (53) trait to be expressed, there must be a copy of the same gene on each

chromosome. Individuals who possess two copies of a dominant gene are _____ (54) for

that gene, and will have the same _____ (55), or characteristic, as those who

possess one dominant and one recessive gene (who are _____ (56)). An X-linked

characteristic is produced by a gene on the X chromosome that is not paired with one on the Y chromosome. If a

recessive gene is located on the X chromosome, the trait it influences is more likely to be seen in

_____ (57); red-green color blindness is an example of a(n) _____

(58) trait. Traits such as height and intelligence are _____ (59), meaning they are

influenced by more than one gene.

During the first half of the 20th century, psychologists came to believe that the _____

(60) was more important in contributing to behavior than genes. By the end of the century, a more balanced

view was adopted. Psychologists now believe that many human behavioral traits are influenced by genes, and

_____ (61) is the behavioral trait whose genetic origins have received the most research

attention. However, it is important to remember that genes control only the production of proteins, so they

influence behavior indirectly through physiological systems.

Locating genes that influence traits is difficult and time-consuming. However, in 2000, several genetics

laboratories published a rough draft of the human _____ (62), which will be useful in

locating specific genes. This effort, known as the International Human Genome Project, has revealed that

humans have between _____ and _____ (63) individual genes, and

that 97% of the genome is made up of "_____" (64) DNA, which are sections of

chromosomes whose function is uncertain, though some of it controls gene expression. Although the map does not tell scientists what each gene does, it will allow them to more easily locate specific genes that contribute to specific traits. For example, although researchers in the 1980s knew that the gene for Huntington's disease was located on chromosome 4 near two _____ (65) genes, it took them ten more years to locate the specific gene. Scientists now predict that they can locate important genes much more quickly because of the map. Such knowledge is expected to lead to genetic-based treatment of many more disorders.

The notion that offspring are like clones of their parents is incorrect. Children inherit _____ (66) of each parent's DNA, and because of the 60 to 70 trillion possible _____ (67) of genes resulting from sexual reproduction; no two individuals are genetically exactly alike (unless they are identical twins!). This variability of traits is the cornerstone of Darwin's theory of _____ _____ (68), which states that organisms possessing traits that are most conducive to survival are more likely to pass their genes on to offspring. Genes are not _____ (69) in their operation. They are not all active at the same time. They may produce more proteins at some times than at others. They may become active during certain _____ (70), such as when an organism is learning. Clearly genes are not the sole dictators of behavior. Instead, they give us predispositions for certain characteristics.

Comparisons between identical and _____ (71) twins allow researchers to estimate the percentage of variation in characteristics due to heredity, or _____ (72). It appears that heritability for intelligence is about _____% (73). Personality characteristics show a heritability of _____ – _____% (74). If half of the variation in behaviors is due to genetics, then the other half must be due to _____ (75). However, it is important to understand that the more similarity there is between people's environments, the _____ (76) the degree of heritability.

Scientists now argue that genes contribute to our predisposition or _____ (77) for certain traits. The genes we inherit may result in a predisposition for a disorder such as schizophrenia, but the disorder will emerge only under certain environmental conditions. Clearly both factors are important.

Short Answer and Essay Questions

Answer the following questions.

5. What do genes do? Describe the ways in which the actions of genes can be variable.

6. What is the rationale for comparing identical and fraternal twins in order to measure the heritability of traits?

7. Janet and Charles are expecting their first baby. They are both highly intelligent, and they assume that their child will inherit their intelligence through the genes it shares with them. They feel that the environment has little or no impact on intelligence. After having read the section "Heredity: Destiny or Predisposition?" what would you tell this couple about the scientific evidence for their claim? (Be sure to address the concept of **predisposition** in your answer.)

Posttest

Use these multiple-choice questions to check your understanding of the chapter.

1. Which of the following did NOT occur during the Decade of the Brain?

    a. Genes contributing to the development of Alzheimer's disease were identified.

    b. It was discovered that neurons conduct electricity.

    c. Drugs that block addiction were discovered.

    d. New treatments for depression were developed.

2. Who among the following is credited with establishing the first psychology laboratory in Germany in 1879?

    a. Wilhelm Wundt

    b. Hermann von Helmholtz

    c. Gustav Fritsch

    d. Franz Gall

3. Dr. Locke is a philosopher who believes that there is no distinction between the physical brain and the mind. This position is known as

    a. materialistic monism.

    b. idealistic monism.

    c. dualism.

    d. materialistic dualism.

4. ___ was a dualist.

a. Aristotle

b. Plato

c. Democritus

d. Descartes

5. According to the hydraulic model of the nervous system,

    a. nerves were like electrical wires that conducted electricity.

    b. nerves were hollow tubes that allowed animal spirits to flow through them.

    c. nerves were not responsible for behavior.

    d. none of the above is correct.

6. Descartes believed that the "seat of the soul" was located in

    a. the frontal lobes of the brain.

    b. animal spirits.

    c. the pineal gland.

    d. the left hemisphere.

7. Through their experiments, Fritsch and Hitzig showed that

    a. the muscle in a frog's leg can be made to move by stimulating the nerve connected to it.

    b. the rate of nerve conduction is about 90 feet per second.

    c. the left hemisphere controls speech.

    d. muscle movement is the result of brain stimulation.

8. Who discovered that nerves conduct electricity at a rate significantly slower than the speed of light?

    a. Hermann von Helmholtz

    b. Rene Descartes

    c. Luigi Galvani

    d. Phineas Gage

9. Broca's mute patient had damage to his

    a. pineal gland.

    b. frontal lobes.

    c. left hemisphere.

    d. motor cortex.

10. The 19th-century belief that over 35 different mental faculties were located in specific parts of the brain was known as

   a. equipotentiality.

   b. extreme localization.

   c. phrenology.

   d. biopsychology.

11. With the exception of egg and sperm cells, all human body cells have

   a. 23 chromosomes.

   b. 46 chromosomes.

   c. 23 genes.

   d. 46 genes.

12. Females have

   a. two X chromosomes.

   b. two Y chromosomes.

   c. one X and one Y chromosome.

   d. one X chromosome.

13. At six weeks after conception, a developing human is known as a(n)

   a. zygote.

   b. ova.

   c. embryo.

   d. fetus.

14. How many different bases make up DNA?

   a. 20

   b. 10

   c. 5

   d. 4

15. Enzymes

   a. are proteins.

   b. are produced as a result of genetic mechanisms.

c. modify chemical reactions in the body.

d. are all of the above.

16. The allele for right-over-left hand clasping preference is recessive. John and Sue both show this hand clasping preference. What preference will their children have?

a. all left

b. half left, half right

c. all right

d. not enough information is given to answer the question

17. Which of the following is FALSE regarding red-green color blindness?

a. It is an X-linked trait.

b. A female cannot be red-green color blind.

c. Males are more likely to have it.

d. It is a recessive trait.

18. George is heterozygous for the dominant allele for hand clasping preference (left-over-right), and his son Jason is homozygous for the dominant allele. Which of the following statements is TRUE?

a. George and Jason have the same phenotype but different genotypes.

b. George and Jason have the same phenotype and the same genotype.

c. George and Jason have different phenotypes but the same genotype.

d. George and Jason have different phenotypes and different genotypes.

19. A trait is polygenic if

a. it is influenced by a gene on the X chromosome.

b. it is influenced by a gene on the Y chromosome.

c. it is influenced by more than one gene.

d. it is influenced only by a single gene.

20. Which of the following is believed to have a genetic basis?

a. sexual orientation

b. drug addiction

c. personality

d. All of the above

21. Which of the following is TRUE of the human genome?

    a. Nearly all of the base-pair sequences have been mapped.

    b. Most of our DNA is directly involved in coding for proteins.

    c. The functions of all genes are well documented.

    d. There are about 80,000 genes.

22. The differential survival of organisms with more adaptive traits is known as

    a. sexual reproduction.

    b. predisposition.

    c. natural selection.

    d. heritability.

23. Which of the following is NOT true of gene activity?

    a. Once a gene becomes inactive, it remains inactive.

    b. Genes may fluctuate in the amount of protein they code for at different times.

    c. A gene may become active at only a certain time of the life cycle.

    d. The activity of a gene may be influenced by experience.

24. Which of the following traits has the HIGHEST degree of heritability?

    a. intelligence

    b. personality

    c. height

    d. occupational interests

25. If people from similar environments are sampled, estimates of heritability for traits will be ___ people from different environments are sampled.

    a. lower than if

    b. higher than if

    c. the same as when

    d. either a or b may be correct

26. The BEST way to think about the relationship among genes, environment, and intelligence is that

    a. genes set the potential range, and environment determines the actual capacity.

    b. environment is more important than genetic inheritance.

c. our genes are more important than the environment.

d. a person's intelligence is equally influenced by each parent's genes.

Answers

Guided Review

1. Neuroscience

2. Brain

3. map

4. Alzheimer's

5. Biopsychology

6. Wundt

7. mind-brain

8. mind

9. monism

10. dualism

11. Aristotle

12. Plato

13. models

14. Descartes

15. pineal

16. soul

17. empiricism

18. electricity

19. Helmholtz

20. localization

21. Phineas Gage

22. frontal

23. Broca

24. left

25. phrenology

26. equipotentiality

27. distributed

28. intelligent design

29. psychotherapy

30. brain

31. consciousness

32. nature versus nurture

33. heredity

34. Genes

35. chromosomes

36. XX

37. XY

38. 46

39. sperm

40. zygote

41. embryo

42. fetus

43. DNA

44. thymine or cytocine

45. cytosine or thymine

46. proteins

47. enzymes

48. DNA

49. cancer

50. alleles

51. type AB blood

52. dominant

53. recessive

54. homozygous

55. phenotype

56. heterozygous

57. males

58. X-linked

59. polygenic

60. environment

61. intelligence

62. genome

63. 20,000 and 25,000

64. junk

65. marker

66. half

67. combinations

68. natural selection

69. rigid

70. experiences

71. fraternal

72. heritability

73. 50

74. 40–50

75. environment

76. higher

77. vulnerability

Short Answer and Essay Questions

1. There are several possible answers, but all must mention that biological psychologists look for a connection between the nervous system and a specific behavior or set of behaviors.

2. Monism assumes that the mind and brain are composed of the same thing or substance. Most monists are materialistic, meaning that they believe everything, including the mind, is physical, and therefore has no separate existence. Dualists, however, believe that while the brain is physical, the mind is also real, although not material, and exists separately from the brain. The problem with dualism is that it cannot explain how something nonphysical (the mind) can affect something physical (the body). The problem with materialistic monism is =explaining how the brain causes subjective, mental experience. Most modern neuroscientists are materialistic monists. They believe that the mind is not a real entity but rather a concept we use to describe what our brains are doing. Therefore, the mind really is the brain or, more precisely, the activity of the brain. However, non-material neuroscientists funded by the Discovery Institute are keeping the brain-body debate alive by arguing that if psychotherapy can change brain function, then the mind must exist to have an impact on the brain. Material monists would argue that this phenomenon demonstrates that the brain affects the brain.

3. It was important because it showed that damage to a particular part of the brain resulted in disruption of some types of functions but not others. Following his accident, Gage was still able to speak and move normally, and he showed no change in memory or intelligence, but his personality changed, and he became impulsive and hard to deal with. This suggested that the part of the brain damaged by his injury was involved in some types of behaviors but not in others.

4. Localization is the theory that different brain areas are in control of different functions. Equipotentiality assumes that the brain as a whole contributes to all functions. Most brain researchers now believe that while

specific functions are located in specific brain regions, several different brain areas work together to produce behaviors and experiences; thus, the brain's functions are both localized and distributed.

5. Genes direct the production of proteins. Genes are variable in their effects, because they may not always be active and because they can vary the amount of a protein that is produced. They may also change functioning as the body ages.

6. Identical twins have the same genes, whereas fraternal twins have about 50% of their genes in common. If we compare identical twins and fraternal twins on some trait such as intelligence, and we find that identical twins are more similar than fraternal twins, then we can assume that genes are responsible for some of the similarity between the identical twins.

7. The evidence suggests that genes and environment are both important. The heritability of intelligence is around 50%, so this means that the environment contributes just as much as genes do. Furthermore, what genes contribute is better thought of as a predisposition; the environment will always have a significant impact.

Posttest

1. b 2. a 3. a 4. d 5. b 6. c 7. d 8. a 9. c 10. c 11. b 12. a 13. c 14. d 15. d 16. c 17. b
18. a 19. c 20. d 21. a 22. c 23. a 24. c 25. b 26. a

2

Communication Within the Nervous System

Chapter Outline

The Cells That Make Us Who We Are

Neurons

APPLICATION: TARGETING ION CHANNELS

Glial Cells

How Neurons Communicate With Each Other

Chemical Transmission at the Synapse

Regulating Synaptic Activity

Neurotransmitters

APPLICATION: AGONISTS AND ANTAGONISTS IN THE REAL WORLD

Of Neuronal Codes, Neural Networks, and Computers

Learning Objectives

After reading this chapter, you should be able to answer the following questions.

1. Describe the structure and function of neurons.

2. How are neurons specialized to conduct information?

3. How do glial cells support the activity of neurons?

4. How do neurons communicate with each other?

5. What strategies do neurons use to increase their capacity for information processing?

6. What are the functions of some of the major chemical transmitters?

7. What are neural networks and why are they important? How are artificial neural networks useful to neuroscientists?

The Cells That Make Us Who We Are

Summary and Guided Review

After studying this section in the text, fill in the blanks of the following summary.

The human brain consists of about 100 billion _____ (1), cells that carry messages and underlie our thoughts, feelings, and behaviors. It also contains many more _____ (2) cells, which have a variety of functions.

Neurons exist in many different forms, but they share similar structures and functions. The _____ (3), or cell body, is where the cell's nucleus containing DNA is located as well as other _____ (4) located in the cytoplasm that carry out the functions of the cell. Branching out from the cell body are _____ (5), structures that receive messages from other cells. A single tail-like structure called the _____ (6) extends away from the cell body and carries messages to other neurons. The end bulbs, or _____ (7) of the axon, contain chemical messengers called _____ (8) that enable the neuron to communicate with other cells. Although axons are quite thin (at most 0.1 mm in mammals), they can be up to _____ (9) m long.

_____ (10) neurons, which are multipolar, carry information to muscle and gland tissue, whereas _____ (11) neurons, which are either unipolar or bipolar, are stimulated by internal or environmental events and transmit information about those events to the brain and spinal cord. Neurons with short or no axons that transmit information between adjacent neurons in the same area of the brain are called _____ (12), and they are the most abundant type.

The membrane of a neuron is composed of a double layer of lipid molecules and contains _____ (13) molecules. Fluid is found both inside and outside the cell. Some molecules, such as oxygen, can pass through the membrane, while others are prevented from getting in; this property is known as selective _____ (14). Because ions (charged particles) are distributed in different concentrations on each side of the membrane, the membrane is _____ (15) (electrically charged). When the cell is at rest, the inside is negatively charged relative to the outside, typically around _____ mV (16). This is known as the _____ (17) potential.

_____ (18) and chloride ions are more concentrated outside the cell, and potassium ions and protein anions are more concentrated inside. Ions are attracted to the side of the membrane where their type is less abundant by the force of _____ (19). Because of _____ (20), ions are also attracted to the side of the membrane with the opposite charge (so positively charged ions are attracted to the negative side of the cell). The _____- _____ (21) pump helps to maintain the balance of ions within and outside of the cell.

Sodium ions are attracted inside the cell by both _____ (22) and _____ (23), but they are kept out because they cannot pass through the membrane. However, if the membrane is stimulated by an activating stimulus, then _____ (24) channels in the membrane will open, allowing sodium into the cell. This results in the cell becoming _____ (25), with the inside less negative than before. If enough sodium enters the cell, its polarity will reach a threshold at which the cell will generate an _____ (26) potential; sodium ions enter so rapidly that the cell becomes suddenly positively charged at the site of the depolarization. Shortly after this, the sodium channels close, and _____ (27) channels open. Potassium moves out by diffusion and as a result of the increasingly positive charge inside the axon. All of this occurs in about 1 _____ (28). Once it occurs, an action potential spreads down an axon, because it causes adjacent sodium channels to open and _____ (29) another portion of the membrane. The outflow of potassium ions restores the resting potential; the displaced ions are eventually returned to their resting locations by the sodium-potassium pump. This wave of action potentials sweeps down the length of the axon until it reaches the axon _____ (30) and signals the next neuron.

Depolarizations and action potentials are not identical. Whereas the initial depolarization or local potential is _____ (31), the action potential is not. Action potentials occur according to the _____ or _____ (32) law, which means that a cell's action potentials are all of the same strength. Also, unlike local potentials, action potentials are _____ (33), meaning they maintain their full strength until they reach the axon terminal.

Immediately after an action potential occurs, the sodium channels are unable to open again, and therefore the cell is unable to produce another action potential right away. This is known as the

_____ (34) refractory period. The cell is also subject to a relative refractory period, when the _____ (35) channels are still open and the inside is slightly more

_____ (36) charged for a short time. In order for an action potential to occur at this time, the stimulus must be _____ (37) than normal. More intense stimuli will produce earlier and, therefore, more frequent action potentials; this is the _____ (38) law.

Puffer fish and snake venoms contain _____ (39) that affect potassium and sodium channels; some animal toxins also affect calcium channels. Sometimes blocking sodium channels can be useful, as is the case with _____ _____ (40), whereas opening potassium channels (causing hyperpolarizations) is one way that _____ _____ (41) work. A new strategy that uses _____ (42) to control ion channels allows more precise targeting of neurons; potential applications range from tracing neural pathways to therapeutic brain stimulation.

Glial cells are an important component of the nervous system. For example, the fatty substance

_____ (43) insulates axons and also increases conduction speed, which allows the nervous system to transmit signals faster without having to produce larger axons. In the central nervous system, myelin is made by _____ (44), while _____ (45) cells produce myelin for the rest of the nervous system. Action potentials occur only at the gaps between myelin cells known as nodes of

_____ (46), where most of the cell's sodium channels are located. The action potential jumps from one gap to the next rather than travelling down the entire length of the axon; this is known as

_____ (47) conduction; it is faster and uses less _____ (48) than conduction in unmyelinated neurons. When myelin is destroyed, as in the disease _____

_____ (49), the neurons cease to function properly.

Glial cells, which are far more numerous than neurons, also perform a number of important functions. By acting as a scaffold, they _____ (50) developing neurons to their destinations. They support and keep mature neurons functioning properly. When deprived of glial cells, neurons lose some of their

_____ (51) with other neurons. Brain complexity in different species is correlated with higher ratios of _____ (52) to neurons.

Short Answer and Essay Questions

Answer the following questions.

1. Identify the key parts of a typical neuron and describe their functions.

2. How are sensory and motor neurons different in terms of their functions and structure?

3. What does it mean that the neural cell membrane is selectively permeable? How do water, oxygen, and carbon dioxide molecules enter the cell? How do ions and other substances necessary for functioning enter the cell?

4. Of all the ions involved in neuronal depolarization, sodium (Na^{+}) ions are most strongly attracted across the membrane. Give two reasons for this.

5. Identify the two "key players" or ions in the action potential. Describe the sequence of events that occur during the action potential.

6. When an axon is depolarized to threshold, it fires an action potential at the site of depolarization. How does that action potential spread to the rest of the axon? Why does that action potential spread in only one direction (toward the axon terminals)?

7. One way in which the intensity of a stimulus is coded or represented in the sensory neuron is by the frequency with which action potentials are generated. For example, a more intense stimulus produces more action potentials per second than a less intense one, although the action potentials themselves are of the same strength. What role does the relative refractory period play in this effect?

8. Explain why action potentials are conducted more quickly, and more efficiently in terms of energy used, in myelinated cells than in unmyelinated cells.

9. What are some functions (other than myelination) of glial cells?

How Neurons Communicate With Each Other

Summary and Guided Review

After studying this section in the text, fill in the blanks of the following summary.

The fact that neurons are not physically attached to one another was discovered by Spanish anatomist

_____ (53) in the 19th century with the help of the _____

_____ (54) that identifies a small number of particular neurons. In the 20th century,

_____ (55) showed that neurons communicate with one another chemically. He did this by

first stimulating the vagus nerve of a frog heart, which resulted in the heart rate _____ (56).

Then he collected the salt solution he had placed in the heart and administered it to another heart, which also

_____ (57) its rate of beating. Later research has shown that neurons can also communicate

by electricity and by gas. At chemical synapses the _____ (58) are located in small sacs in

the axon terminals called _____ (59). When an action potential reaches the axon terminal,

_____ (60) ions enter the cell and cause the vesicles to fuse with the presynaptic cell

membrane, dumping their contents into the synaptic cleft. The neurotransmitter molecules then attach to

receptors on the _____ (61) membrane, causing ion channels to open and producing a

graded potential. An immediate response in the postsynaptic cell is seen when _____ (62)

receptors are opened, while prolonged effects follow the opening of _____ (63) receptors.

Neurotransmitters can affect the postsynaptic cell by causing hyperpolarization (inhibition), or

_____ (64) (excitation). Inhibition in the nervous system is important for many reasons,

including its role in controlling excitation. Neurotransmitters that cause _____ (65)

channels to open lead to EPSPs of the soma and dendrites, whereas those that cause potassium and/or chloride

channels to open lead to _____ (66). EPSPs and IPSPs are _____ (67)

potentials, and when they reach the axon _____ (68), they either increase or decrease the

rate of action potentials. EPSPs may ultimately have inhibitory effects, if they increase output to inhibitory

neurons. The stimulant drug _____ (69) is believed to calm hyperactive children by

increasing frontal lobe activation, which in turns inhibits behavior.

A single cell is continuously receiving messages from as many as _____ (70) other

cells, most of which have only very small effects on the polarity of the cell. The incoming information is

integrated by the postsynaptic neuron. When two or more postsynaptic potentials arrive simultaneously but at

different parts of the cell, _____ (71) summation occurs. Because the effect of a graded

potential takes a while to dissipate, when postsynaptic potentials arrive in close succession,

_____ (72) summation can occur. A good way of thinking about the neuron is that it serves

22

as both an information integrator in handling information from a variety of sources and as a

_____ (73) maker about whether it will fire and at what rate.

Once it has attached to the postsynaptic receptor and had its effect on the postsynaptic cell, the

_____ (74) is inactivated in some way. Often this is accomplished as the presynaptic cell

absorbs it, a process called _____ (75). The neurotransmitter may also be broken down by

the _____ (76) acetylcholinesterase. Also, glial cells absorb some transmitters. Drugs may

affect behavior by interfering with these mechanisms in some way.

Synaptic transmission can be altered by _____ (77) synapses on the terminals, which

affect the release of the neurotransmitter from the presynaptic neuron through presynaptic excitation

or_____ (78). Additionally, _____ (79) on the presynaptic axon

terminals can monitor the amount of neurotransmitter in the synapse and adjust the cell's release of it, and the

postsynaptic membrane regulates the number and sensitivity of its _____ (80).

_____ (81) cells also regulate synaptic activity in a number of ways, including absorbing

neurotransmitter from the synapse and releasing neurotransmitter.

There are many different neurotransmitters, and each may have different effects through different receptor

types. For example, acetylcholine has an excitatory effect at _____ (82) receptors, while at

_____ (83) receptors, it may have excitatory or inhibitory effects. A single neuron can

release more than one type of neurotransmitter at the same synapse. One of these may be

_____ _____ (84) and have an immediate effect on the postsynaptic

cell, while the others (such as neuropeptides) enhance the effects of the first through more prolonged

mechanisms. Some cells appear to release two fast-acting transmitters at the same time, and some release both

excitatory and inhibitory transmitters at different _____ (85).

Many drugs affect neural functioning. Nicotine, for example is an _____ (86) at

acetylcholine receptors. Amazonian Indians tip their darts with an acetylcholine antagonist,

_____ (87) to paralyze animals.

It is difficult to understand how neural activity controls behavior if we limit ourselves to simple trains of

impulses in a chain of individual neurons. However, researchers have been able to record temporal variations in

firing during taste stimulation that form a _____ (88) that can then be duplicated as

electrical pulses to produce the same behavior in other animals. However, complex processing such as color

vision or sound discrimination requires groups of neurons that function together as a _____

_____ (89). Because working with actual groups of neurons is a daunting task, researchers have created _____ _____ _____ (90) on computers. These networks are not programmed to perform a specific task; instead they _____ (91) to carry out their tasks.

Short Answer and Essay Questions

Answer the following questions.

10. Describe the experiment by Otto Loewi. How did he arrive at the conclusion that neurons communicate via chemical transmission?

11. What happens to a cell's polarity and firing rate when an IPSP occurs? Why does the firing rate change?

12. Why is the model consisting of a single chain of neurons inadequate for explaining how the brain works? Give two reasons. (Hint: In your answer, consider both postsynaptic integration and how synaptic activity may be regulated.)

13. Explain temporal and spatial summation.

Posttest

Use these multiple-choice questions to check your understanding of the chapter.

1. Scientists estimate that there are about ____ neurons in the brain.

   a. 1 million

   b. 100 million

   c. 1 billion

   d. 100 billion

2. In the nervous system, which of the following types of cells is MOST numerous?

   a. glial

   b. motor neurons

c. sensory neurons

d. interneurons

3. The nucleus of a neural cell is located in the

a. axon.

b. dendrites.

c. soma.

d. axon hillock.

4. A neuron that transmits information between the central nervous system and a muscle is called a(n)

a. motor neuron.

b. sensory neuron.

c. interneuron.

d. projection neuron.

5. A ___ neuron has an axon and several dendrites projecting away from the cell body.

a. bipolar

b. multipolar

c. unipolar

d. monopolar

6. Which of the following statements regarding interneurons is TRUE?

a. They receive input directly from the external environment.

b. They send information across long distances.

c. They may have no axon at all.

d. They are found only in the brain.

7. The neural membrane is selectively permeable to all of the following substances EXCEPT

a. sodium.

b. potassium.

c. oxygen.

d. chloride.

8. When a neuron is at rest, ___ ions are more plentiful outside of the cell.

a. Na^+

b. K$^+$

c. Anions

d. All of the above

9. The TYPICAL resting potential of a neuron is

a. −70 V.

b. −35 mV.

c. 70 mV.

d. −70 mV.

10. When the cell is at rest, K$^+$ ions are strongly attracted across the cell membrane

a. mostly because of electrostatic pressure

b. mostly because of the force of diffusion.

c. equally because of electrostatic pressure and force of diffusion.

d. neither electrostatic pressure nor force of diffusion.

11. All of the following are able to pass through the membrane under certain conditions EXCEPT

a. Na$^+$

b. Cl$^-$

c. K$^+$

d. A$^-$

12. Which of the following statements regarding the sodium-potassium pump is FALSE?

a. It requires a lot of energy.

b. It works against diffusion.

c. It pumps sodium into the cell.

d. It helps maintain the resting potential.

13. Neurons undergo depolarization when

a. K$^+$ ions enter the cell.

b. Na$^+$ ions enter the cell.

c. either K$^+$ or Na$^+$ ions enter the cell.

d. Cl$^-$ ions leave the cell.

14. Depolarization is MOST similar to

a. hypopolarization.

b. hyperpolarization.

c. action potential.

d. electrical gradient.

15. When the cell is at rest, Na⁺ ions are strongly attracted across the cell membrane because of

a. electrostatic pressure.

b. diffusion.

c. both electrostatic pressure and diffusion.

d. neither electrostatic pressure or diffusion.

16. A neuron will fire an action potential when it is

a. depolarized by 10 mV.

b. hyperpolarized by 10 mV.

c. depolarized by 15 mV.

d. depolarized to its threshold.

17. The outflow of K⁺ ions during an action potential results in

a. hypopolarization.

b. hyperpolarization.

c. depolarization.

d. another action potential.

18. The action potentials generated by a specific neuron

a. are the same strength.

b. occur at the same frequency.

c. are graded.

d. are decremental.

19. Which of the following statements regarding the absolute refractory period is FALSE?

a. The potassium channels are closed and cannot be opened.

b. The sodium channels are closed and cannot be opened.

c. An action potential cannot be generated.

d. The absolute refractory period ensures that the action potential will travel only in one direction.

20. During the relative refractory period,

    a. the neuron is hyperpolarized.

    b. a stronger stimulus may result in another action potential.

    c. potassium channels are open.

    d. All of the above

21. The maximum speed at which a neuron can conduct an action potential seems to be about

    a. 10 m/s.

    b. 1000 m/s.

    c. 120 m/s.

    d. 1.2 m/s.

22. The ___ the axon, the ___ the action potential.

    a. thicker; slower.

    b. thicker; faster.

    c. longer; slower.

    d. thinner; faster.

23. In the brain, myelin is formed by

    a. Schwann cells.

    b. protein.

    c. oligodendrocytes.

    d. vesicles.

24. In myelinated axons,

    a. action potentials occur along the entire length of the axon.

    b. action potentials occur only at the nodes of Ranvier.

    c. action potentials occur only where the myelin is in contact with the axon.

    d. action potentials travel more slowly than on unmyelinated axons.

25. Myelination results in all of the following EXCEPT

    a. increased capacitance.

    b. increased speed of conduction.

c. saltatory conduction.

d. less work required by the sodium-potassium pump.

26. Which of the following was not mentioned as a function of glial cells?

a. Releasing neurotransmitters.

b. Guiding developing axons.

c. Assisting in the development of synapses.

d. Transmitting action potentials.

27. Who discovered that neurons are NOT in contact with each other?

a. Ramón y Cajal

b. Golgi

c. Loewi

d. Dale

28. Who demonstrated that synaptic transmission is chemical?

a. Ramón y Cajal

b. Golgi

c. Loewi

d. Dale

29. When an action potential reaches an axon terminal, ____ ions enter the cell and trigger the release of the neurotransmitter.

a. Na^+

b. K^+

c. $Cl^?$

d. calcium

30. Fast-acting receptors involved in muscle activity and sensory processing are referred to as

a. metabotropic.

b. autroreceptors.

c. ionotropic.

d. presynaptic.

31. Under normal circumstances, the neurotransmitter molecules released by a *single* neuron can do all of the following EXCEPT

    a. cause ion channels to open.

    b. trigger a graded depolarization.

    c. trigger an action potential.

    d. inhibit the postsynaptic cell.

32. An IPSP will occur if

    a. sodium channels open.

    b. potassium channels open.

    c. chloride channels open.

    d. b or c

33. Action potentials are first produced

    a. at the axon hillock.

    b. in the soma.

    c. in the dendrites.

    d. in the axon terminals.

34. In order for spatial summation to occur,

    a. several EPSPs must arrive at the same time.

    b. several EPSPs and/or IPSPs must arrive at the same time.

    c. several EPSPs must arrive in quick succession.

    d. EPSPs and IPSPs must arrive in quick succession.

35. If a neuron has a resting potential of –70 mV and a threshold of –60 mV, which of the following combinations of simultaneous postsynaptic potentials will result in an action potential?

    a. 15 EPSPs of 1 mV each and 20 IPSPs of 1 mV each.

    b. 50 EPSPs of .5 mV each and 20 IPSPs of .5 mV each.

    c. 50 EPSPs of .2 mV each and 15 IPSPs of .2 mV each.

    d. 25 EPSPs of 1 mV each and 20 IPSPs of 1 mV each.

36. Acetylcholine is inactivated by

a. reuptake by the presynaptic neuron.

b. absorption by the postsynaptic neuron.

c. enzymatic deactivation.

d. absorption by glial cells.

37. Neurotransmitters can fit into receptor sites

    a. on both the presynaptic and postsynaptic membrane.

    b. on neither the presynaptic nor the postsynaptic membrane.

    c. on the presynaptic membrane only.

    d. on the postsynaptic membrane only.

38. Which of the following statements regarding nicotinic receptors is FALSE?

    a. They are inhibitory.

    b. They are stimulated by acetylcholine.

    c. They are found in the brain.

    d. They are found in muscles.

39. Regarding the types of neurotransmitters that a neuron can release, which of the following statements

    is FALSE?

    a. A neuron may release more than one fast-acting neurotransmitter.

    b. A neuron may release only excitatory or only inhibitory neurotransmitters.

    c. A neuron may release one fast-acting and one slower-acting neurotransmitter.

    d. A neuron may release one fast-acting and several slower-acting neurotransmitters.

40. Which of the following is an antagonist at acetylcholine receptors?

    a. nicotine

    b. muscarine

    c. naloxone

    d. curare

41. In an artificial neural network, MOST of the processing occurs in which layer of neurons?

    a. input

    b. hidden

    c. output

        d. excitatory

42 The ability of neurons to carry information is increased by

        a. variations in the size of the neural impulse.

        b. its maintenance of the same firing rate regardless of the stimulus.

        c. the neuron's consistency in producing excitation or inhibition.

        d. varied time intervals of neural bursts

43 The solution to the problem that chains of single neurons are inadequate to handle the brain's tasks is

        a. neural networks.

        b. artificial neural networks.

        c. labelled lines.

        d. temporal coding.

Answers

Guided Review

1. neurons

2. glial

3. soma

4. organelles

5. dendrites

6. axon

7. terminals

8. neurotransmitters

9. 1

10. Motor

11. sensory

12. interneurons

13. protein

14. permeability

15. polarized

16. -70

17. resting

18. Na$^+$ or Sodium

19. diffusion

20. electrostatic pressure

21. sodium-potassium

22. diffusion

23. electrostatic pressure

24. sodium

25. hypopolarized or partially depolarized

26. action

27. potassium

28. millisecond

29. depolarize or hypopolarize

30. terminals

31. graded

32. all-or-none

33. nondecremental

34. absolute

35. K$^+$ or potassium

36. negatively

37. stronger

38. rate

39. neurotoxins

40. local anesthetics

41. general anesthetics

42. light

43. myelin

44. oligodendrocytes

45. Schwann

46. Ranvier

47. saltatory

48. energy

49. multiple sclerosis

50. guide

51. synapses

52. astrocytes

53. Cajal

54. Golgi stain

55. Loewi

56. decreasing

57. decreased

58. neurotransmitters

59. vesicles

60. calcium

61. postsynaptic

62. ionotropic

63. metabotropic

64. hypopolarization or depolarization

65. Na^+ or sodium

66. IPSPs

67. graded

68. hillock

69. Ritalin

70. 1,000

71. spatial

72. temporal

73. decision

74. transmitter

75. reuptake

76. enzyme

77. axoaxonic

78. inhibition

79. autoreceptors

80. receptors

81. Glial

82. nicotinic

83. muscarinic

84. fast-acting

85. terminals

86. agonist

87. curare

88. code

89. neural networks

90. artificial neural networks

91. learn

Short Answer and Essay Questions

1. A typical neuron has a cell body or soma, containing the nucleus (which contains the genetic material) and organelles that keep the cell alive and functioning. Dendrites are the receiving components of the cell, whereas the axon carries information to the terminals. The terminals contain transmitters that communicate with the next cell.

2. Sensory neurons carry information about internal and environmental stimuli to the central nervous system, whereas motor neurons carry messages away from the central nervous system to the muscle and glandular cells of the body. Structurally, sensory neurons are usually bipolar or unipolar. Motor neurons are usually multipolar, with dendritic branches extending in several directions.

3. A membrane that is selectively permeable allows only certain substances to pass through it. Neurons can be readily permeated by water, oxygen, and carbon dioxide but not by other substances that they need for proper functioning. Protein channels embedded within the membrane control the flow of ions and various kinds of molecules. These substances can get in only when the protein channels are open.

4. Na^+ ions are more concentrated on the outside of the cell, so they are attracted across the membrane by the force of diffusion. And, because they are positively charged, they are also attracted into the cell because the inside of it is negative relative to the outside (electrostatic pressure).

5. If the excitatory inputs exceed the inhibitory inputs to an adequate degree, the cell will depolarize to a threshold at which sodium channels will open, and sodium will enter, further depolarizing the cell. Potassium

channels will also open, and as potassium leaves the axon the cell will return to the resting potential and actually become hyperpolarized for a time.

6. The action potential spreads because it causes the sodium channels near it to open, thereby depolarizing the adjacent part of the membrane to threshold. This propagates the action potential across the length of the axon. The action potential cannot spread backward toward the soma because once the sodium channels at the site of depolarization close, they cannot be opened for a brief period (the absolute refractory period).

7. During the relative refractory period, a neuron is slightly more negative inside than while at rest, and so it requires a stronger stimulus to initiate an action potential. Therefore, stimuli of stronger intensities will have a greater effect than those of weak intensities. A stronger stimulus will cause the neuron to fire again earlier in the recovery period and, therefore, more frequently.

8. The axons of myelinated cells contain gaps between the myelin where the action potential actually occurs. In between those gaps, the cell undergoes a graded depolarization that spreads more quickly than an action potential. This depolarization then triggers the action potential at the next gap. Because the action potential is generated at fewer points along the axon and transmission is faster between nodes, it travels more quickly. Furthermore, fewer ions are exchanged, and therefore, the cell does not have to work as hard (via the sodium-potassium pump) to restore the resting potential.

9. Glial cells provide support and guidance for developing neurons. They also support synapses (neurons lose synapses in the absence of glial cells). They absorb and recycle neurotransmitter from the synapse. They release glutamate into the synapse, which may alter the function of neurons.

10. First, Loewi isolated the hearts of two frogs and kept them beating. Then he stimulated the vagus nerve of one heart, which caused it to slow down. He transferred fluid from this heart to the other heart, which also slowed down. Then he caused the first heart to speed up, and repeated the procedure of transferring fluid. The second heart also increased its rate of contractions. He concluded that something in the fluid, some chemical released by the nerve he stimulated, had caused the change in heart rate.

11. The cell becomes slightly hyperpolarized, and this makes it more difficult for the neuron to fire. This is because in order for the cell to be depolarized to threshold, a stronger than normal stimulus (perhaps in the form of several additional EPSPs) is required.

12. First of all, a single postsynaptic neuron usually receives information from more than one presynaptic neuron. Therefore, its activity is a result of the integration of excitatory and inhibitory information it receives from all of these different sources. Second, synaptic activity may be modulated by a number of mechanisms, including glial cells, autoreceptors, and presynaptic excitation or inhibition from a third neuron.

13. Temporal summation occurs when two or more postsynaptic potentials occurring in close temporal (time) proximity have a cumulative effect on a neuron. For example, while a single EPSP will not cause a neuron to fire or increase a cell's firing rate, several EPSPs occurring very close together in time will have a cumulative effect. Spatial summation occurs when simultaneous postsynaptic potentials arriving at nearby locations influence the likelihood of firing or the firing rate of a neuron. For example, while a single IPSP may not reduce the frequency of action potentials, several IPSPs occurring together may.

Posttest

1. d 2. a   3. c   4. a   5. b   6. c   7. c   8. a   9. d   10. b   11. d   12. c   13. b   14. a   15. c   16. d   17. b
18. a   19. a   20. d   21. c   22. b   23. c   24. b   25. a   26. d   27. a   28. c   29. d   30. c   31. c   32. d
33. a   34. b   35. b   36. c   37. a   38. a   39. b   40. d   41. b   42. d   43. a

3

The Organization and Functions of the Nervous System

Chapter Outline

The Central Nervous System

The Forebrain

APPLICATION: THE CASE OF PHINEAS GAGE

The Midbrain and Hindbrain

The Spinal Cord

Protecting the Central Nervous System

The Peripheral Nervous System

The Cranial Nerves

The Autonomic Nervous System

Development and Change in the Nervous System

The Stages of Development

How Experience Modifies the Nervous System

Damage and Recovery in the Central Nervous System

IN THE NEWS: IS THE BRAIN TOO FRAGILE FOR SPORTS?

APPLICATION: MENDING THE BRAIN WITH COMPUTER CHIPS

Learning Objectives

After reading this chapter, you should be able to answer the following questions.

1. What are the major functions of each of the cerebral hemispheres?

2. What are the locations and major functions of the thalamus, hypothalamus, midbrain, hindbrain, and cerebellum?

3. Describe the structure and function of the spinal cord.

4. What features of the central nervous system protect it?

5. What structures make up the peripheral nervous system, and what are their functions?

6. What happens in the nervous system during each of the stages of neural development?

7. How does the nervous system change in response to experience?

8. What are the barriers to recovery from damage in the nervous system? What new techniques are being developed to overcome some of these barriers?

The Central Nervous System

Summary and Guided Review

After studying this section in the text, fill in the blanks of the following summary.

The central nervous system (CNS) is composed of the _____ (1) and the

_____ _____ (2). In the CNS a bundle of axons is called a

_____ (3) and a group of cell bodies is known as a _____ (4). In the

peripheral nervous system (PNS), an axon bundle is called a _____ (5) and a group of cell

bodies is a referred to as a _____ (6). Early in development, the CNS begins as a hollow

tube and quickly differentiates into a spinal cord and three brain areas, the _____ (7)

(which in humans becomes the largest area), the _____ (8), and the

_____ (9).

The forebrain contains two _____ (10) hemispheres, the _____

(11), and the underlying _____ (12). The hemispheres are separated by the longitudinal

_____ (13). For the most part, each hemisphere receives information from and controls

movement in the _____ (14) side of the body. The outer layer of the cerebral hemispheres, the _____ (15), is wrinkled in appearance and contains many _____

(16) (ridges) and _____ (17) (grooves). The surface is composed mostly of cell

_____ (18), which accounts for its gray appearance. Its convoluted structure allows for

greater _____ (19) area and more efficient connections for axons. The interior of the

cortex, composed mostly of axons, appears _____ (20). Furthermore, the cortex is arranged

in six _____ (21) in most areas. The layers are organized in _____

(22) that run perpendicular to the cortical surface area; these provide a vertical unity to the layers and are

considered the primary _____ _____ (23) unit in the cortex.

Among humans, having a larger brain is not usually an indication of superior _____

(24). In comparing different species, the overall size of the brain is in proportion to the body, with larger animals

having larger brains. The intelligence of a species appears to be more related to the _____

(25) of the brain rather than its size. Among the most intelligent species, the cortex is

_____ (26) in proportion to other brain areas. The nervous system itself is arranged in a

_____ (27), with complexity in structure and in the behaviors controlled increasing from

the spinal cord up to the cortex.

Each hemisphere is divided into four lobes, and each lobe contributes to somewhat different functions. One

function that the _____ (28) lobes are involved in is movement, as well as some of the

most complex human capabilities. Different parts of the body are mapped onto areas of the

_____ _____ (29), the location of the primary motor cortex, in the

form of a _____ (30), such that the parts of the body that are capable of fine motor

movements (such as the fingers) are represented by a larger portion of the brain. The primary motor cortex also

works with neighboring _____ (31) motor areas and subcortical structures such as the

_____ _____ (32) in the control of movement.

_____ (33) area, another frontal lobe structure, is involved in _____

(34) production and grammar.

The _____ (35) cortex, which is the anterior portion of the frontal lobe and the largest

area of the human brain, contributes to a number of cognitive functions. Damage to this area can lead to many

types of problems, including an inability to plan or organize actions, learn from experience, control impulsive

behavior, or make decisions. It is also believed to be involved in mental illnesses such as schizophrenia and

_____ (36). In the 1940s and 1950s, it was common practice to "disconnect" the prefrontal cortex from the rest of the brain through a procedure known as a _____ (37). Over 40,000

of these were performed in the United States on people with mental illnesses of various types. The success of

this procedure was limited, and it eventually fell into disfavor, especially when effective

_____ (38) treatments become available in the 1950s. The importance of the frontal lobes

was clearly demonstrated in the case of _____ _____ (39) who

suffered specific deficits as a result of an accident in which a dynamite tamping iron pierced his skull and brain.

The parietal lobe contains the postcentral gyrus, which includes the _____ (40) cortex,

onto which the body senses are projected. This area is structured to represent the body in much the same way as

the primary motor cortex. The parietal lobe _____ _____ (41) provide

further processing of sensory information, integrating several different types of sensory input. A person with

damage to this area may experience _____ (42), a condition in which objects, people, and

activity on the side opposite the damage are ignored.

The _____ (43) lobe contains the auditory cortex and (on the left hemisphere)

_____ (44) area, which is involved in language comprehension and production. Visual

identification of objects is carried out in the _____ (45) temporal cortex; people with

damage to this area have difficulty recognizing objects by sight, including familiar people. People have reported

experiencing specific events or memories when parts of the temporal cortex have been stimulated during brain

surgery. Most of this brain stimulation research was conducted by the neurosurgeon _____

(46).

The entire occipital lobe is devoted to the sense of _____ (47). The primary projection

area is organized like a map of the retina (the back part of the eye). The remainder of the occipital cortical areas

process different components of images, such as color, form, and movement.

Other major structures of the forebrain include the _____ (48), which serves as a relay

station for sensory information, and the _____ (49), which is important in emotions and

motivated behavior. The hypothalamus controls the _____ (50) or master gland, which in

turn controls all other glands in the body. Bodily cycles such as sleep are controlled in part by the

_____ (51) gland.

One way in which the hemispheres communicate with each other is via structures such as the corpus

_____ (52), which is found at the bottom of the longitudinal fissure. In cases of severe

epilepsy, the corpus callosum may be surgically disconnected. People who have had this procedure can lead normal lives, but they show that to a certain extent that the two hemispheres have different functions, the left hemisphere being more involved in _____ (53) and the right in _____ (54) tasks and recognizing faces. Fluid-filled cavities called _____ (55) are located in the brain. They contain _____ (56) fluid, which transports nutrients to and wastes away from the CNS.

The midbrain contains several important structures. The superior and inferior _____ (57) are involved in eye movements and locating sounds, respectively. The midbrain also contains areas involved in movement; degeneration of cells in the _____ _____ (58) is implicated in Parkinson's disease. The ventral _____ (59) area plays a role in reward. The tube-shaped midbrain and hindbrain make up the brain _____ (60). The hindbrain includes the _____ (61), which is involved in vital functions such as respiration and keeping the heart beating, and the _____ (62), which is involved in sleep and arousal. The _____ (63) formation is a collection of nuclei running through the core of the midbrain and hindbrain. On the back of the brain stem is the _____ (64), which physically resembles the cerebral cortex and is essential in a number of motor and cognitive activities.

The spinal cord communicates between the brain and the body; it contains _____ _____ (65), which are motor programs for repetitive behaviors such as walking, and is responsible for certain reflexive behaviors. The spinal cord contains ascending _____ (66) tracts, which enter the spinal cord through the _____ (67) roots, and descending _____ (68) tracts, which exit the spinal cord through the _____ (69) roots. Some of the sensory neurons form connections directly or indirectly with motor neurons, which allow for spinal _____ (70).

The CNS is protected in a number of ways. It is covered by the _____ (71) (three-layered membrane), and the _____ (72) fluid cushions the brain. Harmful substances are prevented from entering the brain by the _____-_____ (73) barrier. The cells making up the walls of many of the _____ (74) serving the brain are tightly joined, which keeps many substances from passing through them. One area of the brain that is not protected in this way is the area _____ (75); when toxins are detected here, vomiting occurs.

Short Answer and Essay Questions

Answer the following questions.

1. What is a major advantage of the convoluted structure of the cerebral cortex?

2. Why is brain size alone not a good indication of intelligence of different species of animals (e.g. humans and elephants)? What is a better indication?

3. How are the primary motor and somatosensory cortices organized in relation to the body areas they receive information from or send information to? What determines how much space on the cortex is devoted to a particular area of the body?

4. What is the condition known as *neglect?* What is the likely cause of it?

5. Identify three of the many functions of the temporal lobe.

6. Name three areas in the midbrain and hindbrain that are involved in motor function.

7. Why is the blood-brain barrier important? Explain how the structure of the blood-brain barrier helps keep some harmful substances out of the brain. Why is it advantageous that the area postrema NOT be protected by the barrier?

The Peripheral Nervous System (PNS)

Summary and Guided Review

After studying this section in the text, fill in the blanks of the following summary.

The peripheral nervous system is composed of spinal and _____ (76) nerves; it can be divided into the _____ (77) nervous system, which is involved in the control of movement and carries sensory information to the CNS, and the autonomic nervous system (ANS), which is involved in the control of _____ (78) and glands. Two of these are sometimes considered part of the brain: the _____ (79) nerve, which carries information about smell, and the _____ (80) nerve, which carries information about vision,.

The ANS has two divisions: the _____ (81), which mobilizes bodily resources, and the _____ (82), which helps to restore energy. The sympathetic nervous system is highly coordinated due to the sympathetic _____ _____ (83). Most of the affected organs are stimulated together when this system is activated. In general, the two branches of the ANS have opposite effects on organs. For example, sympathetic activation _____ (84) heart rate, while parasympathetic activation _____ (85) it. However, both branches are active at the same time, but one may have a stronger effect at one time than the other.

Short Answer and Essay Questions

Answer the following questions.

8. From the information provided in Figure 3.19, which cranial nerves appear to be involved in eye movement? Which are probably involved in speaking?

9. Why is the sympathetic nervous system able to act in a more coordinated fashion than the parasympathetic? What advantage is there for the coordinated action of the sympathetic nervous system?

Development and Change in the Nervous System

Summary and Guided Review

After studying this section in the text, fill in the blanks of the following summary.

Once the neural tube has formed, the nervous system develops in stages. During the first stage, _____ (86), new neurons are formed at a high rate in the _____ (87) zone of the neural tube. In the second stage, the new neurons migrate toward the outer layers of the tube with the support of _____ (88) glial cells. During this time, the neurons have the potential to become many different types of neurons. The next stage is _____ _____ (89) formation, during which axons find their way to target cells and form synapses with them. The chemical environment of the developing nervous system is detected by _____ _____ (90) on the ends of the axons; they are attracted to certain locations and repelled from others by the chemicals. The genes _____ (91) 1 and 3 are involved in getting neurons to their final destination. The nervous system produces many more neurons than it needs, and during the next stage of development, _____ _____ (92), synapses are eliminated and neurons die, leaving only those that are functional and useful. A neuron is more likely to survive this stage if it fires at the same time as its neighbors, in part because postsynaptic neurons release _____ (93) that enhance the development of presynaptic neurons. Circuit pruning may occur before birth, even in the absence of environmental input. In the visual system, for example, waves of activity sweep through the _____ (94), strengthening the connections that have been formed. As synapses are formed, most neurons lose _____ (95), or the ability to undergo modification, while others remain flexible throughout the lifespan.

During the formation of the nervous system, disruption of development can have serious consequences. For example, periventricular _____ (96), a genetic disorder, produces a smooth cortex, which usually results in severe epilepsy and mental retardation. Prenatal exposure to _____ (97) consumed by the mother may result in neurons migrating to the wrong place or failing to become appropriately organized. Babies with fetal alcohol syndrome often have small and malformed_____ (98) and are mentally impaired. Ionizing _____ (99) is another environmental agent that can interfere with proliferation and migration, particularly if the mother is exposed between the 8th and 15th week of pregnancy. The nervous system is not considered fully mature until _____ (100) is complete, which happens sometime in late _____ (101) or adulthood. This process begins with the lower areas of the brain, and the last areas to mature are the _____ (102) lobes.

Throughout the lifespan, the nervous system may undergo _____ (103) in response to experience. Through this process, some synapses may be lost while new ones are formed, and areas of the brain devoted to specific functions may actually expand. Reorganization can even violate the doctrine of specific _____ _____ (104), which states that input to a particular sensory area will always result in the same type of sensation. In the blind, for example, some of the visual cortex may be taken over by the _____ (105) system, so the visual cortex actually participates in reading Braille. Sometimes reorganization can have detrimental effects, such as when a limb is amputated and the somatosensory neurons from nearby body parts take over the part of the cortex that was devoted to the missing limb; this is thought to be responsible for _____ (106) pain that amputees sometimes experience. Experiments with cats have revealed that if an animal sees only vertical stripes during early development, it will not be able later to detect objects that are oriented _____ (107).

Recovery from damage in the nervous system is limited. Although in some species, such as

_____ (108), damaged neurons easily regenerate, this is not true in all animals. In mammals, regeneration involving the regrowth of a severed _____ (109) occurs in the _____ (110) nervous system with the help of myelin. In the CNS, however, regrowth is unlikely because of the chemical environment, scar tissue, and the presence of glial and _____ (111) cells. Also, in most parts of the nervous system, new cells are not produced once proliferation ends. However, new cell production, or _____ (112), is seen in the hippocampus and the olfactory bulb, as well as at other sites when disease-related damage occurs. It may be possible to enhance regeneration as a treatment for brain damage.

Many people who suffer brain damage do recover some of the functions lost initially from the damage through the process of _____ (113), in which healthy neurons take over the connections that were lost due to the damage. Reorganization may also occur, such as in the case of _____ (114) (language impairment). Occasionally, researchers encounter a person who suffers from profound structural damage but who shows no apparent behavioral impairment. Examples from the text include cases of periventricular heterotopia, which has been discussed previously, and _____ (115), a condition in which blockage of cerebrospinal fluid can lead to severe retardation if untreated. These cases demonstrate that the nervous system is capable of compensating for even extensive damage, although the processes involved are not understood.

There are some other promising forms of therapy that may result in repairing CNS damage, including spinal cord injury and brain damage. Neuron growth enhancers and providing _____ _____ (116) or scaffolding for axons may promote self-repair of neurons in the CNS. Embryonic _____ (117) cells are pluripotent and may be used in the mature brain to replace cells damaged by injury or disease. Finally, humans with spinal cord injury (like actor Christopher Reeve) may benefit from tissue implants from the patient's own _____ _____ (118).

Short Answer and Essay Questions

Answer the following questions.

10. During neural development, axons often have to grow over extensive distances, and sometimes across hemispheres, in order to reach their target postsynaptic cells. How is this accomplished? Include in your answer the roles of growth cones and the *Robo1* and *Robo3* genes.

11. It is clear that the nervous system starts out with a lot more neurons than it needs. Why do you think it is advantageous for the nervous system to have so many neurons to start with, if many of them are only going to be lost? Keep in mind that the environment an animal encounters is at least somewhat unpredictable.

12. Maria was exposed to high levels of ionizing radiation during her 32nd week of pregnancy. She is concerned that this will have profound negative effects on her fetus, particularly its nervous system. What would you tell her?

13. What is syndactyly? How does surgical correction of syndactyly and the resulting changes in the brain demonstrate neural reorganization?

14. Describe some ways in which the CNS can compensate at the level of the synapse for the loss of neurons in specific locations.

15. Describe some possible treatments that may be used in the future to correct brain and spinal cord injuries.

Posttest

Use these multiple-choice questions to check your understanding of the chapter.

1. A ___ is the name for a bundle of neurons in the PNS.

    a. nerve

    b. tract

    c. nucleus

    d. ganglion

2. The spinal cord is part of the ___ nervous system.

    a. central

    b. autonomic

    c. peripheral

    d. sympathetic

3. Which of the following is the largest division of the mature CNS in humans?

a. forebrain

b. midbrain

c. hindbrain

d. spinal cord

4. The space separating the cerebral hemispheres is called the

    a. lateral fissure.

    b. corpus callosum.

    c. central sulcus.

    d. longitudinal fissure.

5. The surface of the cortex appears gray because it is composed mostly of

    a. unmyelinated axons.

    b. unmyelinated cell bodies.

    c. myelinated axons.

    d. myelinated cell bodies.

6. In the cortex, a ridge is called a

    a. fissure.

    b. gyrus.

    c. tract.

    d. sulcus.

7. What is the name of the 19th-century European anatomist who argued that because women have smaller brains than men, they are less intelligent?

    a. Penfield

    b. Ramón y Cajal

    c. Bischoff

    d. Sperry

8. Animal species that are the MOST intelligent tend to have

    a. bigger brains overall.

    b. more convolutions on the cortex.

    c. a proportionately larger forebrain.

d. b and c

9. The directional term *anterior* means

a. in front of.

b. behind.

c. above.

d. below.

10. The brain area controlling fine motor movement is located on the

a. prefrontal cortex.

b. precentral gyrus.

c. postcentral gyrus.

d. central sulcus.

11. The area of the motor cortex devoted to which of the following body areas is probably the smallest?

a. lips

b. tongue

c. thumb

d. thigh

12. Damage to the prefrontal cortex is LEAST likely to result in problems with

a. decision making.

b. planning.

c. speech comprehension.

d. impulse.

13. Who among the following was a proponent of lobotomies as a treatment for mental illness?

a. Penfield

b. Gage

c. Freeman

d. Bischoff

14. The somatosensory cortex is located in the ___ lobe.

a. frontal

b. occipital

c. temporal

d. parietal

15. Identifying objects by touch is a function of the

    a. somatosensory cortex.

    b. parietal association cortex.

    c. visual cortex.

    d. inferior temporal cortex.

16. Modern computer studies of the skull of Phineas Gage have revealed the extent of damage to the

    a. frontal lobes.

    b. corpus callosum.

    c. parietal lobes.

    d. brain stem.

17. Which of the following is NOT a function of the temporal lobes?

    a. processing auditory information

    b. language comprehension

    c. fine motor control

    d. visual identification of objects

18. Electrical stimulation of the association areas of the temporal lobe may result in the patient experiencing

    a. intense pain.

    b. buzzing sounds.

    c. bright lights.

    d. vivid memories.

19. The occipital lobe processes ____ information.

    a. visual

    b. auditory

    c. somatosensory

    d. a and b

20. The thalamus receives information from all of the sensory systems EXCEPT the system for

a. vision.

b. hearing.

c. smell.

d. taste.

21. The hypothalamus is located ___ the thalamus.

a. above

b. below

c. behind

d. in front of

22. The ___ is the body's "master" endocrine gland.

a. pituitary

b. pineal

c. hypothalamus

d. pons

23. The sleep-inducing hormone melatonin is released by the

a. pituitary gland.

b. pineal gland.

c. hypothalamus.

d. pons.

24. Which statement regarding the corpus callosum is FALSE?

a. It consists of neuron tracts connecting the two hemispheres.

b. It is the only place in the brain where information crosses from one side to the other.

c. It may be severed in order to help control epileptic seizures.

d. It allows the left side of the brain to share information with the right.

25. Which of the following structures is NOT part of the brain stem?

a. lateral ventricle

b. midbrain

c. pons

d. medulla

26. All of the following structures are located in the midbrain EXCEPT the

    a. superior colliculi.

    b. ventral tegmental area.

    c. pons.

    d. substantia nigra.

27. Heart rate and breathing are controlled by the

    a. pons.

    b. cerebellum.

    c. superior colliculi.

    d. medulla.

28. A person with damage to the cerebellum may

    a. be blind.

    b. be unable to recognize familiar objects.

    c. be insensitive to pain.

    d. have problems with movement.

29. The cerebrospinal fluid protects the brain in all of the following ways EXCEPT that it doesn't

    a. provide nourishment to brain cells.

    b. cushion the brain.

    c. remove waste products from the CNS.

    d. prevent toxins from entering the CNS.

30. The skeletal muscles are MOST directly controlled by the ___ nervous system.

    a. autonomic

    b. somatic

    c. sympathetic

    d. central

31. Which of the following cranial nerves is sometimes considered part of the CNS rather than the PNS?

    a. oculomotor

    b. auditory

    c. vagus

d. optic

32. Which of the following is more a result of parasympathetic than sympathetic activation?

    a. increased digestive activity

    b. increased heart rate

    c. increased blood pressure

    d. increased respiration

33. The stage of neural development in which axons grow toward their target connections is called

    a. proliferation.

    b. migration.

    c. circuit formation.

    d. circuit pruning.

34. Cell proliferation occurs

    a. in the innermost layer of the neural tube.

    b. in the outermost layers of the neural tube.

    c. throughout the neural tube.

    d. in the location of a neuron's final destination.

35. Cells that form a scaffold for neural migration are called

    a. astrocytes.

    b. radial glial cells.

    c. myelin cells.

    d. ladder cells.

36. During the first three weeks after birth, the neurons in a monkey's corpus callosum

    a. triple in number.

    b. increase by about 8 million.

    c. decrease by about 8 million.

    d. undergo very little change.

37. Neural plasticity is retained to the greatest extent in adulthood in which of the following brain areas?

    a. primary visual cortex

    b. somatosensory cortex

c. primary motor cortex

d. association cortex

38. Which of the following is NOT a result of fetal exposure to alcohol?

a. improper migration of cells

b. failure of cells to form myelin

c. small brain size

d. mental retardation

39. Which of the following brain areas is among the last to undergo myelination?

a. frontal cortex

b. occipital cortex

c. spinal nerves

d. medulla

40. Which of the following is NOT an example of brain reorganization?

a. larger area of the somatosensory cortex devoted to the index finger in people who read Braille

b. the occipital cortex of people blind from birth responding to somatosensory information

c. phantom limb pain following amputation of a leg

d. regrowth of a severed spinal motor neuron

41. Regeneration is LEAST likely to occur in the

a. CNS of a frog.

b. PNS of a frog.

c. CNS of a mammal.

d. PNS of a mammal.

42. In the adult mammal, neurogenesis is MOST likely to occur in the

a. spinal cord.

b. medulla.

c. hippocampus.

d. hypothalamus.

43. Which of the following is NOT true of hydrocephalus?

a. It results from a blockage of the cerebrospinal fluid.

b. It can be treated using a drainage shunt.

c. Even without treatment, individuals usually have normal intelligence.

d. It affects the development of the CNS.

44. Which of the following is not a problem following stroke?

    a. Edema

    b. Abnormal protein deposits

    c. Excitotosis

    d. Paralysis

45. Which of the following is FALSE regarding traumatic brain injury? It

    a. can produce Alzheimer-like effects even in young brains.

    b. includes concussion as one of its mild forms.

    c. requires a severe blow, due to the brain's cushioning.

    d. can be minimized by 3 weeks of rest.

Answers

Guided Review

1. brain

2. spinal cord

3. tract

4. nucleus

5. nerve

6. ganglion

7. forebrain

8. midbrain

9. hindbrain

10. cerebral

11. thalamus

12. hypothalamus

13. fissure

14. opposite

15. cortex

16. gyri (plural of gyrus)

17. sulci (plural of sulcus) or fissures

18. bodies

19. surface

20. white

21. layers

22. columns

23. information processing

24. intelligence

25. convolutions

26. larger

27. hierarchy

28. frontal

29. precentral gyrus

30. homunculus

31. secondary

32. basal ganglia

33. Broca's

34. speech

35. prefrontal

36. depression

37. lobotomy

38. drug

39. Phineas Gage

40. somatosensory

41. association areas

42. neglect

43. temporal

44. Wernicke's

45. inferior

46. Penfield

47. vision

48. thalamus

49. hypothalamus

50. pituitary

51. pineal

52. callosum

53. language

54. spatial

55. ventricles

56. cerebrospinal

57. colliculi

58. substantia nigra

59. tegmental

60. stem

61. medulla

62. pons

63. reticular

64. cerebellum

65. pattern generators

66. sensory

67. dorsal

68. motor

69. ventral

70. reflexes

71. meninges

72. cerebrospinal

73. blood-brain

74. capillaries

75. postrema

76. cranial

77. somatic

78. organs

79. olfactory

80. optic

81. sympathetic

82. parasympathetic

83. ganglion chains

84. increases

85. decreases

86. proliferation

87. ventricular

88. radial

89. circuit formation

90. growth cones

91. *Robo*

92. circuit pruning

93. neurotrophins

94. retina

95. plasticity

96. heterotopia

97. alcohol

98. brains

99. radiation

100. myelination

101. adolescence

102. frontal

103. reorganization

104. nerve energies

105. somatosensory

106. phantom pain

107. horizontally

108. amphibians

109. axon

110. peripheral

111. immune

112. neurogenesis

113. compensation

114. aphasia

115. hydrocephalus

116. guide tubes

117. stem

118. olfactory mucosa

Short Answer and Essay Questions

1. One advantage is that it increases the surface area of the brain without increasing its size a great deal. This means more cortex can be packed into a small area.

2. If we compare between species, brain size is more related to body size than intelligence; the largest animals tend to have the largest brains. A good way of representing the connection between brain and intelligence is its complexity, particularly the degree to which the forebrain is developed. Humans' forebrains are larger and more extensively convoluted than apes' brains, which are larger and more convoluted than monkeys' brains, etc.

3. These areas of the brain are organized like maps of the body. Sensory neurons from adjacent areas of the body project to adjacent areas of the somatosensory cortex, and neurons from adjacent parts of the motor cortex control movement in adjacent areas of the body. Areas of the body that are either especially sensitive (because they contain a lot of sensory receptors) or capable of fine motor movement are represented by a larger

area of the cortex than areas that are less sensitive or not involved in fine motor movement. For example, the fingers are represented to a greater extent in both cortices than is the back.

4. This is usually the result of damage to the association cortex in the parietal lobe. It occurs because this part of the brain is involved in various spatial tasks, such as being able to tell where things are in the environment and being able to locate one's own body in space. Persons who suffer damage to this area in the right hemisphere may not pay attention to things on the left side of the body; such an individual may not even recognize that an arm or leg belongs to her or him.

5. The temporal lobes are where auditory information is initially processed and most of language comprehension occurs; the lobes also contain auditory and visual association areas responsible for tasks such as recognition of faces and other visual objects.

6. Three areas with a role in motor function in the midbrain and hindbrain are the substantia nigra, the cerebellum, and the reticular formation.

7. The main route for toxins and other substances to get into organs is through the blood stream.. The brain is especially vulnerable (because most adult CNS neurons do not replicate), so it is especially important to keep toxins out of the brain. In many parts of the brain, the capillaries are structured to do just that. The cells that make up the capillary walls are tightly packed together, so that very few substances can pass through them without going through special channels, and the special channels are selective in what they allow through. However, not all brain areas are protected in this manner. In the area postrema, toxins can get in, and it is actually beneficial that they do in some cases. If a toxin is detected in this area, it triggers the vomiting response, and if the source of the toxin is in the stomach, it will be removed from the body.

8. Cranial nerves III (oculomotor), IV (trochlear), and VI (abducens) control eye movement. Cranial nerves X (vagus) and XII (hypoglossal) are probably involved in speech.

9. The sympathetic nervous system consists of components of several of the spinal nerves serving various internal organs. The activity of its neurons is coordinated because many of them are interconnected within the sympathetic ganglion chain just outside the spinal cord, which allows for a coordinated response. No such structure exists in the parasympathetic division. The advantage of the coordinationof the sympathetic division is that it provides a mobilization of most of the body's resources in times of stress.

10. First of all, axons contain a growth cone, which is used to find the correct pathway. The cone is

sensitive to the external chemical environment, and it is attracted to certain places and repelled from others. The sensitivity of the growth cone to different chemicals can also change over time as the axon grows into different areas. The *Robo1* gene produces a chemical that repels axons; so when it is active, axons do not grow across the midline of the brain. Activation of the *Robo3* gene leads to axons being attracted across the midline. Once it is deactivated, the axon is no longer attracted to the midline and continues to grow in that side of the brain.

11. By initially overproducing neurons, the nervous system allows for streamlining (elimination of unused and retention of used connections) to eliminate errors in circuit formation. The alternative to overproduction would be more precise circuit formation, which would require complex chemical and genetic codes. In addition, this strategy allows for adaptation to varied environmental conditions that could not be predicted in advance. An example of such selection occurred in the experiment in which kittens were reared with only horizontal or only vertical stripes.

12. While there may be some detrimental effects, they would probably be worse if she had been exposed earlier, between 8 and 15 weeks of gestation, because that is when proliferation and migration of neurons are occurring at high rates.

13. Syndactyly is a condition in which the fingers are connected by a web of tissue, are of limited usefulness, and are mapped onto overlapping areas of the somatosensory cortex. Within a week following surgical separation, patients' brains showed dramatic changes in that the separated fingers were now represented in distinct locations on the somatosensory cortex.

14. Healthy presynaptic neurons can form new terminals to create replacement connections. Postsynaptic cells can create new receptors to compensate for reduced presynaptic input. And "silent" collaterals, terminals that were inactive, may become active almost immediately following injury.

15. One possibility is introducing new neurons, either from fetal cells or stem cells. The other possibilities involve manipulating the environment of the mature CNS so that it does not inhibit axon regeneration. These mechanisms include providing the nervous system with substances that can promote neural growth, inhibit those substances that inhibit neural growth, serve as scaffolds for developing axons, and/or block the immune response that may be harmful to developing axons. Use of glial and stem cells from the person's own olfactory mucosa may also be helpful in restoration or improvement in function.

Posttest

1. a　2. a　3. a　4. d　5. b　6. b　7. c　8. d　9. a　10. b　11. d　12. c　13. c　14. d　15. b　16. a　17. c
18. d　19. a　20. c　21. b　22. a　23. b　24. b　25. a　26. c　27. d　28. d　29. d　30. b　31. d　32. a
33. c　34. a　35. b　36. c　37. d　38. b　39. a　40. d　41. c　42. c　43. c　44. b　45 c

4

The Methods and Ethics of Research

Chapter Outline

Science, Research, and Theory

Theory and Tentativeness in Science

Experimental Versus Correlational Studies

Research Techniques

Staining and Imaging Neurons

Light and Electron Microscopy

Measuring and Manipulating Brain Activity

APPLICATION: BRAIN IMPLANTS THAT MOVE

Brain-Imaging Techniques

APPLICATION: SCANNING KING TUT

Investigating Heredity

Research Ethics

Plagiarism and Fabrication

Protecting the Welfare of Research Participants

Gene Therapy

IN THE NEWS: A BRAVE NEW WORLD?

Stem Cell Therapy

Learning Objectives

After reading this chapter, you should be able to answer the following questions.

1. What roles do theories and hypotheses play in scientific research, and why are scientists often

tentative in drawing firm conclusions about the results of their studies?

2. How do correlational and experimental studies differ?

3. How are staining, imaging, and microscopic techniques used to study individual cells and their components? What have such techniques revealed?

4. What are the procedures for measuring and manipulating brain activity?

5. What are the procedures for imaging brains?

6. What correlational methods are used for studying heredity in humans?

7. What are the different types of genetic engineering studies?

8. What is plagiarism? Fabrication? Why are these problematic for science?

9. What issues must be considered in research using human participants? Animal subjects?

10. What are the ethical problems associated with gene therapy and stem cell research?

Science, Research, and Theory

Summary and Guided Review

After studying this section in the text, fill in the blanks of the following summary.

Science requires that information be derived from observation, a concept known as

_____ (1). Scientific observations should be objective, so that two or more people

watching the same event will describe it in the same way.

Like many other scientists, biological psychologists are careful about the way they interpret their research

results. Knowledge often undergoes _____ (2) over time; what is thought of as a "fact"

today may be shown to be incorrect in the future. For example, it was recently discovered that axon regrowth

and _____ (3) may occur in the mature primate central nervous system. Many scientists use

_____ (4) to explain observations and guide their research. They generate

_____ (5), which are testable predictions derived from theories. If a hypothesis is found to

be incorrect, then the theory must be revised. The _____ (6) theory of schizophrenia is a 3 good example of the need to alter theories when new data become available

An experiment is a study in which the researcher manipulates at least one _____ (7) variable and measures its effects on one or more _____ (8) variables. Experimenters also eliminate _____ (9) variables that might influence behavior, or equate them across subjects. Causal relationships cannot be determined from correlational studies because when two variables are found to be correlated, there may be a _____ (10) variable that accounts for the relationship between the two. Although experimental studies are most useful for determining cause-effect relationships, they are sometimes more artificial than _____ (11) studies. If a researcher measured the extent of frontal lobe impairment in a large group of people and then examined their records for criminal behavior, they might find that criminals are more likely to have frontal lobe deficits than other individuals. This would be an example of a _____ (12) study. This relationship could not be studied as an _____ (13) study for ethical reasons.

Short Answer and Essay Questions

Answer the following questions.

1. Why do researchers avoid using words like "truth" and "proof" when they discuss the results of their work?

2. If experimental studies are the only ones that allow us to determine cause-effect relationships, why are other studies used at all? What are the limitations of experimental studies?

3. Discuss how the dopamine theory of schizophrenia has evolved. What observations led to the dopamine theory? How was it tested? What were the results of these tests? What is the current status of the theory?

Research Techniques

Summary and Guided Review

After studying this section in the text, fill in the blanks of the following summary.

Brain researchers use a variety of techniques to study brain tissue, including staining and imaging neurons. An early method, invented by Camillo _____ (14) and used by Santiago Ramón y Cajal to examine individual neurons, involved staining brain tissue so that about 5% of the neurons would stand out from the rest. Neural pathways (bundles of axons) can be identified by using _____ (15) stains, whereas groups of cell bodies can be identified with _____ (16) stains. Injection of fluorescent substances such as _____ (17), which is transferred between neurons, also allows researchers to trace pathways between neurons. Injecting radioactively labelled glucose allows researchers to see which brain areas are most active during particular activities; this technique is known as _____ (18). Candace Pert used a similar technique to identify _____ (19) receptors in brain tissue. Immunocytochemistry involves attaching a dye, which is usually fluorescent, to _____ (20) to make receptors, neurotransmitters, or other cellular components visible. Using in situ _____ (21), in which radioactive DNA is paired with messenger RNA, researchers have been able to locate specific sites of gene activity.

Light microscopes magnify cells so that their larger components such as cell bodies, some organelles, axons, and _____ (22), are discernible. Electron microscopes can magnify images up to _____ (23) times by passing electrons through objects and onto photographic film. This technique allows researchers to see such things as synaptic _____ (24). A _____ (25) electron microscope produces a three-dimensional image by inducing the object being observed to emit electrons. Two of the newest examples of advances in microscopic technology are the _____ _____ _____ (26) microscope and the _____ _____ (27) microscope.

Brain activity in the form of waves may be measured using electrodes attached to the scalp; the record of this activity is called an _____ (28). This technique has excellent _____ (29) resolution, but poor spatial resolution, meaning it is difficult to locate the exact area in which changes are occurring. Researchers can present a specific stimulus several times; the EEGs are recorded and then averaged to cancel out the "noise" from the rest of the brain, producing an _____ (30) potential.

When researchers want to locate a specific brain area for recording or manipulation, a _____ (31) instrument is used to insert an electrode or cannula, in a location determined from a stereotaxic _____ (32). A small electrode may be inserted and left in place to determine what effect stimulation of the brain area containing the electrode will have on the subject's behavior. A _____ (33) is used for single-unit recording while the subject is presented with different stimuli or engages in a certain behavior. A narrow tube called a _____ (34) may be inserted for delivering chemicals to specific brain areas or removing brain fluid, a procedure known as _____ (35).

The study of people with brain damage may give scientists clues about which brain areas are involved in which functions, but more precise methods require experimentally damaging specific areas and observing the effects under controlled conditions. Such studies are done with animals. A procedure called _____ (36) involves removing brain tissue; this may be done with more precision using a vacuum to remove the desired tissue, a technique known as _____ (37). Neural tissue may also be _____ (38), or damaged by the use of electricity, heat, or chemicals. Chilling a brain region or using certain chemicals produces a _____ (39) lesion, allowing the researcher to make comparisons before and during damage and following recovery. In humans, a cannula or electrode may be implanted in order to facilitate surgery or to treat certain conditions (such as epilepsy or Parkinson's disease). Implants of electrodes into the human brain have been developed to help control a mechanical arm or keyboard. This would be very useful for people with _____ (40) who eventually become unable to move or speak.

Brain imaging techniques allow for the examination of intact brains; they can reveal areas of damage as well as show which areas are active in response to specific stimulation or during specific behaviors. The first modern imaging technique that was developed was the _____ (41) scan, which takes several X-rays of the brain and combines the different images using a computer; the horizontal "slices" thus form a composite view of the entire brain.. Another technique is _____ _____ (42) imaging, which works by measuring radio-frequency waves from hydrogen (or other elemental) atoms exposed to a magnetic field. A variant of this procedure, _____ _____ (43), imaging measures the movement of water molecules and is useful for identifying brain pathways. Although these techniques produce pictures of the brain, none shows changes over time. Brain activity may be measured by injecting radioactive chemicals such as 2-DG into the bloodstream and then identifying areas of the brain that take up greater amounts of the chemical. This technique is known as _____ (44), and it allows researchers to determine which brain areas are most involved in specific activities. Another measure of brain activity is the _____ (45) MRI procedure (fMRI), which detects differential oxygen increases. Some researchers are concerned about this technique's lower sensitivity and less-than-perfect test-retest reliability. A relatively new non-invasive technique called _____ (46) uses a magnetic coil to induce changes in electrical activity in the brain. Although this procedure shows some promise as a therapeutic tool, at the moment it is most likely to be useful for _____ (47).

The heredity of behavior in humans may be studied in family, adoption, and _____ (48) studies. By comparing the behaviors of related individuals, researchers can determine the extent to which heredity influences traits among related individuals. For example, family studies have revealed that between parents and their children there is a _____ (49) of about .42 in IQ scores and a rate of about _____ (50) for schizophrenia in the offspring of a schizophrenic parent as compared to the general population rate of 1%. However, _____ (51) studies reveal that when children are adopted out, the correlation of their IQ scores with those of their biological parents drops to .22, indicating that some of the similarity between parents and children stems from the environment. One of the best ways of examining the influence of heredity on behavior in humans is through twin studies. _____ (52) twins, who share the same genetic material, are compared to _____ (53) twins; this comparison controls for environment to some extent, although not entirely. Neither twin nor adoption studies eliminate the influence of the _____ (54) environment or of the time from birth to adoption. Twin studies reveal correlations of IQ scores in dizygotic twins to be around _____ (55) whereas that for monozygotic twins is about _____ (56), suggesting a strong genetic component to intelligence. Sometimes researchers use the term _____ (57) rate to refer to the frequency with which relatives are alike in a characteristic or disorder. Studies show that the concordance rates for schizophrenia in monozygotic twins is about _____ (58) times the concordance rates for dizygotic twins.

At present, the experimental manipulation of genes, or _____ (59), is done mostly with nonhuman animals, particularly mice. One way of changing mice's genetic makeup is by inserting non-functioning DNA into mouse embryos and then breeding the offspring, thus creating _____ (60) mice. The _____ _____ (61) procedure is used to alter a gene's activity by blocking the cell's protein building activity. Gene _____ (62) is a procedure in which a gene from another organism is introduced into a recipient's cells; when the gene is inserted into a developing embryo, the result is referred to as a _____ (63) animal. Gene therapy has been used to treat _____ (64) experienced by individuals like Ashanthi, and doctors have had

some success using gene transfer to treat the memory disorder _____ (65).

Short Answer and Essay Questions

Answer the following questions.

4. What is the advantage of autoradiography over Nissl and myelin staining procedures? Give an example of an important discovery that has resulted from the use of autoradiography.

5. How were immunocytochemistry and in situ hybridization used together to identify the likely protein responsible for night-migration in birds? In your answer, be sure to explain how both of these methods work.

6. What are evoked potentials, and how are they obtained? What do they measure?

7. Describe the uses of a stereotaxic instrument.

8. Why do researchers who want to understand brain damage in humans use ablation and lesioning in animal studies?

9. How do CT and MRI scans work? What does each method reveal about the brain, and what are the limitations of each of these methods?

10. How do PET and fMRI scans work? What does each method reveal about the brain, and what are the limitations of each of these methods?

11. Distinguish between adoption and family studies. Why are adoption studies generally better for studying heredity of traits than family studies?

12. Give some examples of genetic engineering that have been used for research and therapeutic purposes.

Research Ethics

Summary and Guided Review

After studying this section in the text, fill in the blanks of the following summary.

Scientists must adhere to guidelines for ethical conduct. These guidelines cover many aspects of scientists' work, including publishing information and using humans and animals in research. One type of ethical violation involves claiming someone else's ideas as one's own; this is known as _____ (66). A more serious violation, in which false or misleading data are published, is _____ (67). These types of violations are potentially damaging for the scientific community.

Scientists are also obligated to treat their human research participants with dignity and respect and to obtain their informed _____ (68) before the individuals participate in the research. This means that participants are fully aware of any potential risks involved in the research. Some behavioral studies, such as the one by Albert Ax described in the book, employ _____ (69), which involves withholding information or giving false information at the outset of a study. Some researchers and subjects' rights advocates say its use is never justified.

Many of the recent advances in medicine would not have been possible without animal research. Animals are used as research subjects for a variety of reasons. Many procedures that are potentially dangerous to humans are performed on animals. Animals' genetic makeup and _____ (70) can be controlled. Consequently, it is easier to interpret results from studies with animals than those from studies with humans. This preference for using animals in potentially harmful studies is considered by some to be a dual ethical standard, which they have labeled _____ (71) Most laboratory animals are _____ (72), and only about 3.5% are _____ (73) (those most closely related to humans). Animal rights _____ (74), people who work on behalf of the welfare of research animals, may cooperate with animal researchers to improve conditions for research animals, or they may damage or destroy labs and threaten to harm or actually harm the researchers themselves. Scientists who use animals in research are obligated to treat them humanely. Animals must be well cared for, and pain and suffering should be _____ (75). Overall, treatment of research animals seems to be improving, and some researchers are using alternative methods such as tissue _____ (76) and _____ (77) simulations.

Perhaps the most controversial area of medical research using humans is in _____ _____ (78). Such research involves altering the genetic makeup or genetic activity of individuals in order to treat specific problems. As the result of a research participant's death in 1999, stricter _____ (79) for such research are expected. There are other ethical concerns with this type of research as well, including its impact on successive generations of human beings. Evidence of the way in which genetic information might be used, or misused, comes from promises of "_____ (80) babies" created in fertility clinics. Similar efforts are occurring in _____ (81) where children are sent to summer camp to be genetically tested in order to predict abilities and recommend appropriate careers.

The use of human _____ (82) cells has also been a controversial area of research. Stem cells have been used to improve heart functioning, and many researchers expect that stem cells will eventually be used to grow human _____ (83) for transplants, and stem cell research will provide a better understanding of the development of disease. Most human stem cells come from "extra" embryos from fertility treatments. The Bush administration _____ (84) federal funding of research with newly-developed stem cell lines, and cells from older lines are of little value for human research. However, _____ (85) reversed this policy in 2009. Because of the complexity of the issue, it is likely that stem cell research will continue to be controversial.

Short Answer and Essay Questions

Answer the following questions.

13. Describe the study by Albert Ax. Why was this study ethically controversial? Would researchers be able to do this study now? Why or why not?

14. If medical research is done to benefit humans, why are animals used as research subjects?

15. What is speciesism?

16. In what way does the movie *GATTACA* reflect concerns in our society about genetic research and genetic manipulation?

17. What is the major ethical controversy of human stem-cell research?

Posttest

Use these multiple-choice questions to check your understanding of the chapter.

1. A theory is

a. an established scientific fact.

b. a prediction that can be tested.

c. an explanation for our observations.

d. All of the above.

2. Which of the following statements is a biological psychologist LEAST likely to make?

   a. These results suggest that people who drink heavily may suffer from memory loss.

   b. These results show that some people who drink heavily suffer from memory loss.

   c. These results prove that heavy drinking results in memory loss.

   d. From these results, it appears that memory loss may be a result of heavy drinking.

3. A detailed study of a single person showing interesting behavior is called

   a. a case study.

   b. an experiment.

   c. a survey.

   d. None of the above.

4. A study that allows researchers to determine if a cause-effect relationship exists between two variables is a(n)

   a. correlational study.

   b. experiment.

   c. naturalistic observational study.

   d. None of the above.

5. Dr. Joy observes the behavior of mice in large colonies, taking particular note of social interactions, but does not interfere with the mice in any way. What type of study is this?

   a. an experiment

   b. a case study

   c. naturalistic observation

   d. a survey

6. Dr. Hagen performs a study in which participants are given different amounts of alcohol and then are tested in a driving simulation. In this study, alcohol is the

   a. dependent variable.

b. correlational variable.

c. confounded variable.

d. independent variable.

7. Research volunteers are given either a placebo pill or a drug containing a small amount of amphetamine. Then, the volunteers are asked to play a game of chess on a computer. The researchers believe that the amphetamine will interfere with the participants' ability to play well. What is the dependent variable in this study?

a. the computer game

b. the placebo

c. the amphetamine

d. performance in the chess game

8. Female and male college students are compared on a mathematical test. This is BEST described as a(n)

a. experiment.

b. independent variable.

c. correlational study.

d. None of the above.

9. The dopamine theory of schizophrenia

a. suggests that the disorder is a result of dopamine overactivity in the brain.

b. was developed after some researchers noticed drug users showing signs of schizophrenia.

c. does not account for all cases of schizophrenia.

d. all of the above.

10. The staining procedure that allowed 19th-century anatomists to study individual neurons was discovered by

a. Santiago Ramón y Cajal.

b. Camillo Golgi.

c. Candace Pert.

d. Henrik Mouritsen.

11. If researchers want to find a nucleus (collection of cell bodies) in the hypothalamus, they are MOST likely to use which of the following techniques?

a. Nissl staining

b. myelin staining

c. in situ hybridization

d. immunocytochemistry

12. ___ is a substance that may be injected into one area of the brain and then transferred to other cells.

   a. Fluorogold

   b. Nissl stain

   c. Golgi stain

   d. Myelin stain

13. Which procedure involves the use of radioactive sugar molecules, which are absorbed by active neurons and then detected on photographic film?

   a. immunocytochemistry

   b. Nissl staining

   c. autoradiography

   d. fluorogold staining

14. Brain researchers discovered opiate receptors using which technique?

   a. Nissl staining

   b. autoradiography

   c. immunocytochemistry

   d. Golgi staining

15. Immunocytochemistry involves the use of ___, whereas in situ hybridization involves the use of ___.

   a. radioactive DNA; dye-labeled antibodies

   b. dye-labelled antibodies; radioactive DNA

   c. dye-labelled antibodies; radioactive sugar molecules

   d. radioactive sugar molecules; radioactive DNA

16. Cryptochromes are proteins that

   a. bind to opiate receptor sites.

   b. impair the immune system's ability to fight infection.

   c. may be responsible for night-migration in some types of birds.

d. interfere with messenger RNA.

17. An electron microscope allows us to see images of objects magnified up to ___ times.

   a. 250

   b. 2,500

   c. 25,000

   d. 250,000

18. The EEG has relatively ___ temporal resolution and ___ spatial resolution.

   a. good; good

   b. poor; poor

   c. good; poor

   d. poor; good

19. Researchers who use evoked potentials to study brain activity are MOST likely interested in

   a. studying patients who are asleep.

   b. identifying how the brain responds to brief changes in stimuli.

   c. recording from single neurons.

   d. injecting chemicals in the brain.

20. A stereotaxic instrument may be used to

   a. place a recording electrode in a specific location in the brain.

   b. place a stimulating electrode in a specific location in the brain.

   c. locate a specific area of the brain in which to inject chemicals.

   d. All of the above.

21. Microdialysis is a procedure for

   a. removing brain fluid for analysis.

   b. injecting chemicals into the brain to destroy neurons.

   c. injecting radioactive substances into the brain to measure activity.

   d. removing neurons from the brain for analysis.

22. Jerry is undergoing a procedure in which several electrodes are attached to his scalp, and the activity of neurons under the electrodes is recorded. What is this procedure called?

a. EEG

b. PET

c. MRI

d. CT

23. Aspiration is BEST thought of as a form of

    a. lesioning.

    b. recording brain activity.

    c. ablation.

    d. reversible lesioning.

24. Which of the following brain imaging techniques involves the use of X-rays?

    a. MRI

    b. fMRI

    c. PET

    d. CT

25. If a brain researcher is interested in studying which brain areas are MOST active during a spatial skills task, the procedure of choice would be

    a. MRI.

    b. PET.

    c. CT.

    d. TMS

26. The effects of heredity and environment on behavior are MOST confounded in

    a. family studies.

    b. adoption studies.

    c. twin studies.

    d. genetic engineering studies.

27. A correlation of –.75 indicates

    a. a weak relationship between two variables.

    b. a strong relationship between two variables.

    c. no relationship between two variables.

d. a mistake; correlations cannot be negative.

28. When researchers look at the IQ scores of children raised by adoptive parents, there is a correlation of about ___ with the IQ scores of their biological parents.

    a. 0.42

    b. 0.47

    c. 0.60

    d. 0.22

29. Compared to identical twins, fraternal twins show ___ concordance for schizophrenia.

    a. a higher

    b. a lower

    c. the same

    d. no

30. The ___ technique of genetic engineering involves preventing or reducing the expression of a particular gene by occupying the cell's ribonucleic acid with a synthetic strand of DNA.

    a. antisense DNA

    b. transgenic

    c. antisense RNA

    d. knockout

31. People with SCID

    a. may die if exposed to a normal environment.

    b. suffer from severe mental disorders.

    c. may be aided by genetic engineering.

    d. a and c

32. Jennifer is a graduate student studying the effects of electrical stimulation on the cingulate gyrus in rat's brains. Her initial results are not what she expected, and because she is worried about finishing her dissertation on time, she changes some of her data so that it fits her hypothesis. Jennifer has engaged in

    a. plagiarism.

b. deception.

c. fabrication.

d. breaking the law.

33. Researchers who use humans as participants

    a. are barred from intentionally deceiving them.

    b. may withhold information from them but may not lie to them.

    c. must fully inform them about all details of a procedure beforehand.

    d. may not withhold information about risks or discomfort that might occur.

34. What percentage of laboratory animals are primates?

    a. more than 90%

    b. about 50%

    c. between 10% and 15%

    d. fewer than 5%

35. Regarding animal research guidelines, which of the following is FALSE?

    a. Procedures involving pain may not be performed on primates.

    b. Stress should be minimized.

    c. Procedures must be approved by an Institutional Animal Care and Use Committee.

    d. Researchers must provide humane housing and medical care.

36. The researcher Edward Taub, whose laboratory at Silver Springs, Maryland, made national headlines in the 1980s,

    a. is currently serving a prison sentence for animal abuse.

    b. received an award from the American Psychological Society.

    c. was able to complete his research after his grant was reinstated by the National Institutes of Health.

    d. none of the above.

37. Which of the following statements regarding gene therapy research is TRUE?

    a. No human has died from gene therapy research.

    b. Some humans have been treated for diseases using gene therapy research.

    c. Gene therapy research with humans is illegal in the United States.

    d. The idea that "designer babies" can be created is science fiction not reality.

Answers

Guided Review

1. empiricism

2. changes

3. neurogenesis

4. theories

5. hypotheses

6. dopamine

7. independent

8. dependent

9. extraneous

10. confounding

11. correlational

12. correlational

13. experimental

14. Golgi

15. myelin

16. Nissl

17. fluorogold

18. autoradiography

19. opiate

20. antibodies

21. hybridization

22. dendrites

23. 250,000

24. vesicles

25. scanning

26. confocal laser scanning

27. two-photon

28. electroencephalogram (EEG)

29. temporal

30. evoked

31. stereotaxic

32. atlas

33. microelectrode

34. cannula

35. microdialysis

36. ablation

37. aspiration

38. lesioned

39. reversible

40. ALS (Lou Gehrig's disease)

41. CT or CAT

42. magnetic resonance

43. diffusion tensor

44. PET (positron emission tomography)

45. functional

46. TMS (transcranial magnetic stimulation)

47. research

48. twin

49. correlation

50. 13%

51. adoption

52. Monozygotic

53. dizygotic

54. prenatal

55. 0.60

56. 0.86

57. concordance

58. three

59. genetic engineering

60. knockout

61. antisense RNA

62. transfer

63. transgenic

64. SCID

65. Alzheimer's

66. plagiarism

67. fabrication

68. consent

69. deception

70. environments

71. speciesism

72. rodents

73. primates

74. activists

75. minimized

76. cultures

77. computer

78. gene therapy

79. guidelines

80. designer

81. China

82. stem

83. organs

84. banned

85. Obama

Short Answer and Essay Questions

1. Knowledge, or what we think we know to be true, changes. Many ideas that are currently accepted as fact may someday be shown to be incorrect. Therefore, scientists are usually careful about drawing such conclusions from their research. They prefer to be tentative about their conclusions.

2. There are many types of questions that cannot be answered using experimental procedures. Researchers are bound by ethical and legal rules that forbid the use of humans for many types of potentially interesting studies. Also, there are many variables that researchers are unable to manipulate, such as age, sex, and other factors that are inherent to individuals.

3. The theory was first developed when some researchers noticed that people using certain drugs that increase dopamine activity in the brain showed symptoms of schizophrenia (but these symptoms disappeared when the drugs wore off). It was suggested that schizophrenia is caused by excess dopamine. One hypothesis

used to test this theory was that schizophrenics should improve when given drugs that decrease dopamine activity. However, not all schizophrenics show this expected result, and therefore the dopamine theory is recognized as being an incomplete explanation of schizophrenia.

4. Autoradiography allows researchers to see which cells are active, whereas other staining methods only show neurons and their parts against the background. One discovery that stemmed from this method was that the visual cortex contains a map of the retina and the visual field. Another discovery was the identification of opiate receptors in the brain.

5. Immunocytochemistry (in which fluorescent antibodies are used to locate specific cell components, including proteins) revealed that cryptochromes were present in both night-migrating and nonmigrating birds during the day, but that these proteins were present at night only in the night-migrating birds. This suggested that cryptochromes were responsible for migration guided by magnetic fields. Before they did this study, the researchers used in situ hybridization (in which radioactively labelled DNA is paired with the cells' own mRNA) to determine which of two cryptochromes to focus on, CRY1 or CRY2. Results showed that CRY2 was constructed in the nuclei, while CRY1 was constructed outside the nucleus; because a magnetoreceptor would likely function outside the nucleus, the researchers focused on CRY1.

6. Evoked potentials are EEG recordings that are taken over a number of trials, during which target stimuli are present or absent. They represent an average response of the brain to specific stimuli, because by looking at several different trials, the change in brain activity in response to the stimulus (which is only weakly detected by the EEG) can be filtered out of the rest of the brain's normal activity (background noise).

7. Stereotaxic instruments are used to hold an animal's head in place and to locate a target in the brain where stimulation or measurement is to take place. The instrument is used to implant electrodes to stimulate the brain or measure activity in neurons, or to insert a cannula to deliver chemicals or collect brain fluids.

8. Researchers often want to know the function of a very specific brain area, and studying humans with brain damage is problematic, because brain damage is rarely limited to the areas of interest. Using animals allows researchers to introduce damage to very specific areas of the brain and to learn about the effects of damage under more controlled conditions.

9. A person receiving a CT scan is injected with a dye, and then X-rays of the intact brain are taken from several different angles; finally, the images are compiled by a computer to show a three-dimensional image. In the past, this procedure has been slow to produce the image, but newer technology allows for faster computing.

The image, of course, is a still shot of the brain, and it cannot show activity or change as the brain functions. MRI scans measure the radio waves given off by hydrogen atoms in the brain when exposed to a magnetic field. Images are formed because of the different concentrations of this element in different structures. No substances such as dyes or radioactive materials need to be given. This procedure is reasonably fast, and it is becoming less expensive (due to advances in technology), but it also produces a static image.

10. PET scans require the administration of radioactively labelled glucose, which is then taken up to differing degrees by different brain areas according to how active they are. Imaging the radioactivity provides a measure of each brain area's activity during stimulation or task performance.. i. This is an expensive procedure, and it only detects brain changes of at least 45 seconds duration. Also, the image of the different amounts of radiation must be superimposed on a scan of the brain, usually from an MRI. Functional MRIs measure differences in brain cells' oxygen consumption. They are relatively safe; the biggest disadvantage of this method is its price.

11. The difference between adoption and family studies is that adoption studies look at children raised in homes by adoptive parents, whereas family studies look at children in intact families. Family studies are inherently confounded, because not only do individuals share genes, they also share an environment. Therefore, any similarities between them may be due to either, or more likely both, factors.

12. Some examples of genetic engineering are the knockout technique, the antisense RNA procedure, gene transfer, gene therapy, and creation of transgenic animals.

13. One part of Ax's experiment involved convincing his participants that they were in physical danger (which they were not) in order to induce fear. Many of the participants indeed seemed very afraid during the procedure. There are two major reasons why this was ethically questionable. First, human research participants should be able to give their informed consent before participating in a research project. This means that they are informed ahead of time of any risks inherent in the procedure and that with this knowledge they voluntarily agree to participate. The second, related, problem is that the participants were deceived. Deception is allowed in research, but only when the potential benefits of the study outweigh the costs of using it. At the time of the study, standards had not been established for deception and informed consent. It is not likely that such a study would be conducted now, because it involved such an extreme manipulation of fear, and because the information divulged while obtaining informed consent would likely make the "threat" unconvincing.

14. There are many procedures that would be unethical to perform on humans. For this reason, procedures

that may eventually be used on humans are tested first on animals. Also, the laboratory animal's environment may be controlled, so it is easier to interpret the results (because many potentially confounding variables can be eliminated).

15. It is the assumption that animals have fewer rights than humans and that procedures that would be unacceptable with humans are acceptable with animals.

16. The movie *GATTACA* concerns a future society in which genetically "superior" individuals are more privileged than others. Although the movie is science fiction, some in our society are concerned that genetic engineering of humans could lead to something similar to this, particularly if people are able to select the most desirable traits for their offspring or to engineer those traits in their children.

17. The primary reason the use of human stem cells in research is controversial is because it destroys the embryo.

Posttest

1. c 2. c 3. a 4. b 5. c 6. d 7. d 8. c 9. d 10. b 11. a 12. a 13. c 14. b 15. b 16. c 17. d 18. c 19. b 20. d 21. a 22. a 23. c 24. d 25. b 26. a 27. b 28. d 29. b 30. c 31. d 32. c 33. d 34. d 35. a 36. b 37. b

5

Drugs, Addiction, and Reward

Chapter Outline

Psychoactive Drugs

Opiates

Depressants

Stimulants

Psychedelics

Marijuana

IN THE NEWS: CONTROVERSY OVER MEDICAL MARIJUANA TAKES A NEW

TURN

Addiction

Addiction and Reward

Dopamine and Reward

Dopamine, Learning, and Brain Plasticity

APPLICATION: IS COMPULSIVE GAMBLING AN ADDICTION?

Treating Drug Addiction

The Role of Genes in Addiction

Separating Genetic and Environmental Influences

What Is Inherited?

Implications of Addiction Research

Learning Objectives

After reading this chapter, you should be able to answer the following questions.

1. What are the physiological and psychological effects of different forms of opiates? How do opiates produce pain relief?

2. What are the different types of depressant drugs, and what are their effects?

3. What are the different types of stimulant drugs, and what are their effects? What do they have in common regarding their effects at dopamine synapses?

4. What are the effects of psychedelic drugs and marijuana?

5. Why are addiction and withdrawal considered independent mechanisms?

6. What brain areas and neurotransmitters are involved in reward? What role is reward believed to play in addiction?

7. What functions besides reward does dopamine have?

8. How are drugs used to treat addiction? What are some examples of each type?

9. How do Type 1 and Type 2 alcoholics differ?

10. How are genes thought to be involved in alcoholism?

11. What are the implications of alcoholism research?

Psychoactive Drugs

Summary and Guided Review

After studying this section in the text, fill in the blanks of the following summary.

Drugs can affect the brain by acting as _____ (1) (mimicking the effects of neurotransmitters), or _____ (2) (blocking or reducing the effects of neurotransmitters). Individuals who become obsessed with obtaining a drug or who use it compulsively are showing signs of _____ (3). When a person stops taking a drug, she or he may experience symptoms of

_____ (4), which are usually opposite to the effects of the drug. With repeated use, the brain may develop _____ (5) to a drug, a result of a reduction in quantity or sensitivity of receptors.

Opiates are drugs that come from opium poppies; these drugs have powerful psychoactive effects, including euphoric, _____ (6), and _____ (7). Morphine has been used clinically for treating the pain of surgery, battle wounds, and _____ (8). Another opiate drug, commonly used as a cough suppressant, is _____ (9). The most commonly abused opiate is _____ (10), because of its intense effects on the nervous system. In a long-term study of heroin addicts, the most common cause of death was _____ (11), yet about half of those surviving were still using heroin at the end of the study. Opiate drugs affect the nervous system because the body produces its own natural opioids called _____ (12), which are internal substances that affect the same receptors as opiates.

Drugs that have inhibitory effects on the central nervous system are called _____ (13). Alcohol, the most commonly abused drug, impairs motor and _____ (14) functions, as well as causing sedation, euphoria, and _____ (15)-reducing effects. Someone with a blood-alcohol level of _____% (16) is considered too intoxicated to drive. At concentrations of 0.5%, a person may go into a coma or _____ (17). Severe withdrawal symptoms such as hallucinations, delusions, and seizures, also known as _____ _____ (18), may occur following prolonged alcohol abuse. Health problems associated with long-term use of alcohol include cirrhosis of the _____ (19) and a form of brain damage called _____ (20) syndrome. _____ (21) drinkers are more likely to be impulsive and have learning and memory deficits. Alcohol affects the central nervous system by inhibiting the release of _____ (22) and by increasing the release of the inhibitory neurotransmitter _____ (23), which acts on receptors to open _____ (24) channels. Exposure to alcohol during prenatal development may result in a cluster of symptoms (including mental retardation, irritability, and facial anomalies) called _____ _____ (25) syndrome.

_____ (26) are depressant drugs that have been used to treat insomnia, epileptic seizures, and _____ (27). They typically produce _____ (28), resulting in increasing dosages and addiction. Because there is a fine line between therapeutic and toxic levels of these drugs, they have mostly been replaced with much safer _____ (29).

_____ (30) are drugs that produce arousal and elevate mood. Cocaine, which is derived from the coca plant, produces euphoria and relieves fatigue. Pure cocaine, or _____ (31), produces especially rapid, intense effects. A less pure and faster acting version of cocaine is called _____ (32). Cocaine blocks the reuptake of _____ (33) and serotonin, which results in removal of cortical _____ (34) of lower structures. Although in the past cocaine was not considered dangerous, it is now recognized as being quite addictive, especially when injected or _____ (35). Cocaine users are markedly impaired in _____ (36) functions and have a high rate of _____ (37) disorders, which makes rehabilitation difficult. Other problems associated with cocaine use include psychotic symptoms and seizures; the seizures are an example of selective _____ (38) in the long-term user. A controlled adoption study revealed that _____ (39) exposure to cocaine is linked to lower IQs and problems with language and attention in children.

Due to their tendency to enhance alertness reduce fatigue, _____ (40) such as Benzedrine and the much more powerful drug _____ (41) are often used by people who want to stay awake for long periods of time. These drugs cause an increase in the release of dopamine and _____ (42) . Psychotic symptoms from prolonged use include _____ (43) and delusions similar to those seen in paranoid schizophrenics.

Nicotine, the addictive psychoactive ingredient in tobacco, has _____ (44) effects when taken in short puffs, but depressant effects when deeply inhaled. Most people find that when they quit smoking, the _____ (45) symptoms such as anxiety and headaches are unpleasant, and they return to smoking. The health risks of smoking are high, but they are due to compounds in _____ (46), not nicotine. Children exposed to nicotine prenatally are more likely to be underweight as infants; their tendency to display _____ (47) disorder and criminal behavior later in life appears, however, to be genetic. In the central nervous system, _____ (48)-releasing neurons are activated by nicotine, leading to cortical arousal. In the periphery, nicoptine stimulates _____ (49) receptors. Caffeine, a milder stimulant than cocaine and amphetamine, affects the nervous system by blocking _____ (50) receptors, which results in an increase in the release of dopamine and _____ (51). Withdrawal symptoms are mild, but common; the most problematic symptom seems to be _____ (52).

Psychedelic drugs cause _____ (53) distortions, such as intensification or changes of visual stimuli and cross-modality perceptions. LSD and drugs derived from the *Psilocybe mexicana* mushroom resemble and stimulate the same receptors as the neurotransmitter _____ (54).

_____ (55) comes from the peyote cactus and may be used legally for religious practices by some Native Americans. MDMA, also known as _____ (56), stimulates the release of serotonin and dopamine; this drug has _____ (57) stimulant effects at lower doses and hallucinatory effects at higher doses. Some studies show a decrease in _____ (58) functioning, with persistent but small effects on _____ (59). Phencyclidine (PCP), also known as angel dust or crystal, was initially developed as a(n) _____ (60). However, this drug often triggers symptoms similar to _____ (61) and shows indications of being addictive.

The psychoactive ingredient in marijuana and hashish is _____ (62), a substance that binds to cannabinoid receptors, which are found on axon terminals. Endogenous cannabinoids such as anandamide are _____ (63) messengers. Marijuana's effects on cognition and time perception may be due to its effects on the _____ (64) cortex, whereas the memory impairment seen with marijuana use probably results from its effects on the _____ (65). Heavy use of marijuana has been associated with temporary loss in _____ (66). Prenatal exposure to marijuana has been linked to various cognitive problems in school-aged children, probably due to impairment of _____ (67) areas. Marijuana has beneficial uses, such as relieving _____ (68) associated with chemotherapy. While federal laws prohibit any use of marijuana, several states have legalized its use and the American Medical Association is calling for a review of the drug's _____ (69) classification. Because withdrawal from marijuana produces very mild symptoms, its compulsive use has often been attributed to _____ _____ (70). However, monkeys will _____-_____ (71) THC when given the opportunity to do so, suggesting that it is an addictive substance.

Short Answer and Essay Questions

Answer the following questions.

1. What is conditioned tolerance? What evidence is there that heroin use may lead to conditioned tolerance?

2. Describe the structure of the GABA$_A$ receptor complex, and compare the mechanisms by which alcohol, barbiturates, and benzodiazepines affect GABA activity.

3. Compare the effects of withdrawal from opiates, alcohol, cocaine, and nicotine. Which drug produces the most serious withdrawal symptoms?

4. Compare the effects of prenatal exposure to the following drugs: alcohol, cocaine, nicotine, and marijuana.

5. Is marijuana addictive? Support your answer.

Addiction

Summary and Guided Review

After studying this section in the text, fill in the blanks of the following summary.

In the past, addiction researchers assumed that addiction to drugs is maintained by the addict's desire to avoid _____ (72) effects. However, this does not explain what motivates drug taking until addiction develops. Initial drug taking apparently depends on the drug's _____ (73) effect, which appears to be a physiologically independent process. Drug researchers have identified the

_____ (74) dopamine system as the major drug reward system. Virtually all abused drugs increase dopamine levels in an area of the system called the _____

_____ (75) and drugs that block dopamine in this area tend to reduce self-administration of amphetamine and _____ (76). Eating, drinking, and _____(77) behavior also increase dopamine levels in this area. Chronic drug users release less dopamine and have fewer dopamine _____ (78), but this condition may precede drug use, producing a

_____ _____ (79) syndrome. Other neurotransmitters are involved in reward as well; for example, the rewarding effect of alcohol is due in part to _____ (80) receptors, and PCP produces reward by blocking _____ (81) receptors on neurons that mediate the dopamine reward system.

Most people agree that while reward is involved in early drug taking, later stages characterized by craving and withdrawal involve life-long changes in _____ (82) functioning. Research on learning has been important in trying to understand drug addiction. Recent studies suggest that dopamine activity signals not only reward but errors in _____ (83). Hence, many drug researchers have replaced the term reward with _____ (84), which refers to any object or event that increases the probability of the events that precede it. Drugs that increase dopamine release also produce anatomical changes in the nucleus accumbens and _____ (85) cortex in rats. In cocaine addicts, the sight of drug paraphernalia evokes _____ (86), which coincides with changes of activity in brain areas involved in _____ (87) and emotion. Researchers believe that these learning processes lead to long-term changes in the brain that underlie addiction. For example, compulsive use of cocaine may be due to pathological changes in the pathway between the _____

_____ (88) and the _____ _____ (89).

_____ (90) addictions, such as gambling, produce at least some of the same types of brain changes as those that occur in drug addiction.

Quitting an addictive substance can be very difficult. The first step is for the body to rid itself of the drug, a process called _____ (91). Withdrawal symptoms during this period can be intense, and in the case of alcohol withdrawal, it may be necessary to administer _____ (92) to prevent life-threatening results. Once the withdrawal symptoms have subsided, abstaining from a drug may involve the therapeutic use of other drugs. For example, _____ (93) is an opiate agonist given to heroin users that has milder effects and can be obtained legally. Antagonist treatments like _____ (94) are used to block the effects of opiates on receptors. _____ (95) reduces dopamine activity in the ventral tegmental area along with people's cravings for cocaine. _____ (96) is an aversive treatment for alcohol addiction; it works by making the person violently ill if alcohol is consumed. A promising area of research involves the use of antidrug _____ (97), which stimulate the immune system to produce antibodies for a drug. Addiction has been correlated with reduced _____ (98) activity, and drugs that increase the level of this neurotransmitter are useful in treating both smoking and _____ (99) addiction. The combination of addiction and other psychological disorders, or _____ (100), makes addiction treatment even more challenging. Many studies suggest that the combination of drug treatment with _____ (101) is quite effective. However, the use of some pharmacological treatments, such as methadone for

_____ (102) addiction, is controversial because it is "too easy."

Short Answer and Essay Questions

Answer the following questions.

6. What are the problems with explaining addiction as the avoidance of withdrawal symptoms?

7. What is reward deficiency syndrome? Why might individuals with this condition be more likely to become drug addicts?

8. How might cocaine-induced brain changes contribute to addiction to the drug?

9. Give an example of each of the following types of treatment for addiction: agonist, antagonist, and aversive. Explain how each works.

10. How might the immune system be manipulated to treat drug addiction? What are the advantages of this approach?

11. Why are pharmacological treatments for drugs controversial? Do you think they should be used? Why or why not?

The Role of Genes in Addiction

Summary and Guided Review

After studying this section in the text, fill in the blanks of the following summary.

Based on results from twin and adoption studies, there appears to be a strong _____ (103) component to alcoholism. The results of Cloninger and colleagues' comprehensive study of Swedish adoptees suggested that there are early and late onset alcoholics. In Type 1 or _____-_____ (104) alcoholics, problem drinking usually emerges after age _____ (105), and these people may alternate between abstinence and _____ (106) drinking. Type 2, or early-onset alcoholics, may begin drinking in adolescence and display a host of personality traits characteristic of _____ (107) personality disorder.

_____ (108)-onset alcoholics are more likely to be hospitalized. The environment seems to have a great impact on the development of alcoholism only in the offspring of _____ (109)-onset alcoholics.

The exact role of genetics in alcoholism is beginning to be understood. For example, mice lacking either _Homer_ or _Clock_ genes are more strongly affected by _____ (110). Moderate alcoholics with the _____ (111) allele of an opioid receptor report greater intoxication and pleasure than those lacking the allele. Furthermore, individuals who are resistant to the _____ (112) effects of alcohol are more susceptible to drinking disorders. The opposite is also true: people who inherit a(n) _____ (113) deficiency, which leads to nausea and other unpleasant effects when drinking, rarely become alcoholics.

Research using EEG has shown that male alcoholics and their children have an abnormal _____ (114) wave, which is a component of the evoked potential elicited by novel stimuli. However, this characteristic is not specific to alcoholism.

Short Answer and Essay Questions

Answer the following questions.

12. Distinguish between early- and late-onset alcoholics in terms of (1) the developmental pattern of the addiction and (2) the personality characteristics of each type.

13. Many alcoholics report that when they started drinking, alcohol seemed to affect them less than others. What genetic and neurological differences may account for this?

14. Describe three ways in which the EEG patterns of alcoholics and those at risk for becoming alcoholics differ from the EEG patterns of nonalcoholics. Why might the EEG be a useful tool for determining who is most at risk for becoming an alcoholic?

15. Imagine you are a scientist who studies the biological basis of alcoholism. You are in the process of seeking a multimillion-dollar grant to fund additional research in this area. The granting agency wants to know why alcoholism should be studied so intensely when there are many other forms of addiction and "more dangerous" drugs. How would you justify your continued study of alcoholism?

Posttest

Use these multiple-choice questions to check your understanding of the chapter.

1. Which of the following is NOT true of heroin use?

   a. It may lead to an addiction that is difficult to overcome.

   b. It may lead to withdrawal symptoms that are life threatening.

   c. Users experience intense euphoria followed by relaxation.

   d. It may lead to conditioned tolerance.

2. Arlene has been smoking marijuana three to four times a week for 2 years. She often worries about running out and occasionally steals small amounts from her friends who smoke. She recently tried to quit, but she started again after 1 month of being off the drug. Arlene is experiencing

   a. withdrawal.

   b. tolerance.

   c. addiction.

   d. depression.

3. Alcohol is BEST classified as a___ drug.

   a. depressant

   b. stimulant

   c. opiate

   d. psychedelic

4. Jerry, a 55-year-old chronic alcoholic, has recently begun experiencing memory loss and motor problems. His doctor informs him that he may be suffering from ___ as a result of his long-term alcohol abuse.

   a. delirium tremens

   b. conditioned tolerance

   c. Korsakoff's syndrome

   d. binge drinking

5. Which of the following drugs influence the activity of GABA?

   a. alcohol

   b. barbiturates

   c. benzodiazepines

   d. all of the above

6. Which of the following is NOT true regarding the early historical use of cocaine?

   a. The freebase form was used by South American Indians for centuries.

   b. It was an ingredient in Coca-Cola until 1906.

   c. In the 1800s, it was used as a local anesthetic.

   d. Sigmund Freud recommended it to his family and friends.

7. Prenatal exposure to cocaine has been linked to which of the following problem(s)?

   a. seizure disorders in children

   b. poor cognitive development

   c. facial abnormalities

   d. All of the above

8. The MOST potent form of amphetamine is

   a. Benzedrine.

   b. Dexedrine.

   c. methamphetamine.

   d. dextroamphetamine.

9. What percentage of people who quit smoking is able to abstain for at LEAST 2 years?

   a. 10%

   b. 20%

   c. 50%

   d. 80%

10. Which of the following is NOT a health problem associated with cigarette smoking or tobacco use?

    a. Buerger's disease

    b. cancer of the mouth

    c. emphysema

d. Korsakoff's syndrome

11. Which stimulant affects dopamine and acetylcholine levels indirectly through its effects on adenosine?

   a. caffeine

   b. cocaine

   c. nicotine

   d. amphetamine

12. Which of the following psychedelic drugs is found in a cactus?

   a. ecstasy

   b. angel dust

   c. mescaline

   d. psilocybin

13. Which of the following psychedelic drugs is MOST closely related to amphetamines?

   a. ecstasy

   b. angel dust

   c. LSD

   d. mescaline

14. The psychoactive ingredient in marijuana affects the same receptor sites as which of the following ligands?

   a. endorphin

   b. anandamide

   c. dopamine

   d. glutamate

15. The cognitive deficits seen in children exposed to marijuana prenatally seem MOST likely due to impairment of which part of the brain?

   a. hippocampus

   b. basal ganglia

   c. cerebellum

   d. prefrontal cortex

16. The MOST compelling reason to believe that marijuana is an addictive substance is that

a. some people experience withdrawal symptoms when they stop using it.

b. many people use it for years.

c. animals will self-administer it.

d. it has negative effects on the fetus.

17. Rats will learn to press a lever in order to inject drugs into which of the following brain structures?

    a. medial forebrain bundle

    b. ventral tegmental area

    c. nucleus accumbens

    d. All of the above

18. Addictive drugs may produce euphoric effects by

    a. stimulating the release of dopamine.

    b. blocking postsynaptic dopamine receptors.

    c. eliminating dopamine from the synapse.

    d. inhibiting the release of dopamine.

19. ESB has its greatest effect

    a. on animals missing a specific subtype of dopamine receptor.

    b. when an animal is also given cocaine or amphetamine.

    c. in brain areas where dopaminergic neurons are highly concentrated.

    d. in brain areas where serotonergic neurons are highly concentrated.

20. There is evidence that people with fewer D_2 receptors

    a. are highly unlikely to become addicted to drugs.

    b. are more responsive to rewards than other people.

    c. experience greater release of dopamine when using drugs than other people.

    d. like the stimulant drug Ritalin more than other people.

21. Opiates are implicated in the rewarding effects of which drug?

    a. alcohol

    b. cocaine

    c. amphetamine

    d. nicotine

22. PCP inhibits the effects of

    a. dopamine.

    b. glutamate.

    c. serotonin.

    d. endorphins.

23. Recent evidence regarding the role of dopamine in learning suggests that

    a. serotonin is actually more important in learning than is dopamine.

    b. serotonin is primarily a signal that an event is rewarding.

    c. dopamine is more likely to be released when a reinforcer is unpredictable.

    d. dopamine is not involved in reward or reinforcement.

24. Cocaine addicts' compulsive drug-using behavior may be a result of

    a. damage to the hippocampus.

    b. damage to the prefrontal cortex.

    c. damage to the ventral tegmental area.

    d. All of the above.

25. When a rat that has learned to press a lever in order to receive a drug reward no longer receives the

    reward, it will stop pressing the lever. However, electrical stimulation of the ___ reinstates the lever

    pressing.

    a. nucleus accumbens

    b. ventral tegmental area

    c. hippocampus

    d. lateral hypothalamus

26. Freud suffered from lifelong addiction to

    a. cocaine.

    b. alcohol.

    c. heroin.

    d. nicotine.

27. Sharon was recently admitted to the hospital because she was suffering severe withdrawal symptoms,

    including seizures. She was given a benzodiazepine to reduce the severity of her symptoms. Which of the following drugs is Sharon MOST likely addicted to?

a. alcohol

b. heroin

c. nicotine

d. cocaine

28. Nicotine gum is an example of an ___ treatment for drug addiction.

a. antagonist

b. aversive

c. agonist

d. antidrug

29. Naltrexone may be used to block opiate receptors in people who abuse

a. nicotine.

b. cocaine.

c. amphetamines.

d. alcohol.

30. Methadone was developed as an analgesic during World War II when ___ was in short supply.

a. morphine

b. heroin

c. codeine

d. endorphin

31. Which of the following statements is NOT true of antidrug vaccines?

a. They lead to the destruction of drug molecules before they can reach the brain.

b. They are more effective than other pharmacological treatments in humans.

c. They result in fewer side effects than other pharmacological treatments.

d. Their effects may be longer lasting than other pharmacological treatments.

32. For heroin addicts,

a. methadone treatment alone is the most effective treatment option.

b. counseling alone has a high rate of success.

c. no treatment method has more than a 50% success rate.

    d. methadone plus counseling is quite effective.

33. The heritability for alcoholism is

    a. 5–10%.

    b. 20–30%.

    c. 50–60%.

    d. 80–90%.

34. Which of the following characteristics typifies early-onset alcoholics?

    a. They tend to feel guilty about drinking.

    b. They tend to be novelty seekers.

    c. They may abstain from alcohol for long periods of time.

    d. They are often emotionally dependent.

35. Which of the following is a characteristic of Type 1 alcoholics?

    a. They begin having problems with alcohol in adolescence.

    b. They tend to behave aggressively when drinking.

    c. They are quite cautious.

    d. All of the above

36. Cloninger's study of early- and late-onset alcoholics indicates that

    a. exposure to alcoholism in the home has more of an impact on the children of late- onset alcoholics than the children of early-onset alcoholics.

    b. exposure to alcoholism in the home has more of an impact on the children of early- onset alcoholics than the children of late-onset alcoholics.

    c. exposure to alcoholism in the home has about the same effect on the children of early- and late-onset alcoholics.

    d. late-onset alcoholics are most likely to have children who are early-onset alcoholics.

37. Genes for which of the following transmitters have been implicated in drug abuse?

    a. GABA

    b. endogenous opioids

    c. anandamide

    d. All of the above

38. Which of the following does NOT indicate a high risk for alcoholism?

    a. being the child of an alcoholic

    b. feeling fewer effects of alcohol when drinking

    c. having ALDH deficiency

    d. showing an abnormal P300 wave

39. ALDH is an enzyme that

    a. breaks down dopamine.

    b. blocks serotonin receptors.

    c. has an agonistic effect on alcohol.

    d. breaks down alcohol.

40. The P300 wave

    a. shows promise for diagnosing those at risk for alcoholism.

    b. occurs in response to a novel stimulus.

    c. occurs in similar ways among family members.

    d. all of the above.

Answers

Guided Review

1. agonists

2. antagonists

3. addiction

4. withdrawal

5. tolerance

6. analgesic

7. hypnotic

8. cancer

9. codeine

10. Heroin

11. overdose

12. endorphins

13. depressants

14. cognitive

15. anxiety

16. 0.08

17. die

18. delirium tremens

19. liver

20. Korsakoff's

21. Binge

22. glutamate

23. GABA

24. chloride

25. fetal alcohol

26. Barbiturates

27. anxiety

28. tolerance

29. benzodiazepines

30. Stimulants

31. freebase

32. crack

33. dopamine

34. inhibition

35. smoked or inhaled

36. executive

37. psychological

38. tolerance

39. prenatal

40. amphetamines

41. methamphetamine

42. norepinephrine

43. hallucinations

44. stimulating

45. withdrawal

46. tobacco smoke

47. conduct

48. dopamine

49. acetylcholine

50. adenosine

51. acetylcholine

52. headache(s)

53. perceptual

54. serotonin

55. Mescaline

56. ecstasy

57. psychomotor

58. serotonin

59. memory

60. anesthetic

61. schizophrenia

62. tetrahydrocanabbinol (THC)

63. retrograde

64. frontal

65. hippocampus

66. IQ

67. prefrontal

68. nausea

69. Schedule I

70. psychological dependence

71. self-administer

72. withdrawal

73. reward

74. mesolimbocortical

75. nucleus accumbens

76. cocaine

77. sexual

78. receptors

79. reward deficiency syndrome

80. opiate

81. glutamate

82. brain

83. prediction

84. reinforcer

85. prefrontal

86. craving

87. learning

88. prefrontal cortex

89. nucleus accumbens

90. Behavioral

91. detoxification

92. benzodiazepines

93. Methadone

94. naltrexone

95. Baclofen

96. Antabuse

97. vaccines

98. serotonin

99. alcohol

100. Comorbidity

101. counseling

102. opiate

103. genetic

104. late-onset

105. 25

106. binge

107. antisocial

108. Early

109. late

110. cocaine

111. G

112. negative

113. ALDH

114. P-300

Short Answer and Essay

1. Conditioned tolerance is a learned tolerance that is specific to the setting where it developed; as a result, the individual shows tolerance to a drug in one context, but not in another. Rats are more likely to die of overdose when given a large dose in a novel environment (64% versus 32% of rats in each group died). Likewise, human heroin addicts may be more likely to overdose when they take the same amount of drug in a novel setting. When in a different environment, those cues that trigger the tolerance response are no longer present, and the same dose may have a more powerful effect.

2. The $GABA_A$ receptor complex has at least five different receptor sites, only one of which responds to the neurotransmitter GABA. When GABA binds to its receptor, chloride channels open and the neuron is inhibited. The other receptor types are affected by various drugs. Alcohol fits a different receptor in the complex, and enhances GABA binding, which produces a stronger inhibitory response. Barbiturates fit yet another receptor in the $GABA_A$ complex, also enhancing the effectiveness of GABA, but at high doses, they can actually open chloride channels without GABA. Benzodiazepines also act at the $GABA_A$ receptor complex in the limbic system, brain stem, hippocampus, and cortex.

3. Opiate withdrawal is like having the flu. Alcohol produces the most serious withdrawal symptoms,

including delirium tremens, convulsions, and even death. Less severe withdrawal symptoms of alcohol include anxiety and mood changes. Cocaine produces mild withdrawal symptoms, including anxiety and loss of motivation and pleasure. Nicotine withdrawal includes anxiety, sleepiness, and headaches.

4. Prenatal exposure to alcohol may result in fetal alcohol syndrome, a cluster of symptoms including facial abnormalities, mental retardation, and irritability. Exposure to cocaine prenatally has been linked to impaired IQ and language development as well as attention problems. Prenatal exposure to nicotine is linked to low birth weight. Marijuana exposure before birth may contribute to behavioral and cognitive deficiencies, but these may not be apparent until after 4 years of age.

5. There is evidence that marijuana is addictive, although it produces only mild withdrawal symptoms. Compulsive use in humans has been documented, and monkeys will self-administer THC, which is usually taken as evidence of addiction.

6. One problem is that withdrawal symptoms occur later, so avoidance of withdrawal cannot be the mechanism that maintains early drug use. Second, addicts intentionally go through withdrawal to adjust their tolerance level. Third, many addicts start using a drug again after having quit for a long period of time and are presumably no longer experiencing withdrawal. Finally, the power of addiction of a drug is not related to the severity of withdrawal. For example, alcohol can cause severe withdrawal symptoms, but heroin or stimulants may not.

7. Some people apparently have fewer D_2 receptors than other people, probably due to genetic differences. Fewer dopamine receptors and reduced dopamine activity are linked to a reduced experience of reward, even among those who are not addicts. These individuals may find drugs that increase dopamine activity, such as cocaine, particularly reinforcing, and they may be more likely to continue using a drug if they start.

8. Learning is associated with synaptic increases in the prefrontal cortex and nucleus accumbens. In addition, the prefrontal cortex also undergoes pathological alterations in dendrites, reduction in dopamine activity, prefrontal deactivation, and reduced behavioral inhibition. As a result of learning, hippocampal stimulation produces a high level of dopamine release and a return to drug seeking behavior; brain changes from learning are considered to be the reason drugs have a lifelong effect.

9. Agonist treatments, such as methadone for heroin addiction, involve the replacement of a more harmful substance with a less harmful one that basically has the same effect on the nervous system. Antagonistic

treatment involves administration of a drug that blocks the effects of the undesirable drug. For example, Baclofen seems to block dopamine activity normally stimulated by several addictive substances. Aversive treatments produce an undesirable reaction when the harmful drug is taken. Antabuse, for example, produces nausea and vomiting when alcohol is consumed, because it inhibits the metabolism of acetaldehyde.

10. Anti-drug vaccines induce the body to produce antibodies to destroy the drug. They appear to be quite effective and may soon be available for use with humans. The advantages of these drugs are that they do not result in the side effects common to drugs that interfere with neurotransmitters, and their effects may be quite long lasting.

11. Pharmacological treatments are controversial because they involve treating drug addiction by giving a person another drug. In the case of methadone, this means substituting a less problematic addiction for a more problematic one. Other drug treatments (such as treatment with Antabuse and possibly with Baclofen) interfere with drug use without leading to addiction. (The argument for these treatments is that they are generally effective, but some people believe that addiction should be overcome by sheer willpower, and that relying on other drugs to do it is taking the easy way out.)

12. Early-onset alcoholics usually begin drinking prior to the age of 25, many of them in their teens. They are more likely to be male, and they often display impulsive, aggressive, and reckless behavior while being socially and emotionally detached from others. This pattern of characteristics is associated with antisocial personality disorder. Late-onset drinkers usually begin having problems with alcohol after the age of 25, following a period of social drinking. They tend to binge drink, which results in guilt feelings; they may abstain from alcohol for long periods. They tend to be cautious and emotionally dependent.

13. Alcoholics who have the A_1 allele for D_2 (dopamine) receptors may actually have fewer of these receptors. Because alcohol stimulates dopamine activity, which is experienced as pleasant or rewarding, such individuals would have to consume more alcohol to feel the same level of effect as someone with more D_2 receptors. Greater consumption puts them more at risk for becoming addicted.

14. First, when not under the influence of alcohol, male alcoholics and their children show more high-frequency waves than nonalcoholics. Also, alcoholics and their children, who are probably at risk for alcoholism, show a reduced "dip" in the P300 waves in response to novel stimuli, and the P300 wave is also delayed. The EEG may be useful for determining who is most at risk for alcoholism, because children of alcoholics who are not alcoholics themselves often show the same pattern of responses as their parents.

15. Alcoholism is a good model for studying drug addiction. Many of the addictive drugs have very similar effects in the brain, mostly through their effects on the dopamine reward system. Therefore, any discoveries made about the genetic and neurological bases of alcohol addiction may be applicable to other forms of addiction. Furthermore, alcoholism is the most problematic addiction in our society. Its use is linked to violence, traffic accidents, and other serious behavioral problems. Because it is a legal drug, there are more alcoholics than people addicted to other drugs. Consequently, it makes sense to attempt to understand and perhaps control or even eradicate it. In doing so, it may be possible to treat other forms of addiction as well.

Posttest

1. b   2. c   3. a   4. c   5. d   6. a   7. b   8. c   9. b   10. d   11. a   12. c   13. a   14. b   15. d   16. c   17. d   18. a   19. c   20. d   21. a   22. b   23. c   24. b   25. c   26. d   27. a   28. c   29. d   30. a   31. b   32. d   33. c   34. b   35. c   36. a   37. d   38. c   39. d   40. d

6

Motivation and the Regulation of Internal States

Chapter Outline

Learning Objectives

After reading this chapter, you should be able to answer the following questions.

1. What are the differences among instinct, drive, incentive, and arousal theories of motivation?

2. What is homeostasis? How does temperature regulation exemplify this concept?

3. What are the two types of thirst, and what mechanism is responsible for each?

4. What are the five primary tastes? How is taste information conveyed in the nervous system?

5. What taste mechanisms help to ensure that we eat a healthy, balanced diet?

6. How does digestion occur? Include in your answer the events of the absorptive and fasting phases.

7. What mechanisms are involved in the stimulation and termination of eating? In controlling body weight?

8. What health problems are associated with obesity? What myths surround obesity?

9. To what extent is heredity believed to be involved in obesity? What specific genetic mechanisms might be involved?

10. What role does metabolism play in obesity? How is obesity treated?

11. What are the characteristics of anorexia and bulimia?

12. What social and biological factors contribute to anorexia and bulimia?

Motivation and Homeostasis

Summary and Guided Review

After studying this section in the text, fill in the blanks of the following summary.

_____ (1) refers to factors that initiate, sustain, and direct behaviors; there are several theories of motivation. Ancient Greeks, as well as some early 20th-century psychologists, proposed that many human behaviors are _____ (2) motivated; a more precisely defined concept continues to be used with animal behavior, but most contemporary psychologists believe instincts have little influence on human behavior. Another explanation for motivation is _____ (3) theory, which proposes that the body attempts to maintain _____ (4), or balance. While this theory helps explain some behaviors, it does not explain behaviors that do not satisfy bodily needs, such as seeking fame or academic excellence. _____ (5) theory accounts for the fact that people are often motivated by external stimuli, such as money. Another theory, _____ (6) theory, suggests that people are also motivated to maintain a preferred level of stimulation, although this level varies from person to person. Perhaps the best way to think about drives is to assume that they represent _____ (7) rather than conditions of the body. This is supported by the fact that many stimuli can motivate a behavior, even in the absence of _____ (8) needs, such as suddenly feeling hungry when smelling food, even after a meal.

A useful way of representing homeostasis and the preferred state of a control system is the _____ (9) point; when conditions deviate too far from this point, the nervous system becomes operative to restore it. For example, all animals must maintain their body _____ _____ (10) within a particular range, or they will die. _____ (11) animals like reptiles rely on the temperature of the external environment, whereas _____ (12) animals like mammals and birds have internal mechanisms that regulate body temperature, although they can also manipulate their environment to maintain a comfortable state. In mammals, body temperature is controlled by the _____ (13) area of the hypothalamus. Here, warmth- and _____-_____ (14) cells respond to the temperature of the blood and to temperature receptors in other parts of the body by initiating physiological activities, such as sweating if the organism is too hot, or _____ (15) if the organism is too cold.

Another drive that nicely fits the homeostatic model is _____ (16). Because water makes up about _____ % (17) of the body, it is essential for the proper function of the bodily systems. Because water is continually lost through urination, defecation, and _____ (18), it is especially important to maintain sufficient liquids in the body. There are two types of thirst: _____ (19) thirst is a result of low intracellular fluid, whereas _____ (20) thirst occurs when blood volume drops. Osmotic thirst is regulated by cells in the _____ (21), along the third ventricle, that detect low levels of intracellular fluid and communicate the deficit to the _____ _____

_____ (22) of the hypothalamus, which initiates drinking. Hypovolemic thirst is detected

by pressure receptors in the _____ (23) that signal the brain via the

_____ (24) nerve to the _____ (25) in the medulla. The

_____ (26) also respond to low blood volume by releasing renin; this increases the level of

_____ (27), which is detected by the _____ (28) organ and induces

drinking via the median preoptic nucleus. Homeostasis is not achieved immediately after ingesting water, so

there must be some kind of _____ (29) mechanism that recognizes when enough water has

been taken and terminates thirst; receptors in the _____ (30) and liver may serve this

purpose.

Short Answer and Essay Questions

Answer the following questions.

1. What is the cause, and what are the consequences, of Prader-Willi syndrome?

2. Why is drive theory alone insufficient to account for motivation?

3. What mechanisms for temperature regulation do ectothermic and endothermic animals have in common?

4. Compare the mechanisms responsible for managing osmotic and hypovolemic thirst. How do researchers know they operate independently?

Hunger: A Complex Drive

Summary and Guided Review

After studying this section in the text, fill in the blanks of the following summary.

As a drive, hunger is more complicated than temperature and thirst, because the _____

(31) can undergo dramatic changes and because there are so many different types of _____

(32) that the body needs.

Humans eat a variety of plant and animal foods, meaning that we are _____ (33); in order to remain healthy, we need to eat a varied diet and at the same time carefully select foods that are not toxic

or spoiled. The sense of _____ (34) helps us select nutritious, safe foods and avoid non-

nutritious, dangerous ones. We have _____ (35) primary taste sensations, each of which

seems to indicate different qualities of food. Foods that taste _____ (36), such as fruits, and

those that taste salty are highly preferred. These types of food typically provide nutrients necessary for survival.

A recently discovered taste, _____ (37), has been described as "meaty" or "savory"; some

researchers believe it could be important in our selection of _____ (38). The other

qualities, _____ (39) and _____ (40), often indicate that food is

spoiled or toxic, respectively, and should therefore be avoided. Sensory information about taste is transmitted

from the taste buds located on the surface of the _____ (41) of the tongue, through the

nucleus of the solitary tract in the _____ (42), and via the thalamus to the

_____ (43), which is the primary gustatory cortex. Information from different taste

receptors travels to the cortex via separate pathways to distinct areas; this is referred to as

_____ (44) coding of stimuli.

   A food particular becomes less appealing as we eat more of it, a phenomenon known as

_____-_____ (45) satiety, which is an important mechanism for

ensuring that we eat a variety of foods. This form of satiety seems to be controlled by the

_____ (46). Taste is an important cue for learning, which foods may be harmful;

experiments with rats have shown that if a certain taste becomes associated with illness, they will

_____(47) items with that taste in the future. Humans also demonstrate these

_____ _____ (48) aversions, although the bouts of sickness are often

not caused by the foods they become associated with, as in the case of children undergoing

_____ (49) who learned to avoid a particular flavor of ice cream. There is even some

evidence that rats will form an aversion to food _____ (50) in thiamine. Taste is also an

important cue for learning which foods to eat when the nutrients themselves may not be detected; for example,

rats deprived of a specific _____ (51) learned to eat a food enriched with it and flavored

with anise. When the anise was switched to a nutrient deficient food, the animals preferred it instead, the rats

switched to that food. This phenomenon is called a _____ (52) taste preference.

_____ (53) begins in the mouth, where _____ (54) is added to

food. In the stomach, pepsin and _____ (55) acid are added to food to break it down. If food contains toxins that irritate the stomach too much, or if toxins reach the area postrema via the blood,

_____ (56) occurs. The first segment of the small intestine, the _____

(57), is where most food is digested. Here, carbohydrates are converted into _____ (58)

such as glucose, and proteins are converted into _____ _____ (59).

Fats are converted to fatty acids and _____ (60) in the intestines and

_____ (61). These basic nutrients are then _____ (62) into the

bloodstream and taken to the liver by the _____ _____ (63) vein.

Excess water is reabsorbed in the large _____ (64). Digestion is controlled by the

_____ (65) nervous system and can be disrupted by arousal, which may lead to nausea,

constipation, or _____ (66).

For the first few hours after a meal, during the _____ (67) phase of the feeding cycle,

recently ingested nutrients provide fuel for the body. This is managed by the parasympathetic nervous system,

which is activated by _____ (68) levels of glucose. Insulin is secreted by the

_____ (69), allowing glucose to be used by the cells. _____ (70) is a

result of not producing enough insulin or being less responsive to it. Glucose is also converted to

_____ (71) for short-term storage. Excess glucose and proteins are converted to

_____ (72) and stored in _____ (73) tissue. When glucose levels in

the blood decline, the body enters the _____ (74) phase of the feeding cycle.

Parasympathetic activity is replaced by _____ (75) activity, resulting in the secretion of

_____ (76) from the pancreas. This substance is instrumental in the conversion of glycogen

to _____ (77) and of fat into fatty acids and _____(78), the latter of

which is converted into glucose for the brain by the _____ (79). Eating and metabolism are

governed by the lateral _____ (80) and the _____ (81).

There are three major signals of hunger; _____ (82) hunger tells the brain that there is

a low level of glucose, _____ (83) hunger indicates a deficit in fatty acids, and the third

signals low levels of nutrients in the _____ (84). Blood levels of glucose and fatty acids are

monitored by the liver; when these levels are low, a message is carried to the medulla via the

_____ (85) nerve. Glucose levels in the brain are monitored directly by the

_____ (86). Next the message is carried to the _____ (87) nucleus,

which in turn sends signals to the PVN and _____ (88) hypothalamus. As the stomach empties during fasting the peptide _____ (89) is released, and stimulates the arcuate

nucleus to cause eating. Excess ghrelin may be involved in the uncontrollable appetite of people with

_____-_____ (90) syndrome. The three hunger signals target neurons

in the arcuate nucleus, which releases _____ (91) and _____-

_____ (92) protein. Both substances excite the PVN and lateral hypothalamus to increase

eating and reduce _____ (93).

    There are a number of satiety signals, including those from _____ (94) receptors in the

stomach that become active when it is full. The stomach and intestines also release a number of

_____ (95) that trigger enzyme release for digestion and also signal the brain. For example,

the duodenal hormone _____ (96) detects fats and triggers the release of bile from the

_____ _____ (97) and initiates a signal in the vagus nerve to the NST

and hypothalamus to stop eating. _____ (98) is another peptide hormone released from the

intestines that inhibits NPY release in the _____ (99) nucleus, which decreases caloric

intake over several hours. Rats with lesions in the _____ (100) hypothalamus overeat in

part because insulin production is increased, which results in nutrients being stored rather than utilized. In

_____ (101) rats in which one was lesioned and one was not, the normal rat reduced its

eating in response to a satiety signal that the lesioned rat was insensitive to. The satiety signal turned out to be

the hormone _____ (102); obese individuals have _____ (103) blood

levels of this hormone. Leptin and insulin decrease eating by inhibiting the NPY/AgRP neurons, but also

activating _____ (104) cells. In turn, these cells reduce feeding by inhibiting the

_____ (105) and the lateral hypothalamus.

Short Answer and Essay Questions

Answer the following questions.

5.   As a drive, why is hunger more complex than the drives of thirst and temperature regulation?

6.   Why is it advantageous for us to prefer sweet and salty foods and to dislike sour and bitter foods?

7.   How does sensory-specific satiety help explain the tendency for some people to overeat at potluck

      meals or buffets where many different types of foods are available?

8. As a child, Shirley became ill and threw up several times in one night. Her family had eaten chilli for dinner that day. Shirley was the only one who became sick, so there must have been some other cause for her illness. However, for the next 10 years, Shirley refused to eat chilli, and even the sight of it made her nauseous. Explain why Shirley stopped eating chilli.

9. Why do diabetics feel hungry, even when their blood sugar is high? What is the role of insulin in this?

10. Why may a diet high in sugar and/or protein lead to weight gain?

11. Identify and describe the three major signals for hunger.

12. What happens when rats are given injections of neuropeptide Y? What effects does it have on appetite? On energy consumption?

13. What signals the end of a meal?

Obesity

Summary and Guided Review

After studying this section in the text, fill in the blanks of the following summary.

Two thirds of adults in the United States are overweight and a third qualify as _____ (106). This condition is increasing in many countries, in part because of the availability of junk food that is high ion calories but now in _____ (107). The degree of obesity is calculated by dividing weight in kilograms by squared height in meters, which yields the _____ (108); the person is considered obese if this value is _____ (109) or higher. Overweight and obese individuals are more at risk for many health problems; for example, in a Swedish study, the more overweight a woman was, the more likely she was to have shrinkage in the _____ (110) lobes. If the trend toward obesity is not reversed, by 2050 the average life expectancy in the United States could _____ (111). On the other hand, dietary restrictions may prolong life. Studies with yeast, roundworms, and rhesus monkeys suggest that inhibition of the protein _____ (112) may play a role in increased longevity and reduced cancer risk.

Obesity seems to be most directly linked to eating high-calorie foods and not getting enough

_____ (113). However, research has not supported the popular opinion that obesity is completely under _____ (114) control or that it results from a maladaptive eating style.

If obesity runs in families, it is more likely due to _____ (115) than environment, as evidenced by the fact that the correlation of BMI scores in identical twins raised apart is _____ (116), only slightly lower than the .74 correlation for those raised together. However, the role of inheritance is complicated, as there are several genes involved, such as the _____ (117) gene on chromosome 6 and the _____ (118) gene on chromosome 4. Coleman used the parabiotic technique described earlier to experimentally study the effects of recessive genes on food intake and weight in mice. The _db/db_ mice produced a signal to stop eating but were insensitive to it, while the _____ (119) mice were sensitive to the signal but did not produce it. It was not until later that researchers discovered that the signalling substance was _____ (120). The _ob_ and _db_ genes are rare and account for few cases of obesity; on the other hand, mutations of the _____ (121) gene may account for 6% of cases of severe childhood obesity. A particular allele of the _____ (122) gene has been implicated in 20% of obese individuals. _____ (123) characteristics are inheritable traits that are unrelated to the individual's DNA sequence. What happens in these cases is that the environment, such as conditions of severe starvation, can turn gene _____ (124) on or off.

A person's basal _____ (125) largely determines how much food is needed to maintain weight, and someone with a higher BMR needs to take in _____ (126) calories than someone with a lower BMR. When a person loses weight, the BMR usually _____ (127), making additional weight loss difficult. The increase in metabolism is variable among people, partly due to nonexercise spontaneous _____ (128), such as fidgeting; these individuals expend more energy and gain less weight than others. Another factor that may make weight loss difficult is that after a person gains weight, she or he may develop a new _____ _____ (129).

Exercise seems to be an important part of losing weight, more because of its effects on one's _____ _____ (130) rate than because of the calories expended during the exercise itself. Some medications have been used to treat obesity; one currently approved drug, _____ (131), inhibits reuptake of the neurotransmitter _____ (132), which reduces carbohydrate craving. The drug _____ (133) blocks fat absorption, but is under review because of reports of liver damage. Treatment with the hormone _____ (134) has been shown to be effective in increasing metabolism and reducing fat while sparing lean mass, but it works only in the 5-10% of obese individuals who lack it. A new approach to understanding and treating obesity is to view overeating as an addictive behavior. One neurotransmitter that plays a key role in both compulsive overeating and addiction is _____ (135). The drug _____ (136) that reduces dopamine has been used experimentally to treat addiction; it also causes weight loss in genetically obese rats. Because drugs and lifestyle changes are not effective with the morbidly obese, surgical procedures such as _____ _____ (137) may be required to save lives. This procedure works by limiting meal size and nutrient absorption in the digestive tract. However, because this surgery has many risks and is expensive, it is often a last resort for weight management.

Short Answer and Essay Questions

Answer the following questions.

14. Why is obesity considered to be a major problem today?

15. Why is it easier to gain than lose weight?

16. Kelly, who does not exercise, recently moved in with a roommate who likes to cook. Before this, Kelly lived by herself and ate small meals at dinner. Now, because of her roommate's influence, she eats lavish dinners and consumes about 500 more calories per day than she used to. However, she is not gaining weight. How might her energy expenditure have increased to prevent weight gain?

17. Discuss the following antiobesity drugs: sibutramine, orlistat, leptin, and vigabatrin. Include in your discussion the mechanism of action, side effects (if mentioned), and limitations of their use.

Anorexia and Bulimia

Summary and Guided Review

After studying this section in the text, fill in the blanks of the following summary.

About 3% of women suffer from anorexia or _____ (138) at some point in their lives, and there are _____ (139) times as many women as men with these t eating disorders.

_____ (140) nervosa is characterized by maintaining weight at an unhealthy low level, which can lead to serious health problems and even death. Anorexics who binge eat and control their weight by vomiting or using _____ (141) are called _____ (142), while _____ (143) are those who simply eat very little food. Health risks associated with anorexia include heart damage, loss of bone density, and reduced _____ (144) matter. Anorexics have elevated _____ (145) and _____ (146), and low leptin levels; suggesting that they are experiencing hunger. Weight in individuals with bulimia is usually _____ (147). Their _____ (148) levels are higher than those of controls.

The social environment plays a role in anorexia and bulimia, including exposure to thin models in the media. After satellite TV became available in _____ (149) in 1995, almost 75% of the teenage girls reported feeling fat, and the number of those who admitted to vomiting to control their weight rose from 3% to _____ % (150). Genetic inheritance also appears to play a role; the concordance rate of anorexia among identical twins is _____ % (151) compared to 12.5% in fraternal twins. Many anorexics and bulimics are _____ (152) for depression.

Bulimics have low levels of the neurotransmitter _____ (153) and antidepressants that increase this transmitter reduce binge eating in bulimics. Anorexics have lower serotonin levels, but only when they are underweight, apparently due to malnutrition. Evidence also points to a dysfunctional _____ (154) system in anorexia. The drug _____ (155) is being tested as a treatment for anorexia; it affects both dopamine and serotonin receptors.

Short Answer and Essay Questions

Answer the following questions.

18. What evidence points to an environmental influence on anorexia and bulimia?

19. Compare purging and restrictive anorexics to bulimics. Include in your answer the role of serotonin.

Posttest

Use these multiple-choice questions to check your understanding of the chapter.

1. Christopher, the person described in the introduction to the chapter, exhibited all of the following EXCEPT

   a. poor impulse control.

   b. short stature.

   c. mental disability.

   d. violent outbursts.

2. Which of the following statements regarding motivation is TRUE?

   a. Motivation is controlled by the thalamus.

   b. Motivations are best thought of as instinctive drives.

   c. Motivation refers to bodily states of need.

   d. Motivation is sometimes confused with emotion.

3. The fact that some people need higher levels of excitement than others is BEST explained by ___ theory.

   a. incentive

   b. arousal

   c. drive

   d. instinct

4. Which of the following animals is ectothermic?

   a. elephant

   b. chicken

   c. cow

   d. snake

5. Endothermic animals can reduce their body temperature by

   a. burrowing into the ground.

   b. finding shade.

   c. sweating.

   d. All of the above

6. Warmth-sensitive and cold-sensitive cells that help mammals regulate their body temperature are found in the ___ of the hypothalamus.

   a. preoptic area

   b. area postrema

   c. ventromedial nucleus

   d. nucleus of the solitary tract

7. Jason has just eaten an entire bag of potato chips and suddenly feels thirsty. What type of thirst is he experiencing?

   a. hypovolemic

   b. osmotic

   c. hypervolemic

   d. endothermic

8. Which of the following does NOT result in loss of extracellular water?

   a. exercise

   b. blood loss

   c. ingesting a lot of salt

   d. vomiting

9. Osmotic thirst

   a. results from activation of baroreceptors in the heart.

   b. results from the release of renin by the kidneys.

   c. is controlled by the subfornical organ.

   d. is disrupted when the OVLT is lesioned.

10. Which of the following statements is TRUE?

    a. The set point for temperature is less variable than the set point for hunger.

    b. The set point for thirst is more variable than the set point for hunger.

    c. The set point for temperature is more variable than the set point for hunger.

    d. Once we reach adulthood, the set point for hunger becomes stable.

11. A species of animal that eats only berries and leaves is a(n)

    a. carnivore.

b. omnivore.

c. herbivore.

d. endovore.

12. Of all of the primary taste qualities, ___ is the MOST recently discovered.

   a. umami

   b. sour

   c. bitter

   d. salty

13. Foods that provide the ions necessary for neural transmission are MOST likely to taste

   a. sweet.

   b. salty.

   c. bitter.

   d. sour.

14. Foods that contain toxins tend to taste

   a. sweet.

   b. sour.

   c. salty.

   d. bitter.

15. The taste buds send signals to the ___ area of the cortex.

   a. olfactory

   b. auditory

   c. gustatory

   d. somatosensory

16. Learned taste aversion accounts for all of the following EXCEPT

   a. bait shyness in rats.

   b. coyotes' refusal to eat lamb after consuming a tainted carcass.

   c. rats' decreased responsiveness to glucose placed on the tongue after receiving a glucose injection.

   d. children avoiding certain flavors of ice cream eaten while undergoing chemotherapy.

17. Which of the following statements regarding taste preferences is TRUE?

a. Rats are better at "listening to what their bodies need" than humans.

b. Rats deprived of a vitamin can develop a preference for a food high in that vitamin.

c. Rats' behavior does not change when their diet is missing critical nutrients.

d. Rats find the taste of cinnamon aversive.

18. Which of the following is released by the stomach as an aid to digestion?

a. pepsin

b. leptin

c. insulin

d. cholecystokinin

19. Most of digestion occurs in the

a. large intestine.

b. small intestine.

c. liver.

d. stomach.

20. Glycerol is a product of the transformation of

a. fats.

b. proteins.

c. carbohydrates.

d. All of the above.

21. After nutrients are absorbed into the bloodstream, they are transported to the ___ by the hepatic portal vein.

a. kidneys

b. liver

c. brain

d. large intestine

22. During the absorptive phase of the feeding cycle,

a. recently eaten food may be stored.

b. recently eaten food is used for energy.

c. the parasympathetic nervous system is activated.

d. All of the above

23. Which of the following statements regarding insulin is TRUE?

    a. Brain cells can import glucose without it.

    b. All body cells can import glucose without it.

    c. Diabetics produce too much of it.

    d. Its production is activated by the sympathetic nervous system.

24. Which of the following contributes to adipose tissue?

    a. excess protein

    b. excess glucose

    c. fat

    d. all of the above

25. Which of the following statements regarding glucagon is FALSE?

    a. It is secreted by the pancreas.

    b. It transforms proteins to fatty acids.

    c. It transforms glycogen to glucose.

    d. It converts stored fat to glycerol.

26. A rabbit injected with 2-deoxyglucose into its hepatic portal vein will

    a. start eating but will eat only a small amount.

    b. not eat for several hours.

    c. start eating and eat more than usual.

    d. enter a diabetic coma.

27. Which of the following statements regarding neuropeptide Y is FALSE?

    a. It is released by the preoptic area of the hypothalamus.

    b. It stimulates eating.

    c. It is released in response to low glucose.

    d. It may help an animal conserve energy.

28. Satiety may be signaled by

    a. stretch receptors in the stomach.

    b. the release of cholecystokinin.

c. the presence of nutrients in the liver.

d. All of the above

29. Rats injected with CCK over several days will

   a. gain a lot of weight.

   b. lose a lot of weight.

   c. stay at the same weight.

   d. lose a little bit of weight but then gain it back when the injections are withheld.

30. In Hervey's parabiotic rats, the rat without a lesion lost weight because

   a. the lesioned rat was digesting all of the food that both rats consumed.

   b. the lesioned rat continually produced a satiety signal that inhibited eating only in the nonlesioned rat.

   c. the nonlesioned rat became insensitive to hunger cues.

   d. the lesioned rat refused to eat.

31. As leptin ___, neuropeptide Y ___.

   a. increases; increases

   b. increases; decreases

   c. decreases; decreases

   d. increases; remains the same

32. Which of the following is NOT a health risk associated with obesity?

   a. loss of bone density

   b. colon cancer

   c. Alzheimer's disease

   d. heart disease

33. A body mass index (BMI) of ___ is considered moderately risky.

   a. 20–25

   b. 30–35

   c. 25–29

   d. 36–40

34. Correlations for BMI are HIGHEST for

131

a. identical twins raised together.

b. identical twins raised apart.

c. fraternal twins raised together.

d. fraternal twins raised apart.

35. A rat of normal weight is MOST likely to starve to death when biotically paired with a(n) ___ rat.

    a. *db/db*

    b. *ob/ob*

    c. *db/db* or *ob/ob*

    d. normal

36. Basal metabolism accounts for energy used to fuel the brain and other organs and for

    a. exercise.

    b. digestion.

    c. maintaining body temperature.

    d. physical activity.

37. Mavis, who does not exercise, has reduced her calorie intake by 25% and expects to lose a lot of weight. What is likely to happen?

    a. She will lose as much weight as she wants.

    b. Her metabolism will increase.

    c. Her metabolism will decrease.

    d. It is impossible to predict.

38. Someone who responds to increased caloric consumption by fidgeting a lot

    a. will probably gain a lot of weight.

    b. may gain little or no weight.

    c. will probably lose weight.

    d. may develop other nervous habits.

39. In some obese people, carbohydrate consumption

    a. elevates mood.

    b. leads to depression.

    c. reduces serotonin levels.

d. a and c

40. Which of the following drugs blocks the absorption of fat?

   a. leptin

   b. sibutramine

   c. PYY

   d. orlistat

41. Serotonin-enhancing drugs are LEAST likely to be useful for treating

   a. obesity.

   b. bulimia.

   c. purging anorexia.

   d. restrictive anorexia.

42. Leptin seems to

   a. increase appetite.

   b. increase metabolism.

   c. decrease appetite.

   d. b and c

43. Based on recent research, the neurtransmitters most involved in anorexia and bulimia are

   a. dopamine and norepinephrine.

   b. serotonin and norepinephrine.

   c. serotonin and dopamine.

   d. dopamine, norepinephrine, and serotonin.

44. The difference between bulimics and purging anorexics is that

   a. bulimics are usually of normal weight.

   b. purging anorexics purge by using laxatives, whereas bulimics rely on vomiting.

   c. purging anorexics are usually male.

   d. bulimics, but not purging anorexics, tend to be impulsive.

Answers

Guided Review

1. Motivation

2. instinctively

3. drive

4. homeostasis

5. Incentive

6. arousal

7. brain states

8. tissue

9. set

10. temperature

11. Ectothermic

12. endothermic

13. preoptic

14. cold-sensitive

15. shivering

16. thirst

17. 70

18. sweating

19. osmotic

20. hypovolemic

21. OVLT

22. median preoptic nucleus

23. heart

24. vagus

25. NST (nucleus of the solitary tract)

26. kidneys

27. angiotensin II

28. subfornical

29. satiety

30. stomach

31. set point

32. nutrients

33. omnivores

34. taste

35. five

36. sweet

37. umami

38. proteins

39. sour

40. bitter

41. papillae

42. medulla

43. insula

44. labeled line

45. sensory-specific

46. NST

47. avoid

48. learned taste

49. chemotherapy

50. deficient or low

51. nutrient

52. learned

53. Digestion

54. saliva

55. hydrochloric

56. vomiting or regurgitation

57. duodenum

58. (simple) sugars

59. amino acids

60. glycerol

61. liver

62. absorbed

63. hepatic portal

64. intestine

65. autonomic

66. diarrhea

67. absorptive

68. high

69. pancreas

70. Diabetes

71. glycogen

72. fats

73. adipose

74. fasting

75. sympathetic

76. glucagon

77. glucose

78. glycerol

79. liver

80. hypothalamus

81. PVN (paraventricular nucleus)

82. glucoprivic

83. lipoprivic

84. stomach

85. vagus

86. medulla/NST

87. arcuate

88. lateral

89. ghrelin

90. Prader-Willi

91. NPY (neuropeptide Y)

92. agouti-related

93. metabolism

94. volume or stretch

95. peptides

96. CCK (cholecystokinin)

97. gall bladder

98. PYY (peptide YY_{3-36})

99. arcuate

100. ventromedial

101. parabiotic

102. leptin

103. higher

104. POMC/CART

105. PVN

106. obese

107. nutrients

108. BMI (body mass index)

109. 30

110. temporal

111. decline

112. TOR (target of rapamycin kinase)

113. exercise

114. impulse or voluntary

115. genetics

116. .62

117. obesity (*ob*)

118. diabetes (*db*)

119. *ob/ob*

120. leptin

121. *MC4R*

122. *FTO*

123. Epigenetic

124. expression

125. metabolism

126. more

127. decreases

128. activity

129. set point

130. basal metabolism

131. sibutramine

132. serotonin

133. orlistat

134. leptin

135. dopamine

136. Vigabatrin

137. gastric bypass

138. bulimia

139. ten

140. Anorexia

141. laxatives

142. purgers

143. restrictors

144. gray

145. NPY

146. ghrelin

147. normal

148. ghrelin

149. Fiji

150. 11

151. 44

152. comorbid

153. serotonin

154. dopamine

155. olanzapine

Short Answer and Essay Questions

1.   This disorder is caused by the failure of a section of the father's chromosome 15 to be incorporated into the fertilized egg. The results of the absence of this genetic material include a number of impulsive behaviors (such as extreme overeating), short stature, and learning disabilities.

2.   Drive theory explains behaviors resulting from tissue deficits, such as eating and drinking, but not other forms of behavior such as sex, striving for achievement, thrill seeking, and even eating when we are not hungry. Most researchers conceptualize motivation in terms of brain states, which can account for all of these forms of motivation.

3. Ectotherms and endotherms can sun themselves, find shade, burrow in the ground, build nests or shelters, and take other external actions to control their body temperature. Only endotherms can regulate their body heat by internal means such as sweating or changing their metabolism.

4. Osmotic thirst is regulated by cells in the OVLT that detect low levels of intracellular fluid. When an

animal whose OVLT is lesioned is given an injection of salt water, it will increase its water intake to a lesser degree than one without the OVLT lesion. Hypovolemic thirst is regulated by receptors in the heart, which signals the hypothalamus via the vagus nerve, and the kidneys, which initiate increases in renin and then angiotensin II, which in turn stimulates the SFO. An animal whose SFO is lesioned will not drink in response to the presence of angiotensin II, but will drink if its intracellular fluid levels fall too low.

5. First of all, the set point for hunger fluctuates to a greater extent than that for the others. The second difference has to do with the fact that thirst is satiated by water, while satiation of hunger requires a variety of nutrients.

6. Naturally sweet foods are generally nutritious, and those that are salty contain salt, which is converted to ions that we need. Sour foods are often rotten or spoiled, and bitter foods may contain toxins. In both cases, we could become sick from eating them.

7. When we eat a lot of the same food, it becomes less appealing. However, having a variety of foods (and tastes) available seems to maintain one's appetite, and therefore interest in eating. For example, the study by Rolls et al. suggested that more food will be consumed if a greater variety of food is offered.

8. Shirley developed a learned taste aversion to chilli. Her illness, although not caused by the chilli, was associated with it because she happened to get sick within a few hours of eating it. Through learning, chilli became repulsive to her.

9. People with diabetes either have low levels of insulin or are less sensitive to it than others. Because insulin is needed to allow cells to utilize glucose, diabetics cannot use glucose as efficiently as other people. Therefore, they essentially "starve" their cells of glucose, even though it is available in the blood.

10. Because excess amounts of either of these types of nutrients is stored as fat.

11. The three major signals for hunger are low levels of glucose (glucoprivic hunger), low levels of fats (lipoprivic hunger), and the release of ghrelin synthesized in the stomach (low level of stomach nutrients).

12. This stimulates the appetite, and they will eat more than normal. There is also evidence that it may reduce energy consumption, because these rats gain weight disproportionately to the amount of food they eat. Under severe deprivation conditions, NPY can reduce body temperature and inhibit sexual behavior, thereby conserving energy.

13. All of the following play a role in satiety: stretch or volume receptors in the stomach, release of CCK

141

in response to food in the duodenum, PYY released in the intestine, leptin secreted by fat cells, and insulin released by the pancreas.

14. Rates of obesity have dramatically increased in both the U.S. and the rest of the world, causing the World Health Organization to view it as a global epidemic. The number of people who are malnourished is now double those who are undernourished, because they are getting their calories from junk food that is low in nutritional value. There are significant health problems related to obesity such as diabetes, heart disease, stroke, cancer, and even brain degeneration. Certainly obesity has negative effects on life expectancy.

15. The body seems to be programmed to hold on to weight. Under survival conditions this is adaptive, because in times of deprivation the body conserves fat. Although the body for the most part maintains weight around a set point, it is less likely to inhibit weight gain than weight loss.

16. According to information presented in the text, spontaneous activity such as casual walking, fidgeting, and posture maintenance may contribute to an increase in energy expenditure. It is possible that her level of spontaneous activity has increased, and her BMR also could have increased in response to the additional calorie intake.

17. Sibutramine inhibits serotonin reuptake. This works in some people because it inhibits carbohydrate craving (because the drug enhances serotonin, which reduces NPY activity). Orlistat blocks the absorption of fat by about 30%. It also blocks the absorption of water and leads to cramping and diarrhea. Leptin may work for obese people who are sensitive to but deficient in leptin. Increasing leptin levels reduces the sensitive individual's hunger. Vigabatrin is an experimental drug being used to treat drug addiction. It decreases dopamine and it produced weight loss in animal studies.

18. These disorders are more common in cultures where the media tend to portray thin people as beautiful. In Fiji, when television was introduced in the 1990s, the rates of anorexia and bulimia rose very quickly among adolescent girls, supposedly in response to seeing thin Western actresses.

19. Both purging anorexics and bulimics are more likely to display impulsive behavior, and they also show low levels of serotonin. Purging anorexics are typically much thinner than bulimics, however. Restrictive anorexics, on the other hand, are in some ways more like people with OCD. Following weight gain, they have higher levels of serotonin than purgers or bulimics; starvation may be a means of reducing serotonin and reducing obsessive concerns.

Posttest

1. c 2. d 3. b 4. d 5. d 6. a 7. b 8. c 9. d 10. a 11. c 12. a 13. b 14. d 15. c 16. c 17. b

18. a 19. b 20. a 21. b 22. d 23. a 24. d 25. b 26. c 27. a 28. d 29. c 30. b 31. b 32. a

33. c 34. a 35. a 36. c 37. c 38. b 39. a 40. d 41. d 42. d 43. c 44. a

7

The Biology of Sex and Gender

Chapter Outline

Hormonal Influence

Brain Structures

The Challenge of Female Homosexuality

Social Implications of the Biological Model

Learning Objectives

After reading this chapter, you should be able to answer the following questions.

1. What occurs during the four phases of the cycle of sexual arousal and satiation?

2. What role does testosterone play in sexual behavior?

3. What brain structures and neurotransmitters are involved in sexual behavior?

4. What sensory signals appear to influence sexual behavior?

5. How is olfactory information transmitted in the nervous system?

6. How does an individual become male or female?

7. What effects does prenatal exposure to hormones have on the brains of males and females?

8. What biological factors might account for the gender differences in verbal skills, spatial abilities, and aggression?

9. What are the characteristics and causes of male pseudohermaphrodism? Of female pseudohermaphrodism?

10. What do studies of behavior in pseudohermaphrodites suggest about the roles of hormones in brain development?

11. What does the case study involving ablatio penis suggest about the formation of gender identity? What are the limitations of this study?

12. What genetic and hormonal factors may contribute to homosexuality in males? What brain structures may be involved in male homosexuality?

13. What evidence is there for a biological basis for homosexuality in females?

14. What are the social implications of the biological model of homosexuality?

Sex as a Form of Motivation

Summary and Guided Review

After studying this section in the text, fill in the blanks of the following summary.

Sex shares some similarities with other forms of motivation, such as cycles of arousal and

_____ (1) and regulation by hormones and specific brain areas, but unlike hunger and

thirst, there is no homeostatic _____ (2) need for sex.

The cycle of sexual arousal and satiation in humans was studied extensively by the researchers

_____ and _____ (3) in the 1960s. They described four phases:

_____ (4), during which physiological arousal increases sharply;

_____ (5), during which arousal levels off; _____ (6), marked by

intense pleasure, vaginal contractions in females, and _____ (7) in males; and

_____ (8), during which the body returns to its resting state. Whereas

_____ (9) can re-enter the excitement phase immediately after orgasm, men have a

_____ (10) phase during which time they cannot be aroused or have another orgasm.

Among some animals, a male will return to arousal more quickly if he is exposed to a novel female rather than

the one with which he has most recently mated; this phenomenon is known as the _____

(11) effect.

The role of hormones in sexual behavior is often studied in nonhuman animals, in part because hormones

control their behavior to a _____ (12) extent than in humans. The method of

_____ (13) involves removing the gonads, the source major of sex hormones; this is done

to determine what effects exposure to hormones has on behavior. Occasionally humans undergo castration, and

those who do often experience a _____ (14) in sexual interest and behavior, although there

is a great deal of variability. Some male criminals have volunteered to undergo castration, which reduces

_____ (15), in order to curb their violent or sexual behavior; additionally, drugs that

_____ (16) testosterone are quite effective in reducing harmful sexual behaviors.

Apparently, in human males just a small amount of testosterone is needed to maintain sexual interest and

behavior.

In many animal species, females will mate only while they are in _____ (17), when they are ovulating and estrogen levels are high. Human females will engage in sex throughout the reproductive cycle, although they are more likely to initiate sex around the time of _____ (18), which corresponds with peaks in _____ (19) and, possibly more important, testosterone. Postmenopausal women's sexual behavior seems to be most closely tied to _____ (20) levels.

Research with animals has revealed several brain areas involved in sexual behavior that probably work in conjunction with one another. The _____ (21) of the hypothalamus is active during copulation in both male and female rats, and studies with monkeys indicate that it is more involved in sexual _____ (22) than motivation. Lesioned monkeys would masturbate but not _____ (23). The _____ (24) amygdala is responsive to sexual stimuli and is also active during copulation. In male rats, when the _____ (25) of the MPOA is lesioned, the result is reduced sexual activity. In female rats, when the _____ (26) hypothalamus is lesioned, they are less likely to copulate. Many neurotransmitters are involved in sexual functioning. _____ (27) activity in the MPOA increases during sexual activity. In males, as DA levels rise, they initially stimulate D_1 receptors, activating the parasympathetic response of _____ (28); later, _____ (29) receptors are activated, leading to ejaculation under _____ (30) control. Dopamine activity in the nucleus _____ (31) may be responsible for the Coolidge effect, as a recently mated male presented with a new female will show an increase in activity there. The refractory period in males appears to be influenced by D_2 receptor activity and the neurotransmitter _____ (32); drugs that inhibit reuptake of this neurotransmitter may reduce sex drive in humans.

External factors are also involved in sexual motivation and behavior; in humans, the role of _____ (33) has recently received research attention. Humans may use scent to recognize relatives or people with similar genes, in particular genes in the major _____ (34) complex (which is involved in immune functioning and may be related to fertility), and avoid selecting those people as mates. Other effective stimuli might be _____ (35), airborne chemicals released by an animal that have physiological or behavioral effects on another animal of the same species. Airborne odorous materials are detected by receptors in the _____ (36) cavity. Axons from the olfactory receptors pass through openings in the base of the skull and enter the _____ _____ (37); the information then travels to the olfactory cortex in the temporal lobes. Our ability to distinguish between _____ (38) different odors seems to be a result of the combination of a few hundred neurons that are active. Most pheromones are detected by the _____ (39) organ, also located in the nasal cavity. Some researchers believe that this organ has evolved to a diminished size in humans, and that the _____ (40) that are responsible for its receptors are no longer functional. This organ sends messages to the _____ (41) and the ventromedial nucleus of the hypothalamus, as well as to the _____ (42). Studies indicate that pheromones may be involved in _____ (43) synchrony in women living together in dorms but the findings have been difficult to replicate. Men preferred the scent of T-shirts worn by women who were in the middle of their menstrual cycle, when they would be expect to be _____ (44) and, therefore, fertile. PET scans suggest that pheromones from the T-shirts might activate the _____ _____ (45) area, where structures important for sexual behavior are located.

Mating in prairie voles involves the release of the neurotransmitter _____ (46) and the neuropeptide _____ (47), which is more important in females and _____ (48), which is more important in males. In humans, oxytocin facilitates bonding and plays a role in muscle contractions in lactation and _____ (49). Oxytocin also contributes to social _____ (50), which is necessary for developing mate preferences.

Short Answer and Essay Questions

Answer the following questions.

1. Compare hunger and sex as forms of motivation. Point out their similarities and differences.

2. Name the four phases of sexual response described by Masters and Johnson.

3. What role does testosterone play in sexual motivation in men and women? Discuss the research that indicates this hormone's importance for sexual arousal and for behavior in men and in women.

4. Identify the brain areas most important for sexual behavior in males and females, based on animal studies.

5. What are pheromones? Give an example of how they might affect reproductive function, sexual behavior, or attraction?

The Biological Determination of Sex and Gender-Related Behavioral and Cognitive Differences

Summary and Guided Review

After studying these sections in the text, fill in the blanks of the following summary.

The term "sex." which refers to the biological characteristics that distinguish males and females, should not be confused with _____ (51), which refers to the behavioral characteristics associated with being male or female, or gender _____ (52), which is the sex an individual identifies herself or himself as being. Sometimes a person's sex does not match the gender or gender identity.

The first step in the determination of sex occurs during _____ (53), when the egg and sperm cells, each containing only 1 chromosome from each of the 23 pairs of chromosomes, combine. The sex of the fetus is determined by the combination of sex chromosomes. The mother always contributes an _____ (54) chromosome. If the sperm cell contains an X chromosome, the fetus will be _____ (55), and if it contains a Y chromosome, the fetus will be _____ (56). Fetuses of both sexes initially possess identical sexual tissue that will later differentiate into male or female sex organs. In XX fetuses, the primitive gonads become _____ (57), the uterus develops from the _____ (58) ducts, the _____ (59) ducts are absorbed, and the external structures form the _____ (60), part of the vagina, and the _____ (61). In XY fetuses, the _____ (62) gene on the Y chromosome transforms the gonads to become _____ (63). These produce _____ _____ (64) hormone, which causes these ducts to degenerate, and _____ (65), which transforms the Wolffian ducts into the _____ (66) vesicles and vas deferens. _____ (67) causes the external structures to form into a penis and _____ (68). These effects of male hormones are called _____ (69) effects, because they occur early in development and produce changes that will last throughout the lifespan. Hormones also have _____ (70) effects, which cause reversible changes later in development. In humans, sexual maturation is completed during _____ (71), when gonadal hormones are again released in large amounts. Puberty is accompanied by both organizing effects, such as maturation of the _____ (72); and

activating effects, such as breast and muscle development, the release of _____ (73), and

production of sperm cells;.

In many species, sex hormones are largely responsible for sexual behavior. There are

_____ (74) periods during development when exposure to a particular hormone alters the

brain and thus influences future behavior. In rats, for example, a newborn male that is castrated will be more

likely to engage in _____ (75) (presenting its hindquarters for mounting) as an adult. A

young female rat exposed to _____ (76) will perform male-typical mounting more often as

an adult. The hormone _____ (77) is critical both for feminizing female brains and

masculinizing male brains (through aromatization of testosterone).

Behavioral sex differences in humans are less clear than they are in other animals, in part because of the

limitations of research in this area. However, _____ and _____ (78)

concluded in a 1974 review of the research literature that there were consistent differences between males and

females. In cognitive performance, girls tended to be better at _____ (79) tasks, whereas

boys tended to be better at visual-spatial tasks and _____ (80). Boys were also found to be

more _____ (81) than girls. These findings have been controversial because there is

considerable _____ (82) between males and females in these characteristics.

The source of these differences has been debated. There is evidence that experience contributes to them, in

that the differences have been decreasing over the last few decades, particularly in the area of

_____ (83). The dramatic differences in aggression rates in countries suggest that there is a

strong _____ (84) component to aggression. However, there is evidence that biological

factors contribute to some of the differences. Most researchers attribute the gender differences to hormonal

exposure during _____ (85). Males who produce low levels of testosterone during the

developmental years have lower _____ (86) ability later in life. Male transexuals who take

estrogen gain in _____ performance (87) but decrease in _____ (88)

performance. The opposite is true for female transsexuals taking _____ (89). Elevated

testosterone is associated with aggression, but it is unclear whether the hormone is the cause or result of the

behavior. For example, winning at sports _____ (90) testosterone, and losing decreases it.

Some researchers explain gender differences in traits by referring to brain anatomy and organization. One

explanation for women's superiority on verbal tasks is that they use both _____ (91) of the brain during the tasks, not just the language-based hemisphere (usually the left). In terms of spatial rotation

tasks, women rely more on _____ (92) areas, whereas men use _____

(93) areas. Brain activation patterns also differ between the genders during learning tasks, stress, and pain.

Males are also more likely to experience disorders like _____ (94), Tourette's syndrome,

and attention deficit hyperactivity disorder. while women are more likely to suffer from

_____ (95).

Short Answer and Essay Questions

Answer the following questions.

6. Which of the different sex organs and structures in females and males develop from the same primitive

    tissue? What factors are responsible for transforming these primitive structures into the male-typical

    structures? Be sure to include both internal and external structures.

7. Distinguish between organizing and activating effects of hormones, and give an example of each.

8. Compare the sexual behavior of normal female rats to those that have been "masculinized."

9. What evidence is there that differences in estrogen levels may be partly responsible for the gender

    differences seen in verbal abilities?

10. Why does the author refer to males and females as "other" rather than "opposite" sexes?

Sexual Anomalies

Summary and Guided Review

After studying this section in the text, fill in the blanks of the following summary.

Studies of people with naturally occurring variations in human sexual development can reveal valuable

information about the roles of experience and biology on sex and gender. For example, many of the physical

differences between males and females are clearly the result of the effects of hormones on development.

_____ (96) are born with ambiguous genitalia, although these individuals have

_____ (97) that match their chromosomal sex. (True hermaphrodites, who possess both

_____ (98) and testicular tissue, are extremely rare.) One cause of male

pseudohermaphrodism is the lack of the enzyme _____ (99) that converts testosterone into

_____ (100); males with this condition appear female at birth but undergo some

masculinization at puberty due to a surge of _____ (101). A similar condition, caused by

the lack of 5α-reductase, has a genetic basis; many individuals with this condition live in the

_____ (102). In most cases, the individual is reared25

as a girl, but she begins questioning her gender during childhood. When masculine characteristics develop

in puberty, most of these individuals will adopt a male gender role. Although this suggests that hormones are

largely responsible for our sense of gender, the fact that males are more valued in this society indicates that

_____ (103) may play a role as well. A third condition that produces male

pseudohermaphrodites is _____ _____ (104) syndrome; due to a

genetic mutation, these individuals lack androgen receptors and develop as apparent females, although they have

undescended _____ (105). They undergo further feminization at puberty due to estrogen

from the testes and adrenal glands, developing _____ (106), for example.

Female pseudohermaphrodism typically results from exposure to high levels of _____

(107) during fetal development. These individuals have internal female structures, but externally they resemble

males; the clitoris is enlarged, resembling a _____ (108), and the

_____ (109) may be partially or completely fused. One cause of female

pseudohermaphrodism is congenital _____ _____ (110), which

involves excessive androgen production by the adrenal glands. Parents may decide to raise the baby as a boy or

a girl, and _____ (111) surgery may be performed to alter the appearance of the genitals to

match the baby's assigned sex. Some researchers believe that we need to recognize more than two categories for

sex, including _____ (112) for individuals who are between males and females. This

ambiguity was recently highlightedin the case of athlete Caster Semnya. Following suspicions over her strong

performance and masculine physique Semenya underwent extensive _____ (113) testing.

Despite rumors that Semenya had testes triple the normal amount of _____ (114), she was

cleared to compete as a woman. One major result of this case is the realization that the International Association

of Athletic Federations does not have a definition of _____ (115).

Hormones may be involved in behavioral differences as well, through their influence on brain development.

For example, androgen insensitive individuals are like females in terms of their higher

_____ (116) ability and lower _____ (117) ability, as compared to

males. Androgen insensitive males are decidedly _____ (118) in their sexual orientation.

Although 95% of women with congenital adrenal hyperplasia who are reared as girls accept a

_____ (119) identity, they are somewhat more likely to display masculine characteristics

and define their sexual orientation as _____ (120) or _____ (121).

Furthermore, women exposed to the anti-miscarriage drug _____ (122) during fetal

development report increased _____ (123) behavior and fantasies.

But what about gender identity in individuals without hormonal anomalies? The debate between "neutral-

at-birth" and "_____ (124)-at-birth" theorists is played out in the case of a young boy

whose penis was accidentally destroyed during _____ (125) at the age of 8 months. Later,

the child underwent corrective surgery and was reassigned and reared as a girl. Money, who followed this case,

reported that "Brenda" was a well-adjusted, feminine child. However, when "Brenda" discovered the truth at the

age of 14 after several years of feeling like a male, he began living as a male, took the name David, married, and

adopted a typically masculine role. Sadly, David committed suicide in 2004. Two other cases of

_____ _____ (126) had different outcomes: In one, the individual

reverted to a male identity, and in the other, the individual remained female (although she was somewhat

masculine and had sexual contact with both _____ and _____

(127) and her sexual fantasies were predominately about women. It is important to keep in mind that these are

case studies, and we must be careful about any conclusions we draw from them.

Short Answer and Essay Questions

Answer the following questions.

11. If androgen-insensitive males are raised as females, look female even after puberty, and typically adopt a female gender identity without question, how may their condition be discovered?

12. Will a female with CAH have a uterus? Why or why not?

13. What accounts for the fact that androgen-insensitive males perform more poorly on tests of spatial skills than their sisters and other females?

14. Describe the case of Semenya that demonstrates the difficulties with gender determination and how this

seriously affected her career

15. Does CAH cause women to engage in homosexual activity? Support your answer.

16. Why are the conclusions that can be drawn about the influence of biology and experience on gender from the ablatio penis studies so limited?

Sexual Orientation

Summary and Guided Review

After studying this section in the text, fill in the blanks of the following summary.

Identifying the basis of sexual orientation is difficult. However, if we can understand why some people are attracted to members of the same sex, this may tell us something about why people are generally attracted to members of the other sex. Gays and lesbians are usually exclusively _____ (128). People who are not exclusively heterosexual or homosexual are _____ (129). It is important to understand that many more people have homosexual experiences than are considered homosexuals. The rate of homosexuality in the population is not known, although a 1994 study suggests it is probably less than 3% for men and less than 1.5% for women. Furthermore, an estimated 1% express no interest in sex at all, and are referred to as _____ (130).

There is evidence that homosexuality develops early in life; about _____% (131) of homosexuals recall feeling different in their early years, suggesting that for many, same-sex attraction is a lifelong pattern. Those who become homosexual are more likely to display gender _____ (132) during development, preferring companions of the other sex and activities typical of the other sex.

There is strong evidence for a genetic component in homosexuality. For example, identical twins show higher _____ (133) rates than other siblings, but the actual figures may be inaccurate due to the "volunteer effect". One researcher, Hamer, claims to have found an area of DNA on the _____ (134) chromosome that contributes to homosexuality in males. Hamer's study group included pairs of gay brothers with gay relatives on the _____ (135) side of the family, and _____% (136) of the brother pairs had identical genotypes in the region in question. The idea that homosexuality is a heritable trait runs counter to _____ (137) theory, which

155

argues that traits that promote survival and reproduction are the ones more likely to be passed on; recent evidence indicates that male homosexuality may be related to an _____ (138) process known as imprinting that involves inhibition of one of the mother's X chromosomes rather than inheritance of "gay genes."

Some animal studies support early hormonal influences on later homosexuality. Experimental manipulation of hormone levels in other species can produce _____-_____ (139) preferences. Critics argue that these animals display homosexuality only when isolated from members of the other sex, but a few studies indicate that homosexuality occurs spontaneously in some species, such as gulls and _____ (140). The evidence for hormonal influences in humans is weak, but there is evidence that early hormonal factors may alter the structure and _____ (141) of the brain, which in turn may contribute to homosexuality.

Some research reveals differences in brain structure between gay and heterosexual men. Simon _____ (142) found that the third interstitial nucleus of the _____ _____ (143) is smaller in gay men and heterosexual women than in heterosexual men. In one study the _____ (144) nucleus was larger in gay men than in heterosexual men and contained more _____ (145) releasing cells. Finally, in another study the anterior _____ (146) was larger in gay men and heterosexual women compared to heterosexual men. Whether these areas contribute to sexual behavior in humans is unclear. The differences in the size of the anterior commissure may be related to differences between gay and heterosexual men on cognitive tasks; gay men tend to score higher on _____ (147) tasks and lower on _____ (148) tasks than heterosexual men, which may result from prenatal hormonal feminization (or undermasculinization) of the brain. _____ (149) individuals feel that they have been born into the wrong sex, and they often undergo surgery for sex reassignment. However transsexuals are not necessarily _____ (150). One brain characteristic that might distinguish transsexuals is the _____ (151), which is smaller in women than men, and female sized in _____ (152) transsexuals.

Understanding female homosexuality also represents a challenge. But, aside from the evidence that _____ (153) women are more likely to display homosexuality, there is little evidence that the brains of lesbians have been _____ (154). Two ways in which lesbians resemble heterosexual men have been discovered: their _____ to _____-

_____ (155) ratios and the strength of click-evoked _____ (156) emissions. Because both of these traits are influenced by prenatal exposure to _____ (157), it may be that the timing of exposure results in masculinization of mechanisms for sexual orientation but not verbal and _____ (158) skills.

The social implications of the biological model are important. If sexual preference is something that can be a _____ (159), then those who display homosexuality do not qualify for minority civil rights status. However, if sexual preference is not chosen, as many homosexuals claim, then their status should be protected. Although the majority of homosexuals believe that one is born being homosexual or heterosexual, some are opposed to the _____ (160) model because of its association with a disease explanation, and their fear of efforts to "cure" homosexuality at the _____ (161) level. Other homosexuals embrace the biological model, because they think it will make homosexuality more _____ (162) in society, an assumption that has some empirical support.

Short Answer and Essay Questions

Answer the following questions.

17. What can studying homosexuality tell us about heterosexuality?

18. What evidence is presented for the social learning hypothesis of homosexuality? What are the problems with interpreting this evidence?

19. Why is homosexuality difficult to explain from an evolutionary standpoint? What evidence is there that homosexuality may be the result of epigenetic processes?

20. One criticism of the studies of brain differences in homosexuals is that they rely too much on older individuals and those who have died from AIDS. Why is this a problem? What limitations do these samples place on the conclusions that can be drawn from the results?

21. Why are some members of the homosexual community opposed to the biological model of homosexuality?

Posttest

Use these multiple-choice questions to check your understanding of the chapter.

1. As forms of motivation, how are hunger and sex different?

   a. Sex, but not hunger, involves arousal and satiation.

   b. Hunger, but not sex, is under the influence of hormones.

   c. Hunger, but not sex, represents a homeostatic tissue need.

   d. Sex, but not hunger, is entirely under the control of external stimuli.

2. Penile and clitoral erection first occur in the ___ phase of the sexual response.

   a. excitement

   b. plateau

   c. orgasm

   d. resolution

3. Which of the following statements regarding the refractory phase of the sexual response is TRUE?

   a. Females have a shorter refractory phase than males.

   b. During the refractory phase, orgasm cannot occur.

   c. Males typically have a refractory phase of 3–5 hours.

   d. All of the above

4. Anti-androgen drugs

   a. may block the production of testosterone.

   b. may reduce deviant sexual behaviors.

   c. may reduce sexual fantasies.

   d. All of the above

5. Which of the following statements regarding sexual activity in females is TRUE?

   a. Only female humans will engage in sexual activity when they are not ovulating.

   b. Women on birth control pills are less likely to initiate sex midcycle than at other times.

   c. In women, the increased likelihood of initiating sex corresponds with an increase in sex hormone levels.

   d. Women are less likely to engage in sexual intercourse during ovulation than at other times of the cycle.

6. Which of the following brain areas is involved in sexual activity in female, but not male, rats?

   a. medial preoptic area

   b. medial amygdala

   c. sexually dimorphic nucleus

   d. ventromedial nucleus

7. Which of the following neurotransmitters increases in the nucleus accumbens during sexual activity?

   a. dopamine

   b. serotonin

   c. norepinephrine

   d. endorphin

8. Which of the following statements regarding the major histocompatibility complex is FALSE?

   a. Couples with similar MHCs may have more fertility problems.

   b. People who are unrelated are more likely to have similar MHCs.

   c. The MHC includes genes involved in the immune system.

   d. All of the above are false.

9. Which of the following statements regarding olfactory receptors is TRUE?

   a. Humans can distinguish approximately 1,000 odors.

   b. Humans have more genes for them than mice.

   c. Humans have 500–750 genes for odor receptors.

   d. There are as many different odor receptors as odors that can be detected.

10. Receptors in the VNO project to which TWO of the four areas of the hypothalamus listed below?

    a. lateral geniculate nucleus

    b. sexually dimorphic nucleus

    c. medial preoptic area

    d. ventromedial nucleus

11. Which of the following statements regarding pheromones in humans is FALSE?

    a. Women's menstrual cycles may be synchronized by pheromones.

    b. Men wearing pheromones are more likely to engage in intercourse than controls.

    c. Pheromones have been linked to sexual behavior, but not non-sexual behaviors like aggression.

    d. Women wearing pheromones are more likely to engage in intercourse than controls.

12. Oxytocin

    a. plays a role in bonding.

    b. is important in social recognition.

    c. causes muscle contractions involved in lactation and orgasm.

    d. All of the above

13. Which of the following statements regarding egg cells is TRUE?

    a. They contain both X and Y chromosomes.

    b. They contain only Y chromosomes.

    c. They contain only X chromosomes.

    d. They contain either an X or a Y chromosome.

14. Which of the following internal structures must be actively inhibited in order for the normal pattern of

    male genitalia to form?

    a. Müllerian ducts

    b. Wolffian ducts

    c. ovaries

    d. testes

15. The penis in males and the ___ in females develop from the same embryonic tissue.

    a. vagina

    b. labia

    c. uterus

    d. clitoris

16. What hormone(s) is (are) responsible for masculinization of the external genitalia in males?

    a. testosterone

    b. dihydrotestosterone

    c. Müllerian inhibiting hormone

    d. a and b

17. Which of the following represents an activating effect of a hormone?

    a. maturation of the genitals at puberty

b. the enlargement of the SDN in male rats

c. production of a mature egg cell during ovulation

d. masculinization of the genitals during prenatal development

18. Which of the following statements regarding sexual behavior in rats is TRUE?

    a. Among male rats, castration does not affect sexual behavior because it occurs after birth.

    b. Androgenized females will mount other rats but do not display lordosis.

    c. Castrated males do not display lordosis.

    d. Normal females occasionally mount other females.

19. Which is NOT true of the hormone estradiol?

    a. It is critical for masculinization of the male brain.

    b. It is critical for feminization of the female brain.

    c. It can be converted by the aromatization of testosterone.

    d. It is only found in females.

20. Which of the following gender differences has NOT been found in the research literature?

    a. Females are more emotional than males.

    b. Females tend to score better on verbal tasks than males.

    c. Males tend to score better on spatial tasks than females.

    d. Males tend to be more aggressive than females.

21. Which of the following is NOT a sex difference reported in the literature?

    a. Males are more susceptible to autism.

    b. Women are more affected by stress than males.

    c. Females are genetically more resistant to pain than males.

    d. Attention deficit disorder is more common in males.

22. Which hormone may be linked to enhanced verbal fluency?

    a. testosterone

    b. estrogen

    c. progesterone

    d. dihydrotestosterone

23. Which hormone may be linked to enhanced spatial skills?

a. testosterone

b. estrogen

c. progesterone

d. dihydrotestosterone

24. Which of the following statements regarding sex differences in aggression is FALSE?

   a. The cultural influence on aggression is weak compared to other factors.

   b. Studies indicate that males are much more likely than females to kill another person.

   c. Studies indicate that aggression is moderately heritable.

   d. Studies indicate that testosterone is related to aggression.

25. Which of the following will NOT result in male pseudohermaphrodism?

   a. 17 α-hydroxysteroid deficiency

   b. androgen insensitivity syndrome

   c. 5 α-reductase deficiency

   d. congenital adrenal hyperplasia

26. Which of the following statements regarding female pseudohermaphrodites is TRUE?

   a. They are always raised as girls.

   b. They have ovaries.

   c. The external genitalia are clearly male in appearance.

   d. They lack testosterone receptors..

27. Which of the following groups tends to score the LOWEST on spatial tasks?

   a. CAH females

   b. female pseudohermaphrodites

   c. normal females

   d. normal males

28. Regarding the case of "Bruce-Brenda-David," which of the following is TRUE?

   a. Brenda wanted to become a boy before she knew her true sex.

   b. Brenda was comfortable with her feminine role until adolescence.

   c. Brenda's identical twin brother also exhibited many feminine characteristics.

   d. This case clearly demonstrated that the "neutral-at-birth" position is incorrect.

29. The study of male pseudohermaphrodites in the Dominican Republic found that

    a. the source of the condition was androgen insensitivity.

    b. most individuals developed a sexual preference for male partners.

    c. although raised as girls, most of the individuals adopted male gender identities.

    d. All of the above

30. An early study indicated that, compared to other females, CAH females

    a. were more oriented toward male-typical occupations.

    b. were less likely to engage in same-sex erotic contact.

    c. were more feminine as children.

    d. were more likely to want to have children.

31. Which of the following statements regarding sexual orientation is TRUE?

    a. Gay men are more likely to be bisexual than lesbians.

    b. Lesbians make up a larger proportion of the population than do gay men.

    c. Gay men and lesbians are usually bisexual to a certain degree.

    d. Many more people engage in homosexual behavior than are considered homosexual.

32. Which of the following is TRUE about sex, gender, and sports?

    a. Sports organizations have successfully established a definition for gender in its rules.

    b. Currently physical examination and chromosome testing are acceptable measures for determining
       gender.

    c. Sports organizations have regarded women with strong athletic performance and a male physique
       with suspicion.

    d. All of the above

33. Gender nonconformity includes

    a. early heterosexual experiences.

    b. a childhood preference for friends of the other sex.

    c. a preference for activities usually associated with the other sex.

    d. b and c

34. According to Figure 7.15, the concordance rate for homosexuality in identical twins is

    a. much higher in lesbians than gay men.

b. about the same in lesbians and gay men.

c. much higher in gay men than lesbians.

d. low in both gay men and lesbians.

35. Homosexuality in other species

a. occurs only under controlled laboratory conditions.

b. results only from the manipulation of hormones during development.

c. sometimes resembles heterosexuality (e.g., pair bonding, parenting).

d. is never observed.

36. LeVay's study of brain anatomy showed that the INAH3 is largest in

a. heterosexual males.

b. homosexual males.

c. heterosexual females.

d. homosexual females.

37. Lesbians resemble heterosexual men in which of the following ways?

a. They perform more poorly on verbal tasks than heterosexual women.

b. They perform better on spatial tasks than heterosexual women.

c. They have a larger anterior commissure than heterosexual women.

d. They have a greater ring-to-index finger ratio than heterosexual women.

38. About what percentage of the homosexual population believes that homosexuality is inborn?

a. 10%

b. 25%

c. 50%

d. 75%

Answers

Guided Review

1. satiation

164

2. tissue

3. Masters & Johnson

4. excitement

5. plateau

6. orgasm

7. ejaculation

8. resolution

9. women

10. refractory

11. Coolidge

12. greater

13. castration

14. decline

15. testosterone

16. block

17. estrus

18. ovulation

19. estrogen

20. testosterone

21. MPOA (medial preoptic area)

22. performance/behavior

23. copulate

24. medial

25. SDN (sexually dimorphic nucleus)

26. ventromedial

27. Dopamine

28. erection

29. D_2

30. sympathetic

31. accumbens

32. serotonin

33. odors

34. histocompatability

35. pheromones

36. nasal

37. olfactory bulbs

38. 10,000

39. vomeronasal

40. genes

41. MPOA

42. amygdala

43. menstrual

44. ovulating

45. anterior thalamic

46. dopamine

47. oxytocin

48. vasopressin

49. orgasm

50. recognition

51. gender

52. identity

53. fertilization

54. X

55. female

56. male

57. ovaries

58. Müllerian

59. Wolffian

60. clitoris

61. labia

62. *6*

63. testes

64. Müllerian-inhibiting

65. testosterone

66. seminal

67. Dihydrotestosterone

68. scrotum

69. organizing

70. activating

71. puberty

72. genitals

73. ova/eggs

74. critical

75. lordosis

76. testosterone

77. estradiol

78. Macoby & Jacklin

79. verbal

80. mathematics

81. aggressive

82. overlap

83. mathematics

84. cultural

85. gestation/pregnancy

86. spatial

87. verbal

88. spatial

89. testosterone

90. increases

91. hemispheres

92. frontal

93. parietal

94. autism

95. depression

96. Pseudohermaphrodites

97. gonads

98. ovarian

99. 17α-hydroxysteroid

100. dihydrotestosterone

101. testosterone

102. Domincan Republic

103. society/culture/environment

104. androgen insensitivity

105. testes

106. breasts

107. androgens

108. penis

109. labia

110. adrenal hyperplasia

111. reconstructive

112. intersexes

113. gender

114. testosterone

115. gender

116. verbal

117. spatial

118. female

119. female

120. homosexual

121. bisexual

122. DES (diethylstilbesterol)

123. homosexual

124. sexuality

125. circumcision

126. ablatio penis

127. males and females

128. homosexual

129. bisexual

130. asexuality

131. 70

132. nonconformity

133. concordance

134. X

135. maternal

136. 64

137. Darwin/evolutionary

138. epigenetic

139. same-sex

140. sheep

141. function

142. LeVay

143. anterior hypothalamus

144. suprachiasmatic

145. vasopressin

146. commissure

147. verbal

148. spatial

149. Transsexual

150. homosexual

151. BSTc

152. male

153. CAH

154. masculinized

155. index-ring-finger

156. otoacoustic

157. testosterone

158. spatial

159. choice

160. biological

161. genetic

162. acceptable

Short Answer and Essay Questions

1. Sex and hunger are similar in that they are under the regulation of the brain and hormones, and they both involve arousal and satiation. However, there are important differences. Usually, we eat to reduce hunger, but we seek out stimuli that will increase sexual arousal. Hunger is also more controlled by internal conditions, including tissue needs, whereas sexual arousal is relatively more responsive to external conditions.

2. The phases are: excitement, plateau, orgasm, and resolution

3. Testosterone seems to be required for sexual motivation in both men and women, although only a low level appears to be necessary. However, sexual activity also increases testosterone levels, so the picture is somewhat complicated. In both men and women, castration leads to a reduction of sexual functioning. Men who are voluntarily castrated or are given testosterone-blocking drugs show reduced aggression and sexual

tendencies. In women, testosterone levels are correlated with initiating sexual activity. When given testosterone, women show more sexual responsiveness.

4. For females and males, the important brain areas are the MPOA and the medial amygdala. For males, the paraventricular nucleus and the sexually dimorphic nucleus (SDN, in the MPOA) are also involved. In females, the ventromedial hypothalamus plays a role in sexual behavior.

5. Pheromones are airborne chemicals released by an animal that affect the behavior and physiology of members of the same species. They exert their effects mostly via the vomeronasal organ, though there is evidence for some pheromone receptors in the olfactory system. Some research shows that pheromones might be involved in menstrual synchrony in women living together in dorms, and both men and women have reported increased sexual activity when exposed to underarm extracts (presumed to contain pheromones). Also, pheromones in women's sweat (the T-shirt study) may be more attractive to men when she is in mid-cycle.

6. Internally, the primitive gonads develop into either ovaries or testes; development of testes is dependent on the presence of the *SRY* gene on the Y chromosome. Without the presence of dihydrotestosterone, the external genitalia will become a clitoris, outer segment of the vagina, and labia, which is typical for females. If dihydrotestosterone is present, as it is in males, then the external structures become a penis and scrotum.

7. Organizing effects typically occur when the developing individual is first exposed to the hormone, either before or shortly after birth. This exposure leads to permanent changes in bodily structures. One example is how dihydrotestosterone changes the primitive external genital structures into a penis and scrotum, but there are many other examples in the book. Activating effects can occur any time in the life span after the initial exposure when hormone levels change, and they are reversible. An example is the development of breast tissue in females during puberty, but there are other examples in the book as well.

8. Normal female rats typically engage in lordosis, although they will occasionally mount other females. In females that have been masculinized, mounting occurs much more frequently.

9. The book cites a study by Miles et al. that showed transsexual males taking estrogen supplements scored higher on verbal tasks than those not taking estrogen.

10. He uses the term "other" to reflect the fact that males and females are not really opposite. There are some consistent differences, but even in these there is a great deal of overlap between the sexes. Overall, males and females share more similarities than they do differences. (And later in the chapter you will see that the lines

between "male" and "female" as *sexes* are not as clear as you might think.)

11. Because they do not have ovaries, they do not menstruate and they certainly cannot become pregnant. So during adolescence or early adulthood, they will probably discover their condition if they try to determine the source of problems with their reproductive systems. If diagnosis does not occur at that time, it may after the individual engages in sex and realizes she has a shallow vagina.

12. Yes, because the development of the uterus is determined by the absence of Müllerian inhibiting hormone, which CAH females are not exposed to.

13. They are insensitive to the effects of masculinizing hormones. Even females outperform them on spatial tasks because their brains are capable of responding to the small amount of androgens their bodies produce.Othe

14. After Semenya won the gold medal in a key track event, some people became suspicious about her gender due to her strong performance and masculine appearance. Her sports participation remained in jeopardy for a year while the International Association of Athletic Federations evaluated the results of her gender testing. Eventually, she was cleared to participate as a woman. This case demonstrated to the IAAF that they need to have a definition of gender in their gender verification policy.

15. It may influence some women, as evidenced by the fact that more CAH women reported homosexual contact than a control group of women. However, we can't ignore that some of the normal women behaved like the minority of the CAH women who had homosexual contact and that most of the CAH women did not report homosexual contact. Clearly, CAH is not the only factor.

16. Each case involves only a single individual, so generalizing to others is very difficult. Another problem is that these were not experiments, and there was virtually no control over the many factors influencing gender.

17. Studying those whose orientation differs from the majority of humans, in particular the ways in which their brains differ, can help us discover what the determinants are of sexual orientation; thus, it will tell us not only why some people are homosexual, but also why others are heterosexual.

18. The social learning hypothesis suggests that people who have early homosexual experiences will be more likely to become homosexual later. There is evidence for this; for example, individuals who reported having other-sex friends, masturbating in the presence of or being masturbated by a same-sex partner, and having homosexual contact prior to age 18 were more likely to be homosexual as adults. But an alternative

interpretation is that these experiences are early manifestations of an underlying homosexual tendency rather than the origin of homosexuality.

19. It seems unlikely that natural selection would favor a trait such as homosexuality that reduces the likelihood of reproduction. Homosexuality may result from an epigenetic process, rather than inheritance of "genes for homosexuality."

20. A problem with studying the brains of older homosexuals is that they have been practicing homosexual behavior for a longer period of time, so it is unclear whether any brain differences found would be the cause of sexual orientation or the result of homosexual experience. Also, gay men who have died from AIDS may have brains that look different as a result of the disease.

21. They are concerned that if a biological basis to homosexuality is discovered, it will be understood in terms of a physical abnormality that can be corrected medically to "cure" homosexuality or genetically to prevent it.

Posttest

1. c 2. a 3. b 4. e 5. c 6. d 7. a 8. b 9. c 10. c & d 11. c 12. d 13. c 14. a 15. d 16. b
17. c 18. d 19. d 20. a 21. c 22. c 23. a 24. a 25. d 26. b 27. c 28. a 29. c 30. a 31. d
32. c 33. d 34. b 35. c 36. a 37. d 38. d

8

Emotion and Health

Chapter Outline

Emotion and the Nervous System

Autonomic and Muscular Involvement in Emotion

The Emotional Brain

The Prefrontal Cortex

    APPLICATION: WHY WON'T I JUMP OUT OF AN AIRPLANE?

The Amygdala

Hemispheric Specialization in Emotion

Stress, Immunity, and Health

Stress as an Adaptive Response

Negative Effects of Stress

    APPLICATION: ONE AFTERMATH OF 9/11 IS STRESS-RELATED BRAIN DAMAGE

Social and Personality Variables

Pain as an Adaptive Emotion

Biological Origins of Aggression

Hormones and Aggression

The Brain's Role in Aggression

Serotonin and Aggression

Heredity and Environment

    IN THE NEWS: AGGRESSION, GENES, AND THE LAW

Learning Objectives

After reading this chapter, you should be able to answer the following questions.

1. How does the case of Jane at the beginning of the chapter demonstrate the importance of emotions in regulating behavior?

2. How is the autonomic nervous system involved in emotions?

3. How do the James-Lange and cognitive theories differ in their explanation of emotions? What evidence is there for these positions?

4. What are the roles of the hypothalamus, insular cortex, basal ganglia, anterior cingulate cortex, prefrontal cortex, and amygdala in emotion?

5. What are the different contributions of the two hemispheres to emotion?

6. In what ways is stress an adaptive response?

7. What are the negative effects of stress?

8. How are social and personality variables related to immune functioning?

9. Why is pain considered to be an emotion?

10. How are hormones related to aggression?

11. What brain areas are involved in aggression?

12. How is serotonin involved in aggression? (Include in your answer a discussion of serotonin's interactions with alcohol and testosterone.)

13. How do genes and environment interact to influence aggression?

Emotion and the Nervous System

Summary and Guided Review

After studying this section in the text, fill in the blanks of the following summary.

Emotions enrich our lives and _____ (1) our behavior. For example, anger intensifies _____ (2) behavior and accelerates flight, whereas happiness encourages the behavior that produces it. Emotions make experiences more _____ (3), so we are likely to repeat

behaviors that bring joy and avoid those that produce pain. Jane was unable to _____ (4)

from her emotional experiences, due to damage to her _____ (5) cortex. As Damasio would

have said about this case, reason without _____ (6) is inadequate for making the decisions

that guide our lives.

Emotions involve subjective "feelings," expressions, and behavior, all of which are rooted in the nervous

system. For example, the autonomic nervous system is intimately involved in emotional responding; activation

of the _____ (7) branch produces arousal, and the _____ (8) branch

helps to reduce activity and restore bodily resources. _____ (9) is an important hormone

released from the adrenal glands in times of stress, due to activation of the sympathetic nervous system.

In the late 1900s an American psychologist and a Danish physiologist independently proposed what has

become known as the _____-_____ (10) theory of emotion, which

states that emotional experience results from the physiological arousal that precedes it. In an experiment in

which subjects were made angry or frightened, the two emotions were accompanied by

_____ (11) patterns of physiological activity. Years later, Schacter and Singer interpreted

these results based on _____ (12) theory, stating that the _____

(13)of the emotion is based on cognitive assessment of the situation, and physiological arousal only determines

the emotion's intensity. This theory is supported by the finding that similar patterns of arousal can be interpreted

differently, based on the _____ (14) context. More recently, studies of facial expression in

emotion have added support for the James-Lange theory. Ekman found that posed facial expressions can

actually produce the _____ (15) of the intended emotion. When a woman's facial muscles

are paralyzed with injections of _____ (16) it affects the ability not only to produce facial

expressions of emotion, but to experience them as well; this has been verified by fMRI evidence of reduced

activation of the amygdala while trying to imitate angry expressions. Feedback from emotional expressions may

also help us _____ (17) other people's emotions, which is critical to social

communication. Special cells in the brain called _____ (18) neurons may be involved in

our ability to show _____ (19) for others, based on the finding that observation of other

people's emotions activate our own "emotional brain" pathways. People with _____ (20)

have difficulty understanding the emotions of others; they can imitate expressions but the mimicry is delayed.

There are several brain structures that play important roles in emotions. Many of these areas are located in the _____ (21) system, which also contributes to learning, memory, and motivation. In humans undergoing brain surgery, Heath found that electrical stimulation of the _____ (22) elicited autonomic arousal, and patients reported feeling different emotions, depending on the placement of the electrode. Sexual interest seems to be at least in part a result of stimulation of the _____ (23) area. Recent brain imaging studies indicate that the _____ (24) cortex and _____ _____ (25) are involved in disgust. Because it combines emotional, attentional, and bodily information, the anterior _____ (26) cortex is believed to be important for cognitive processing of emotion, and possibly _____ (27). This structure is also larger on the right side in people who manifest _____ (28) avoidance; which involves worry about possible problems, fearfulness, and shyness. Although research has linked emotions to particular brain areas, it is important to remember that no emotion can be linked to a _____ (29) part of the brain.

Patients with damage to the prefrontal cortex have difficulty making rational _____ (30). When damage includes the _____ (31) cortex, people show a lack of responsiveness to a gambling task; their skin _____ (32) response is not affected by risk, and they do not learn to avoid making risky choices. In _____ (33) seekers, brain scans have found strong connections in a loop involving the hippocampus, amygdala, and striatum. But in _____ (34) dependent individuals the strongest connections are between the striatum and the _____ (35) areas.

The _____ (36), a limbic structure that sends information to the prefrontal cortex, is especially involved in the negative emotions of fear and _____ (37). Rats with damage to the amygdala display no _____ (38) of cats, and humans with damaged amygdala are very trusting of others and have difficulty identifying fearful _____ _____ (39) in others. Furthermore, they seem incapable of learning to recognize harmful situations or experiencing emotional responses to rewards and _____ (40).

There are hemispheric differences in emotion; the left hemisphere seems to be more involved in _____ (41) emotions, while the right hemisphere is more involved in _____ (42) emotions. Right hemisphere damage has been linked to impairment of emotional responses and perception of emotions in others, perhaps because people with such damage have diminished _____ (43) response. People with right hemisphere damage often speak in an unemotional _____ (44), and have trouble recognizing emotion from a person's speech.

Short Answer and Essay Questions

Answer the following questions.

1. Many people believe that decision making should be guided by rationality and that emotion leads to bad decisions. After reading this section of the chapter, do you agree with this view? Why or why not?

2. Compare the James-Lange and cognitive theories of emotion.

3. Identify key brain areas involved in emotion. How do the right and left hemispheres differ in the role they play in emotion?

4. Give an example of how emotional experiences are adaptive (how they promote survival).

Stress, Immunity, and Health

Summary and Guided Review

After studying this section in the text, fill in the blanks of the following summary.

The term _____ (45) is used to refer to external events that challenge an organism as well as internal responses to the challenge. The internal experience of stress is highly variable; not everyone feels stress under the same conditions.

Usually, the internal changes associated with stress are positive and _____ (46). These include activation of the _____-_____-_____ (47) axis, a mechanism responsible for the release of stress _____ (48) that prepare the body for "fight or flight" via their effects on circulation and energy availability. For example, the stress hormone _____ (49) converts proteins to glucose and increases both fat availability and _____ (50); this provides more energy for a longer period of time than _____ (51) nervous system arousal alone. Changes also occur in the _____ (52) system, which protects the body against foreign substances that could be introduced during injury. There are several types of _____ (53), including macrophages, T cells, and antibody-producing _____ (54). Another type of immune cell,

_____ _____ (55) cells, destroy cancer and viral-infected cells. In autoimmune disorders, such as multiple _____ (56), the immune system attacks cells produced by the body (in this case myelin). In AIDS, _____ (57) fail to detect invaders and the person dies of an infectious disease.

If the stress response continues over a long period of time, considerable harm can occur, including memory_____ (58), motivational changes, mood changes, and immune system impairment. People in the vicinity of the Three Mile Island nuclear accident continued to experience reduced immune functioning as long as _____ (59) years after the event. In another study, volunteers exposed to cold viruses were more likely to develop _____ (60) if they had experienced stress for longer than a month.Increased vulnerability to stress may produce cardiovascular disease, as evidenced by the fact that children who were more reactive to having their hands placed in _____ _____ (61) were more likely to have high blood pressure as adults. There is even evidence that acute stress can lead to sudden _____ _____ (62). For example, on the day of the 1994 earthquake in Southern California, the number of deaths due to _____ (63) was five times higher than average. Stress may also contribute to brain damage in victims of torture or abuse, particularly in the _____ (64), perhaps due to prolonged exposure or greater sensitivity to cortisol. Three years after the 9/11 attack, people living near the site showed exaggerated activity in the _____ (65) when they viewed facial expressions of fear, and they had reduced gray matter in several locations. Cardiac events can increase during _____ (66) events, as well as during the first few days after the change to _____ _____ (67) time in the autumn.

Several social and _____ (68) variables are linked to stress-related health problems as well. For example, people who are _____ (69) are more likely to suffer from heart disease, and among _____ (70) patients, those who lose hope or accept their disease have a lower survival rate than those who display a fighting spirit. Individuals with greater left prefrontal activity (associated with positive emotion) developed more antibodies following _____ (71) vaccination. Introverted HIV-positive men had _____ (72) viral loads than extroverts. However, these studies are correlational, so personality may not be the cause of differences in immune response. It is suggested that because introverts have higher sympathetic nervous system activity, high _____ (73) levels may contribute to both the introversion and increased HIV virus multiplication.

Like stress, _____ (74) is in many ways an adaptive response. People with congenital _____ (75) to pain have difficulty learning to avoid injuries and may die prematurely. Pain can be considered an _____ (76) as well as a sensation. How people experience pain varies on an individual and cultural basis. For example, in the United States _____ (77) is considered more painful than it is in some other cultures. A study of World War II soldiers wounded in combat revealed that they reported very little pain compared with patients undergoing _____ (78). Also, pain that is inflicted by others _____ (79) hurts more than pain caused by accident.

Pathways that carry messages about pain connect with the _____ (80) cortex and the anterior cingulate cortex, which is connected to several limbic structures. Studies suggest that the _____ _____ (81) cortex is involved in the emotional component of pain. The _____ (82) cortex is also involved in emotional responses to pain, and it is implicated in cases of pain insensitivity disorders in which people are able to feel pain but are not bothered by it.

Short Answer and Essay Questions

Answer the following questions.

5. List the four types of immune cells discussed in the book, and explain the function of each.

6. Discuss the role of personality factors in cancer survival. Why is it difficult to determine if factors such as introversion are directly responsible for reduced immune functioning?

7. Why is pain considered to be adaptive? What would your life be like if you could not feel, or were not bothered by, pain?

8. Discuss the role of the anterior cingulate cortex in pain. How do researchers know that it is involved in the emotional response to, but not the sensation of, pain?

Biological Origins of Aggression

Summary and Guided Review

After studying this section in the text, fill in the blanks of the following summary.

Aggression is sometimes, but not always, an adaptive response, involving both motivation and

_____ (83). There are many different forms of aggression, including

_____ (84) aggression, which is characterized as an unprovoked attack on another

individual; _____ (85) aggression, which involves responding physically to a threat; and

_____ (86) aggression, which occurs when an animal kills another for food. Human

aggression can be classified as reactive, which is impulsive, provoked, and emotional, and aggression that is

premeditated, unprovoked and relatively emotionless, called _____ (87).

The sex hormones seem to be especially involved in _____ (88) aggression,

particularly in rats. In humans, studies suggest that increased aggression is linked to _____

(89) syndrome in some women, and violent male criminals have higher _____ (90) levels.

However, the causal relationship between hormones and aggression is not clear, because it has been shown that

testosterone _____ (91) while watching one's team win a sports event and even after

receiving the MD degree.

Defensive and predatory aggression in cats involve different brain pathways in the amygdala,

hypothalamus, and _____ (92) gray. In humans, the hypothalamus, amygdala, and

_____ (93) region are involved in aggression. For example, seizures in the

_____ (94) are linked to increased aggression, whereas damage to this structure is linked to

decreased aggression. Reactive and proactive aggression also involve different brain activation patterns, based

on PET scans. Reactive aggression in murderers is associated with reduced activity in the

_____ (95) cortex. People with _____ _____

(96) are more likely to have reduced prefrontal gray matter. Proactive aggression is also associated with

_____ (97), a condition in which people show lack of remorse for their actions and less

autonomic responding to stress and aversive stimuli.

Serotonin activity, which can be measured via the metabolite _____ (98) in the

cerebrospinal fluid) and by _____ (99) scans, is also related to aggression. People with

_____ (100) aggression have decreased serotonin activity in the prefrontal cortex and

anterior cingulate gyrus. Evidence for serotonin's causal role in aggression comes from a study in which men

deprived of _____ (101), a serotonin precursor, displayed more aggression in a mock

competition than controls. Some researchers believe high _____ (102) levels and low

_____ (103) levels interact to produce aggression. This is supported by animal studies as well as human data: violent alcoholic offenders have _____ (104) testosterone levels and

_____ (105) serotonin levels. In fact, low serotonin levels and alcohol consumption create

a deadly cycle of craving and aggression. Drugs that inhibit _____ (106) reuptake at the

synapse, such as the antidepressant fluoxetine, reduce alcohol intake and aggressiveness.

Aggression is genetically influenced; about _____ (107) % of the variation among

people in aggression is genetic in origin. The genes for three types of serotonin _____

(108) have also been implicated in impulsive aggression. The environment also plays a role in aggression. For

example, inadequate _____ (109) may contribute to violent criminality in both men and

women. Several studies suggest that genes and environment interact. The *MAO-L* _____

(110) of the *MAOA* gene results in low levels of the enzyme; this allele was discovered in a Dutch family with a

large number of violent males. The allele has also been found to predict males' membership in

_____ (111) and their use of weapons. However, low levels of the MAOA enzyme initially

result in high serotonin, so why are these individuals more aggressive? Most likely the brain compensates by

reducing its sensitivity to _____ (112). The interaction of genes and environment in

aggression is demonstrated by the finding that the *MAO-L* allele only produced violence in males who had been

subjected to childhood physical abuse. An Italian court recently administered a lighter sentence in a murder case

because the defendant had the *MAOA-L* allele. Researchers urge caution in using genetic information to make

such decisions when we know so little about how genes affect a particular individual. Furthermore,

environmental factors clearly contribute to aggression.

Short Answer and Essay Questions

Answer the following questions.

9. Distinguish between offensive, defensive, and predatory aggression. Give an example of each.

10. Identify the specific nuclei of the amygdala, hypothalamus, and periaqueductal gray involved in defensive and predatory aggression.

11. What are the characteristics of people with antisocial personality disorder? What brain anomaly may account for this disorder?

12. Describe how Moeller and colleagues demonstrated a causal relationship between low serotonin levels

and aggression in humans. From this study, can we say for sure that low serotonin causes aggression in humans? Why or why not?

13. Explain how serotonin and alcohol may interact in contributing to aggression.

Posttest

Use these multiple-choice questions to check your understanding of the chapter.

1. In the gambling task described in this chapter, individuals with ventromedial prefrontal damage

    a. produce a skin conductance response to the risky piles but do not learn to avoid choosing from the risky card piles.

    b. do not produce a skin conductance response but learn to avoid choosing from the risky card piles anyway.

    c. do not produce a skin conductance response and do not learn to avoid choosing from the risky card piles.

    d. produce a skin conductance response and learn to avoid choosing from the risky card piles.

2. Sympathetic arousal involves all of the following EXCEPT

    a. increased heart rate.

    b. increased blood pressure.

    c. increased respiration.

    d. increased digestion.

3. According to the James-Lange theory, emotional experiences occur in which order?

    a. stimulus-arousal-emotion

    b. stimulus-emotion-arousal

    c. stimulus-appraisal-emotion

    d. stimulus-arousal/appraisal-emotion

4. Which of the following is NOT true about mirror neurons?

    a. They respond both when we engage in a specific act and when we observe the same act in others.

    b. They show increased activity in autism.

c. They most likely play a role in the emotion of empathy.

d. They were discovered when researchers noted that the same neurons responded when monkeys reached for food and when they saw the researcher pick up food.

5. Studies of physiological changes during negative emotions indicate that

   a. there are no differences in autonomic arousal patterns for different negative emotions.

   b. blood pressure increases more during anger.

   c. heart rate increases more during sadness than fear.

   d. fear involves less motor activation than sadness.

6. Facial expressions

   a. are probably less important in emotional feedback than autonomic arousal.

   b. are all learned from one's family.

   c. can evoke emotions consistent with the expression.

   d. None of the above

7. Which of the following structures is NOT considered part of the limbic system?

   a. amygdala

   b. cingulate gyrus

   c. hippocampus

   d. medulla

8. In an early study by Heath with humans, stimulation of the septal area evoked

   a. pleasure.

   b. fear.

   c. anxiety.

   d. sadness.

9. Someone with heightened activity in the amygdala would be MOST likely to experience

   a. pleasure.

   b. anxiety.

   c. anger.

   d. sadness.

10. People with damage to the amygdala

a. are completely fearless.

b. often exhibit fits of rage.

c. have difficulty learning to avoid harmful situations.

d. suffer from antisocial personality disorder.

11. People with prefrontal damage can probably do all of the following EXCEPT

a. experience any emotion at all.

b. learn to avoid venomous snakes.

c. experience negative emotions.

d. learn to avoid risky investments.

12. People with right hemisphere damage have difficulty with all of the following EXCEPT

a. recognizing facial expressions in others.

b. recognizing emotion in others' voices.

c. understanding verbal expressions of emotion.

d. displaying nonverbal signs of emotion.

13. Cortisol is released by the

a. hypothalamus.

b. pituitary gland.

c. adrenal glands.

d. All of the above

14. Cortisol is responsible for all of the following EXCEPT

a. increased oxygen transport to muscle cells.

b. conversion of protein to glucose.

c. increase in fat availability.

d. increase in metabolism.

15. Immune system cells that work by ingesting foreign substances and then displaying their antigens are called

a. T cells.

b. B cells.

c. macrophages.

d. natural killer cells.

16. Antibodies are produced by

    a. T cells.

    b. B cells.

    c. macrophages.

    d. natural killer cells.

17. Following the Three Mile Island accident, nearby residents displayed

    a. reduced immune cells.

    b. a higher cancer rate.

    c. reduced ability to concentrate.

    d. a and c

18. Children who showed the greatest amount of reactivity (in terms of blood pressure increase) when placing their hands in cold water were MORE likely to develop

    a. cancer as children.

    b. cancer as adults.

    c. high blood pressure as children.

    d. high blood pressure as adults.

19. Sudden cardiac death may be linked to

    a. stress.

    b. bereavement.

    c. joy.

    d. a and b

20. On the day of a major earthquake in Southern California, the number of people who died from a heart attack was ____ times the average.

    a. 50

    b. 25

    c. 5

    d. 1/5

21. Brain damage in posttraumatic stress may be due to increased sensitivity to

a. cortisol.

b. norepinephrine.

c. epinephrine.

d. all of the above.

22. The personality factor of hostility is MOST strongly associated with

    a. cancer.

    b. heart disease.

    c. ulcers.

    d. reduced immune functioning.

23. Greater prefrontal right-hemisphere activity is associated with

    a. greater antibody production following vaccination.

    b. greater T-cell levels among AIDS patients.

    c. lower antibody production following vaccination.

    d. lower T-cell levels among AIDS patients.

24. Introversion is associated with

    a. increased natural killer cell activity.

    b. higher levels of HIV.

    c. higher cancer rates.

    d. a and b

25. Which of the following statements regarding pain is FALSE?

    a. It is both a sensation and an emotion.

    b. Situational factors may influence how strongly it is felt.

    c. The ability to experience pain is not adaptive.

    d. Some people are unable to experience pain.

26. The emotional component of pain is MOST directly linked to activity in the

    a. somatosensory cortex.

    b. anterior cingulate cortex.

    c. prefrontal cortex.

    d. insular cortex.

27. People who underwent prefrontal lobotomy for pain that failed to respond to other treatments

    a. no longer experienced pain.

    b. were no longer bothered by the pain.

    c. experienced more pain than before the procedure.

    d. were often paralyzed as well as rendered insensitive to pain.

28. Which of the following is an example of offensive aggression?

    a. two male elk fighting over a female in estrus

    b. a cheetah chasing down and killing an antelope

    c. a woman killing an attacker in self-defense

    d. a man hunting deer for meat

29. Allopregnanolone is a metabolite of ___ that may be linked to aggression in females.

    a. estrogen

    b. testosterone

    c. progesterone

    d. serotonin

30. Among prisoners, testosterone would probably be LOWEST in those convicted of which of the following crimes?

    a. drug offenses

    b. rape

    c. murder

    d. armed robbery

31. Which of the following statements regarding hormones and aggression in humans is FALSE?

    a. The hormonal changes accompanying PMS may be associated with increased aggression in women.

    b. Winning a sporting event increases testosterone.

    c. High testosterone is linked to aggression in men but not women.

    d. Male prisoners with higher testosterone are rated as tougher by their peers.

32. Which of the following structures is NOT part of the pathway for predatory aggression in cats?

    a. amygdala

b. hypothalamus

c. thalamus

d. periaqueductal gray

33. In humans, aggression is linked to

    a. excessive prefrontal activity.

    b. seizures in the amygdala.

    c. hypothalamic tumors.

    d. b and c

34. In humans, affective, but not premeditated, murder is linked to

    a. underactivity in the prefrontal cortex.

    b. tumors in the hypothalamus.

    c. seizures in the amygdala.

    d. tumors in the septal area.

35. The impulsiveness displayed by people with antisocial personality disorder may result from abnormalities of the

    a. amygdala.

    b. prefrontal cortex.

    c. medial hypothalamus.

    d. lateral hypothalamus.

36. Proactive aggression

    a. is associated with psychopathy.

    b. is premeditated, unprovoked, and lacks emotional intensity.

    c. is similar to predatory aggression in animals.

    d. All of the above

37. 5-HIAA is a(n) ____ of serotonin.

    a. precursor

    b. antagonist

    c. metabolite

    d. agonist

38. Men who drank a substance that inhibited tryptophan

    a. were more likely to physically attack their opponents.

    b. were more likely to lose points to their opponents.

    c. were more likely to take points away from their opponents.

    d. showed reduced 5-HIAA levels.

39. Prozac (fluoxetine) reduces all of the following EXCEPT

    a. alcohol cravings.

    b. serotonin levels.

    c. aggression.

    d. alcohol consumption.

40. Monkeys with high testosterone and low 5-HIAA levels would MOST likely

    a. tend to be cautious.

    b. tend to be extremely aggressive.

    c. engage in dominance-related aggression only.

    d. show little hostility toward other monkeys.

41. Heredity accounts for about ___% of the variability in aggression.

    a. 50

    b. 75

    c. 25

    d. 15

42. Which of the following genes has been implicated in aggression, and this information was used in a

    court case to determine sentencing?

    a. the *MAOA-L* gene

    b. the *5-HIAA* gene

    c. the *MC4R* gene

    d. all of the above

Answers

Guided Review

1. motivate

2. defensive

3. memorable

4. learn

5. prefrontal

6. emotion

7. sympathetic

8. parasympathetic

9. cortisol

10. James-Lange

11. different

12. cognitive

13. identity

14. environmental

15. experience3

16. botox

17. recognize/understand

18. mirror

19. empathy

20. autism

21. limbic

22. hypothalamus

23. septal

24. insular

25. basal ganglia

26. cingulate

27. consciousness

28. harm

29. single

30. judgements

31. ventromedial

32. conductance

33. novelty

34. reward

35. prefrontal

36. amygdala

37. anxiety

38. fear

39. facial expressions

40. punishments

41. positive

42. negative

43. autonomic

44. monotone

45. stress

46. adaptive

47. hypothalamus-pituitary-adrenal

48. hormones

49. cortisol

50. metabolism

51. sympathetic

52. immune

53. leukocytes

54. B cells

55. natural killer

56. sclerosis

57. T cells

58. impairment

59. 6

60. infections

61. cold water

62. cardiac death

63. heart attacks

64. hippocampus

65. three

66. sports

67. daylight savings time

68. personality

69. hostile

70. cancer

71. influenza

72. higher

73. norepinephrine

74. pain

75. insensitivity

76. emotion

77. childbirth

78. surgery

79. intentionally

80. somatosensory

81. anterior cingulate

82. prefrontal

83. emotion

84. offensive

85. defensive

86. predatory

87. proactive

88. offensive

89. premenstrual

90. testosterone

91. increases

92. periaqueductal

93. septal

94. amygdala

95. prefrontal

96. antisocial personality

97. psychopathy

98. 5-HIAA

99. PET

100. reactive or impulsive

101. tryptophan

102. testosterone

103. serotonin

104. high

105. low

106. serotonin reuptake

107. 50

108. receptors

109. parenting

110. allele

111. gangs

112. serotonin

Short Answer and Essay

1. Answers may vary on this question. However, the author makes a compelling argument against the distinction between rationality and emotion. In particular, the studies of people whose emotional capacities are impaired suggest that without emotion, we would not make very good decisions. For example, people like Jane who have prefrontal damage seem to be unable to learn from the emotions that normally accompany rewards and punishment, and so their behavior is often impulsive.

2. The James-Lange theory states that emotional experience results from the physiological arousal that precedes, and different emotions are the result of different patterns of arousal. The cognitive theory of emotion stated that the identity of the emotion is based on the cognitive assessment of the situation, and physiological arousal contributes only to the emotion's intensity.

3. The important systems are the parts of the limbic system, including the hypothalamus, septal area, insula, anterior cingulate cortex, amygdala, and pre-frontal cortex. The right hemisphere seems more important in negative emotions, whereas the left hemisphere is more active during positive emotions.

4. There are many possible answers, but a correct response should refer to the role of emotions in decision-making, communication, preparation or motivation for a response, or learning.

5. Macrophages are a type of leukocyte that engulf and ingest invading microorganisms, and then display the antigens of the invader, attracting T cells. The T cells than multiply and destroy the invaders. B cells produce antibodies that fight off specific intruders. Natural killer cells target cancer cells and virus-infected cells; they are less specific than T and B cells.

6. Cancer survival is higher among patients with a fighting spirit and lower among those who are depressed. However, this research is correlational, which makes cause and effect difficult to determine. A good example comes from the association between introversion and HIV levels in AIDS. The introverted patients had high levels of sympathetic activity. Increased sympathetic activity is caused by epinephrine and norepinephrine, both of which are high in introverted individuals, and norepinephrine increases HIV virus multiplication in the laboratory. Thus, norepinephrine may be responsible for both the introversion and the HIV virus proliferation in the subjects; personality characteristics and emotional states may be more of a marker for physiological activity that results in the health condition rather than a causal influence.

7. Pain is adaptive because it lets us know when we have done something that is harmful, and therefore, we can learn to avoid such behaviors. People who are insensitive to or are not bothered by pain do not respond to the warning signals of pain, and are subject to greater injury; and, lacking the emotional deterrent, they have difficulty learning to avoid behaviors that can lead to injury.

8. The anterior cingulate cortex appears to mediate the emotional aspect of pain. When a painful stimulus is presented several times and participants feel increasing unpleasantness (but the stimulus remains the same), there are changes in the anterior cingulate cortex, but not the somatosensory cortex. Also, when participants under hypnosis are instructed that a painful stimulus is becoming more unpleasant (again, without any change in

the stimulus), the same result occurs.

9. Offensive aggression involves an unprovoked attack, such as when a male lion kills the offspring of a rival male. Defensive aggression involves a response to a threat or attack and is motivated by fear. An example of this is when an animal attacks another animal that has threatened it. Predatory aggression involves killing another animal for food and generally lacks the emotional components seen in the other forms of aggression. (There are many other possible examples that could be given.)

10. Defensive aggression: medial nucleus of amygdala to the medial hypothalamus to the dorsal periaqueductal gray. Predatory aggression: lateral and central nuclei of amygdala to the lateral hypothalamus to the ventral periaqueductal gray.

11. People with antisocial personality disorder tend to display impulsive behavior and generally have difficulty getting along with others, because they do not follow the "rules" of social conduct. Furthermore, they apparently lack the capacity for remorse or guilt over their disruptive and destructive behavior. People with antisocial personality disorder are more likely to have smaller prefrontal areas. Furthermore, people with damage to this area (e.g., due to injury) show many of the same characteristics.

12. In this study, one group of men drank a mixture that reduced tryptophan and, it was assumed, would also reduce serotonin, because tryptophan is a precursor for this neurotransmitter. The control group drank another mixture that had no effect. The men in the first group displayed more aggression by subtracting more points from a competitor's score. The first limitation of this study is that no mention is made of whether 5-HIAA was measured; it is assumed that lowered tryptophan would reduce serotonin. Another problem is the nature of the aggression measure. This is not physical aggression, so even if the men deprived of tryptophan indeed had lower serotonin levels, all we can say from this study is that they displayed one form of aggression more than the control subjects, but it is not clear if this would occur with other forms of aggression.

13. Both alcohol and low levels of serotonin are associated with increased aggression. Furthermore, alcohol reduces serotonin. Therefore, alcohol probably enhances aggression through its reduction of serotonin.

Posttest

1. c 2. d 3. a 4. b 5. b 6. c 7. d 8. a 9. b 10. c 11. d 12. c 13. c 14. a 15. c 16. b 17. d

18. d 19. a 20. c 21. a 22. b 23. c 24. b 25. c 26. b 27. b 28. a 29. c 30. a 31. c 32. c

3. d 34. a 35. b 36. d 37. c 38. c 39. b 40. b 41. a 42. a

9

Hearing and Language

Chapter Outline

Hearing

The Stimulus for Hearing

The Auditory Mechanism

Frequency Analysis

Locating Sounds With Binaural Cues

APPLICATION: COCHLEAR AND BRAINSTEM IMPLANTS TO RESTORE HEARING

Language

Broca's Area

Wernicke's Area

The Wernicke-Geschwind Model

Reading, Writing, and Their Impairment

Mechanisms of Recovery From Aphasia

A Language-Generating Mechanism?

Language in Nonhumans

Neural and Genetic Antecedents

Learning Objectives

After reading this chapter, you should be able to answer the following questions.

1. How is sensory information transmitted to the nervous system?

2. What are the characteristics of sound stimuli?

3. What are the components and functions of the: outer ear; middle ear; inner ear?

4. What brain areas are involved in processing sound?

5. How is sound frequency analyzed by the nervous system?

6. How are we able to locate the source of a sound?

7. What brain areas are involved in language? How does damage or impairment of these areas account for different types of language deficits such as aphasia and dyslexia?

8. In what ways is the brain specialized for language?

9. What language capabilities do nonhuman animals possess, and what does this indicate about the evolution of language in humans?

Hearing

Summary and Guided Review

After studying this section in the text, fill in the blanks of the following summary.

_____ (1) is the first step in information processing that allows us to interact with the external environment. When we encounter environmental stimuli, our _____ (2), often-specialized neurons, respond to specific types of stimuli and convert sensory information such as light or sound into neural signals. Then the sensory information is interpreted, a process known as _____ (3). It is the amplitude and timing, or _____ (4), of the neural impulses that makes sensory information meaningful.

Our sense of hearing is highly complex. The auditory stimulus is the vibration of molecules in a conducting medium, which may be air, _____ (5), and even the skull. These vibrations can be represented graphically as number of cycles or _____ (6) per second, with their frequency expressed in _____ (7). _____ (8) is our *experience* of the frequency of a sound. The range of frequencies that humans are most sensitive to is _____ - _____ Hz (9). A sound with a single frequency is a _____ (10). Most sounds are complex, because they contain many frequencies.

_____ (11), or height of the wave, represents the physical intensity of sound, which we *experience* as _____ (12).

    To hear, we must get information about the sound; this involves sound reception, _____ (13), and conversion of sound waves into neural impulses. The _____ (14), or outer ear, captures sound waves and amplifies them by directing them into the smaller auditory canal. Then sound waves reach the first part of the middle ear, called the _____ (15) membrane or eardrum. Its vibration transmits the sound energy to the second part of the middle ear, the _____ (16), which is made up the tiny _____ (17) called the hammer, anvil, and stirrup. The next structure involved is the _____ (18) of the inner ear, which is a small coiled object about 35 mm long in humans containing three fluid-filled canals. The stirrup rests against the oval window, a thin membrane on the face of the _____ (19) canal, which is the point of entry into the cochlea. This canal connects with the _____ (20) canal at the far end of the cochlea. Activity in these canals bathes the cochlear canal, where the auditory _____ (21) are located. Conversion of sound waves to neural impulses occurs when vibrations reach the organ of Corti, which rests on the _____ (22) membrane. The organ of Corti consists of four rows of _____ (23) cells, their supporting cells, and the shelf-like _____ (24) membrane. Vibration of this membrane causes the hair cells to bend, which opens _____ (25) channels, depolarizing the hair cell membrane, which sets off impulses in the _____ (26) neuron. The inner hair cells, which are less numerous than the _____ (27) hair cells, are apparently responsible for most of what we hear, as is evidenced by the observation that mice lacking inner hair cells due to a mutant gene are _____ (28).

    Cochlear neurons project to the primary auditory cortex in the _____ (29) lobe via the auditory nerves, passing through the brain stem, inferior colliculi, and the _____ _____ (30) nucleus of the thalamus. Most, but not all, of the fibers from the auditory nerves cross to the opposite hemisphere. Some of the functions of the auditory cortex of each hemisphere are specialized: _____ (31) in the left, some aspects of music in the right. The auditory cortex is also _____ (32) organized, as neurons from adjacent sites on the basilar membrane project to adjacent points on the cortex. Sound information is conveyed to areas beyond the primary auditory cortex; the _____ (33) stream processes information about the spatial location of a sound, and the _____ (34) stream processes information about what an object is.

In converting sound waves into neural impulses, the auditory system codes for the intensity and frequency of stimuli. A 19th-century theory of frequency coding advanced by _____ (35) postulated that auditory neurons fire at the same rate as the frequency of sound that stimulates them. This so-called _____ (36) theory was tested in 1930 by Wever and Bray, who found evidence to support it. But they recorded from a cat's auditory _____ (37) rather than a single neuron, and Wever later hypothesized that several neurons cooperatively produced volleys of signals, thus following the original stimulus. However, volleying can reproduce frequencies only below about _____ (38) Hz; some other mechanism must be responsible for coding higher frequencies.

The 19th-century scientist Helmholtz proposed a _____ (39) theory of frequency coding that suggested that vibration of the _____ (40) membrane varies along its length with the frequency of the sound; thus the auditory mechanism identifies sound frequency according to *place* of maximal vibration. This theory is still widely accepted. This selective responsiveness helps explain why the cortex contains a _____ (41) map corresponding with different points along the basilar membrane, and why one can hear through _____ (42) conduction. However, the place theory does not account for sounds below about _____ (43) Hz. Currently, most researchers believe that the _____-_____ (44) theory is the most accurate account of auditory frequency processing.

Intensity coding is simpler. With low-frequency sounds, more intense stimuli produce responses in more neurons; for higher-frequency sounds, intensity is coded by the _____ (45) of neural impulses.

Most of the sounds that we hear are complex, containing several frequencies. Research suggests that the ear performs a _____ (46) analysis of complex sounds, in which the sound is analyzed into sine wave components. The _____ (47) membrane carries out this analysis by responding simultaneously along its length to the component frequencies of the sound. We must also explain why we are capable of picking out a target sound among several competing sound sources, such as when we attend to a particular conversation among many different conversations at a party (known as the _____ _____ (48) effect). Such selective attention involves both selecting parts of the auditory environment to pay attention to and _____ (49) irrelevant background information. It is as if the brain is capable of producing an _____

_____ (50), a representation of a target sound source, which helps us track that source among competing noises. Sound localization also helps us distinguish among auditory objects. Recognition of voices of different people involves secondary auditory cortex in the _____ (51) temporal area, whereas recognizing different environmental sounds requires _____ (52) temporal areas. Suppressing irrelevant information typically involves sending stimulation to lower levels of the sensory pathway, in particular by changing the length of _____ (53) hair cells to make localized tension adjustments in the organ of Corti.

Much of our ability to locate sounds involves automatic processing of sounds within the nervous system. Animals with two ears use three different binaural cues to locate sounds: phase differences, _____ (54) differences, and time-of-arrival differences at the two ears. The farther apart the ears are, the easier it is to locate sounds. Phase differences, which help us locate sounds below _____ (55) Hz, and intensity differences, which help us locate sounds above _____-_____ (56) Hz, are detected by cells in the _____ _____ (57) nucleus. Time-of-arrival cues have been studied extensively in the barn owl. Neurons called _____ (58) detectors, which are located in the nucleus laminaris (a structure analogous to the superior olivary nucleus), fire most when they receive input from both ears at the same time.

Short Answer and Essay Questions

Answer the following questions.

1. Why do we need different terms for the physical properties of sound (frequency, intensity) and for the experience of sound (pitch, loudness)?

2. Describe Rutherford's telephone theory of frequency analysis. How did Wever and Bray test this theory? What was wrong with their procedure?

3. How do frequency theory and place theory account for our ability to process low- frequency and high-frequency sounds, respectively? Why is neither theory sufficient to explain all frequency analysis?

4. What is the possible role of the outer hair cells in selective attention?

5. Explain how phase- and intensity-difference cues help in locating the source of a sound.

6. How does the organization of neural input from auditory neurons to coincidence detectors account for the ability to locate sounds based on time-of-arrival cues?

Language

Summary and Guided Review

After studying this section in the text, fill in the blanks of the following summary.

Language, which includes spoken, _____ (59), and gestural communication, is of central importance in human behavior. There are many brain areas involved in language, and damage to them impairs different language functions. For example, in the 19th century Broca and Wernicke identified different forms of language impairment, or _____ (60), resulting from damage to different areas of the _____ (61) hemisphere of the brain.

Broca's aphasia, also referred to as _____ (62) expressive aphasia, is the result of damage to Broca's area, which is located on the _____ (63) lobe anterior to the motor cortex. People with Broca's aphasia have difficulty expressing themselves. They often display _____ (64) (halting) speech, _____ (65) (difficulty finding the right word), difficulty with articulation, and _____ (66) speech (lacking function words). They also have problems with reading and writing, and _____ (67) is impaired for grammatically complex sentences.

Wernicke's aphasia, sometimes referred to as _____ (68) aphasia, is the result of damage to Wernicke's area, located on the left posterior _____ (69) lobe. People with Wernicke's aphasia can articulate words, but their utterances, described as _____ _____ (70), have little meaning. As the term receptive aphasia implies, they also have difficulty understanding language.

According to the _____ - _____ (71) model, language processing (answering a question) occurs along a pathway from the auditory cortex to Wernicke's area to _____ _____ (72) and then to the facial area of the _____ _____ (73) (for a spoken response), or to the _____ _____ (74) (for a written response). When a person reads aloud the route is from angular gyrus to _____ (75) and on to Broca's

areas for speech production. However, damage to areas outside this pathway—including other areas of the

cortex and subcortical structures such as the basal ganglia and _____ (76) also results in

language impairment, indicating how widespread language processing is. Using different types of words

activates brain locations appropriate to the word's type; for example, naming tools and imagining hand

movements activates the left _____ (77) cortex, which then sends output to the motor

cortex. The various language functions are scattered throughout the four lobes; however, the Wernicke-

Geschwind model is essentially correct in that temporal areas are most important for comprehension and frontal

areas are most important for _____ (78).

Damage to the _____ (79) gyrus, which connects the visual projection area with

auditory and visual association areas, can result in _____ (80) (the inability to read) and

_____ (81) (the inability to write). _____ (82), the most common type

of learning disorder, also involves reading and writing difficulties. This disorder can be

_____ (83), through damage, but its origin is more often developmental. Its heritability is

estimated to be between _____ and _____ (84) percent. Several genes

have been identified: what they have in common is that they affect neuron guidance and

_____ (85). People with dyslexia also show disruption in the development of the left

_____ _____ (86). The most common symptoms of dyslexia involve

_____-_____ (87) problems, in which words are read backward,

letters are confused, and words seem to move around on the page. These problems are thought to be the result of

deficits in the _____ (88) visual pathway. The competing _____ (89)

hypothesis argues that difficulty with processing phonemes underlies dyslexia. Studies indicate that dyslexics

have low activity in Wernicke's area and the _____ _____ (90) during

phonological tasks.

Recovery from aphasia, which is more pronounced for Broca's than for Wernicke's aphasia, results in part

from a decrease in the _____ (91) that occurs along with brain damage. Reorganization of

the brain is also involved. For example, there is evidence that if the left hemisphere is damaged before age

_____ (92), the right hemisphere takes over language functions. For damage occurring

later, other areas in the left hemisphere may become involved in language processing. The right hemisphere is

important in incorporating _____ (93) (intonation and rhythm) and emotion into speech as well as in understanding _____ (94) rather than literal meaning of words.

Because language is readily learned by almost all children, including those born deaf who are exposed to sign language, some theorists believe that the brain contains a language _____ (95) device, that the language structures are dedicated to acquiring language. Regardless of the form of language children learn, they all show the same stages of language development, including early _____ (96) through either speech or gestures. Most people show left hemisphere dominance for language, and several left hemisphere structures, including Broca's area, the _____ (97) fissure, and the planum temporale are larger than their counterparts in the right hemisphere. Prenatal and early postnatal differences in structure and function of the left hemisphere have been observed, suggesting that the left hemisphere in most people is designed to support language. A striking example of the newborn's sensitivity to language is that the rhythm of their _____ (98) is consistent with that of their parents' language. Even though it is a visual language, _____ (99) language activates left hemisphere structures similar to those used in spoken language. People who have learned two languages early in life show activation of the same areas for both languages, while those who acquired a _____ (100) language after childhood show activation of somewhat different areas, but still within Broca's and Wernicke's areas. Although it is clear that language involves specific structures, it is not clear if these structures evolved specifically for language or if they originally served a more general purpose and were later taken over by language.

Studying language abilities in other species allows us to speculate on the evolutionary basis of language in humans, although the results of such studies must be interpreted with caution, because it is often difficult to determine whether an animal who uses a language symbol truly understands the meaning of that symbol. Language abilities in _____ (101) have been studied the most intensively, although because of limitations to the vocal apparatus, they are unable to speak. The chimpanzee Washoe was exposed to American _____ _____ (102) from an early age, and she learned _____ (103) signs in four years. She and other signing chimps then taught some of these signs to her adopted son Loulis. The Rumbaughs used a different approach involving symbols on a panel. The pigmy chimpanzee Kanzi first began using the symbols as an _____ (104) when his mother was being trained on it. Savage-Rumbaugh claims that Kanzi's use of symbols is about as sophisticated as that of a _____ (105)-year-old child. Remarkable language abilities have also been demonstrated by Alex, an African _____ _____ (106), who was able to give the name, color, quantity, and shape of objects.

There is also evidence that the brains of some species are lateralized in ways similar to humans. The lateral fissure and planum _____ (107) are larger in the left hemisphere in chimpanzees. Japanese macaques show a _____ (108) hemisphere dominance for responding to the calls of other Japanese macaques but not to those of other monkey species. Dolphins and chimpanzees demonstrate faster learning of symbols when the symbols are presented to the left hemisphere. _____ (109) with left hemisphere lesions are unable to sing normally. However, an important difference is that the _____ _____ (110), which connects Wernicke's area to Broca's area, is much smaller in chimpanzees than humans. _____ (111) neurons may be important in the ability to imitate the movements and sounds of others; these cells are found in language areas of human and animal brains as well as in other areas. One gene that has been implicated in language is the _____ (112). In humans, this gene differs slightly from its counterpart in chimpanzees, and people with a mutated form of the gene show several language-related deficits.

Short Answer and Essay Questions

Answer the following questions.

7. Compare the language limitations observed in people with Broca's and Wernicke's aphasias.

8. How does the Wernicke-Geschwind model account for your ability to write a response to an oral question? To read aloud?

9. What is the Wada technique, and what is it used for?

10. In terms of acquisition and brain mechanisms, how are American Sign Language and spoken language similar?

11. What were the criticisms of the claims that Washoe was using language? How did subsequent work with Washoe and Loulis and the project with Kanzi address these criticisms?

Posttest

Use these multiple-choice questions to check your understanding of the chapter.

1. ____ is defined as the acquisition of sensory information.

a. Perception

b. Sensation

c. Conversion

d. Translation

2. The range of human hearing is about

a. 20–200,000 Hz.

b. 2–20,000 Hz.

c. 20–20,000 Hz.

d. 200–2,000 Hz.

3. Sound may be conducted through

a. air.

b. water.

c. bone.

d. All of the above

4. We experience the frequency of a sound as

a. pitch.

b. loudness.

c. amplitude.

d. intensity.

5. A pure tone is MOST likely to be produced by a(n)

a. clarinet.

b. tuning fork.

c. air conditioner.

d. flute.

6. Humans are MOST sensitive to sounds with frequencies in the range of

a. 1,000–3,000 Hz.

b. 200–400 Hz.

c. 2,000–20,000 Hz.

d. 2,000–4,000 Hz.

7. Which of the following causes the eardrum to stretch or relax in response to different levels of sound?

   a. tensor tympani

   b. incus

   c. pinna

   d. tympanic membrane

8. Which of the following does NOT contribute to amplification of sound waves in the ear?

   a. outer ear

   b. eardrum

   c. stapes

   d. malleus

9. Which of the following structures is (are) NOT part of the auditory system?

   a. cochlea

   b. ossicles

   c. pinna

   d. semicircular canals

10. Vibrations are initiated in the cochlea by movement of the ___ against the oval window.

    a. stapes

    b. malleus

    c. incus

    d. helicotrema

11. The organ of Corti is located in the ___ canal.

    a. vestibular

    b. tympanic

    c. cochlear

    d. auditory

12. Hair cells rest on top of the

    a. helicotrema.

    b. tectorial membrane.

    c. basilar membrane.

d. tympanic membrane.

13. When hair cells bend, ___ channels open, causing depolarization.

    a. sodium and chloride

    b. potassium and calcium

    c. calcium and sodium

    d. chloride and calcium

14. The primary auditory cortex is located on the ___ lobe.

    a. temporal

    b. frontal

    c. parietal

    d. occipital

15. Neurons from the left ear project

    a. exclusively to the right hemisphere.

    b. exclusively to the left hemisphere.

    c. mostly to the right hemisphere.

    d. mostly to the left hemisphere.

16. At low frequencies, sound intensity is coded by

    a. the number of neurons responding.

    b. the volley pattern of neurons.

    c. the point on the basilar membrane responding.

    d. None of the above

17. The volley theory was proposed by

    a. Rutherford.

    b. Helmholtz.

    c. Békésy.

    d. Wever.

18. ___ discovered that the basilar membrane is stiffer at one end than at the other.

    a. Rutherford

    b. Helmholtz

c. Békésy

d. Wever and Bray

19. A 15,000-Hz tone will produce the greatest vibrations at which point along the basilar membrane?

   a. near the base

   b. at the apex

   c. near the apex

   d. in the middle

20. Which sound frequency does NOT seem to produce maximal vibration at a specific point on the basilar membrane?

   a. 20,000 Hz

   b. 2,400 Hz

   c. 1,200 Hz

   d. 20 Hz

21. The outer hair cells may be involved in

   a. suppressing response to background noise.

   b. processing high- but not low-frequency sounds.

   c. processing sounds related to language but not music.

   d. All of the above

22. Which of the following animals probably would you expect to have the MOST difficulty locating sounds?

   a. elephant

   b. alligator

   c. mouse

   d. owl

23. A sound with a frequency of 50 Hz is located by which of the following cues?

   a. phase difference

   b. intensity difference

   c. time-of-arrival difference

   d. a and c

24. In humans, binaural cues for localizing sound are processed by cells in the

    a. planum temporale.

    b. nucleus laminaris.

    c. superior olivary nucleus.

    d. medial geniculate nucleus.

25. Broca's area lies anterior and adjacent to the

    a. motor cortex.

    b. auditory cortex.

    c. somatosensory cortex.

    d. visual cortex.

26. In MOST people, Wernicke's area is found on the ___ lobe.

    a. left frontal

    b. right frontal

    c. left temporal

    d. right temporal

27. Which of the following is NOT a characteristic of Broca's aphasia?

    a. impairment in writing

    b. word salad

    c. agrammatic speech

    d. difficulty with articulation

28. People with Wernicke's aphasia

    a. have difficulty saying words.

    b. have difficulty understanding others.

    c. produce utterances that have no meaning.

    d. b and c

29. The inability to write is called

    a. agraphia.

    b. alexia.

    c. anomia.

d. aphasia.

30. The angular gyrus connects the visual projection area with the

    a. auditory association areas.

    b. visual association areas.

    c. motor cortex.

    d. a and b

31. Abnormalities in the magnocellular visual pathway are implicated in ___ problems in dyslexics.

    a. visual-perceptual

    b. phonological

    c. aphasic

    d. All of the above

32. A phonological symptom of dyslexia is

    a. difficulty translating letters into sounds.

    b. confusing mirror-image letters like *b* and *d*.

    c. reading words backward.

    d. difficulty tracking words on a page.

33. According to the Wernicke-Geschwind model, when we give a spoken response to an oral question, what is the sequence of brain activation?

    a. auditory cortex to Broca's area to Wernicke's area

    b. Broca's area to Wernicke's area to auditory cortex

    c. auditory cortex to Wernicke's area to Broca's area

    d. Wernicke's area to Broca's area to auditory cortex

34. Someone with damage to the premotor cortex would MOST likely have difficulty

    a. producing articulate speech.

    b. using verbs.

    c. using nouns.

    d. reading out loud.

35. There is evidence that the right hemisphere may assume left-hemisphere language functions

    a. in adults who have suffered strokes or other brain injuries.

b. in adults who learn a second language.

c. in children under five who suffer brain injury.

d. in children who acquire two languages simultaneously.

36. Babies exposed to American Sign Language

a. will babble in gestures, but only if they are deaf.

b. babble in gestures, but at a later age than that at which babies exposed to spoken language begin babbling in sounds.

c. babble in gestures at about the same age as babies exposed to spoken language babble in sounds.

d. are at a disadvantage for language learning, because sign language is not a true language.

37. Which of the following is TRUE?

a. Left-handed people are more likely to show left-hemisphere dominance for language than right-hemisphere dominance for language.

b. All right-handed people show left-hemisphere dominance for language.

c. Left- and right-handed people are equally likely to show left-hemisphere dominance for language.

d. People are completely either right- or left-hemisphere dominant for language.

38. Based on information in the text, which language capability in animals is most questionable?

a. Use signs and symbols to communicate with humans.

b. Use signs and symbols to communicate with each other.

c. Produce grammatically correct sentences.

d. Teach their offspring signs and symbols.

39. Which of the following species has NOT demonstrated a possible capacity for language?

a. pygmy chimpanzee

b. African gray parrot

c. Japanese macaque

d. dolphin

40. Mirror neurons

a. are found only in humans.

b. are active only during language use.

c. are found only in nonhuman animals.

d. are active during observation and imitation.

Answers

Guided Review

1. Sensation

2. receptors

3. Perception

4. patterning

5. water

6. waves

7. hertz (Hz)

8. Pitch

9. 2000-4000

10. pure tone

11. Amplitude

12. loudness

13. amplification

14. pinna

15. tympanic

16. ossicles

17. bones

18. cochlea

19. vestibular

20. tympanic

21. receptors

22. basilar

23. hair

24. tectorial

25. potassium

26. auditory

27. outer

28. deaf

29. temporal

30. medial geniculate

31. language

32. topographically

33. dorsal

34. ventral

35. Rutherford

36. telephone

37. nerve

38. 5200

39. place

40. basilar

41. tonotopic

42. bone

43. 200

44. frequency-place

45. rate

46. Fourier

47. basilar

48. cocktail party

49. suppressing

50. auditory object

51. superior

52. posterior

53. cochlear

54. intensity

55. 1500

56. 2000-3000

57. superior olivary

58. coincidence

59. written

60. aphasia

61. left

62. expressive

63. frontal

64. nonfluent

65. anomia

66. agrammtic

67. comprehension

68. receptive

69. temporal

70. word salad

71. Werkicke-Geschwind

72. Broca's area

73. motor cortex

74. angular gyrus

75. Wernicke's area

76. thalamus

77. premotor

78. articulation

79. angular

80. alexia

81. agraphia

82. Dyslexia

83. acquired

84. 40 and 60

85. migration

86. planum temporale

87. visual-perceptual

88. magnocellular

89. phonological

90. angular gyrus

91. swelling

92. five

93. prosody

94. figurative

95. acquisition

96. babbling

97. lateral

98. crying

99. sign

100. second

101. chimpanzees

102. Sign Language

103. 132

104. infant

105. two

106. gray parrot

107. temporale

108. left

109. canaries

110. arcuate fasciculus

111. Mirror

112. *FOXP2*

Short Answer and Essay

1. While pitch varies with frequency and loudness varies with intensity, neither relationship is precise.

Our sensitivity is not the same across the range of sounds; for example, we are more sensitive to sounds between 2,000 and 4,000 Hz, and we can detect smaller changes in amplitude in that range. Thus, a sound of a particular intensity and frequency will not have the same loudness at another frequency, and it will not have the same pitch at a different intensity.

2. Rutherford proposed that auditory neurons fire at the same frequency as sounds that stimulate them, so that the brain received signals that matched or followed the frequency of sounds in the environment. Wever and Bray tested this theory by recording from the auditory nerve of a cat while it was exposed to sounds and amplifying the signal so that it could be heard; the result was very faithful to the original sound. However, this wasn't an adequate test of the theory, because Wever and Bray were not recording from a single neuron. Individual neurons cannot fire fast enough to follow the frequency of most environmental sounds; they found frequency following only because the combined firing of many neurons was able to follow the frequency of the sounds used.

3. Frequency theory accounts for low-frequency sounds, as neurons do fire at the same rate as low-frequency sounds. Place theory accounts for higher-frequency sounds, as different points along the basilar membrane are most responsive to particular frequencies and many auditory neurons are frequency specific. However, neither theory alone is sufficient to account for all frequency analysis. Frequency theory is limited by the physical property of neurons that prevents them from firing more than a few hundred times per second, and place theory cannot account for processing low frequency sounds, because sounds below 200 Hz cause the entire basilar membrane to vibrate equally.

4. The outer hair cells may be involved in a mechanism for selective attention. Messages along the descending auditory pathway suppress activity in the inner hair cells, but this may occur via the outer hair cells. When the length of the outer hair cells changes, the rigidity of the organ of Corti changes. This may allow the organ of Corti to zero in on a particular sound source (with a particular mix of frequencies) and tune out others with different frequencies. (Note: Be sure to check the Web link for the "Dancing Hair Cell" video.)

5. Phase-difference cues involve the point at which a sound wave stimulates the ear. If a sound is coming from any direction such that it reaches each ear at different points in the wave, this difference will be detected by cells in the superior olivary nucleus. Intensity-difference cues work because the head produces a sound shadow. The ear closer to the source of sound will receive a more intense sound than the other ear; this difference is also detected by specialized neurons in the superior olivary nucleus.

6. Coincidence detectors receive input from neurons from both ears. However, the length of the input neurons connected to a specific coincidence detector from each ear differs. When a sound occurs, it will reach the closer ear first and the farther ear later, but the two signals will arrive at a particular coincidence detector simultaneously because the length of the neuron from the closer ear compensates for the delay in the sound reaching the distant ear. Which coincidence detector is responding most indicates the sound's location relative to the two ears.

7. In Broca's aphasia, people have difficulty recalling the appropriate words, their speech is halting and impaired in articulation, and function words are missing. Their understanding is also impaired by their inability to process function words. Reading and writing are disrupted as well. People with Wernicke's aphasia, on the other hand, often speak fluently, but their utterances make little sense, and they have difficulty understanding what others are saying to them.

8. According to this model, when you write an answer to an oral question, the pattern of activation begins in the auditory cortex, then moves to Wernicke's area, and then to the angular gyrus to elicit the visual pattern. When reading out loud, the visual system sends input through the angular gyrus to Wernicke's area, and then to Broca's area.

9. The Wada technique involves administering an anesthetic to one hemisphere of a person's brain to suppress its activity and then giving the person tasks to perform. This is used along with electrical stimulation to determine the location of different functions (such as language) prior to surgery.

10. Babies exposed to sign language seem to progress in language development along the same lines as babies exposed to speech. Both babble at about the same time, and the babbling seems to have the same function in each case (although it is of a very different form). Furthermore, similar areas of the left hemisphere are involved in both spoken language and sign language.

11. Terrace claimed that chimpanzees do not form sentences, that the utterances lacked grammatical structure and were simply strings of words. Loulis acquired signs from Washoe and other chimps and used these signs to communicate with other chimps, suggesting that the signs are being used like language. The Rumbaughs' work with Kanzi indicates that chimpanzees are capable of spontaneously making complex utterances and understanding complex directions.

Posttest

1. b   2. c   3. d   4. a   5. b   6. d   7. a   8. b   9. d   10. a   11. c   12. c   13. b   14. a   15. c   16. a   17. d
18. c   19. a   20. d   21. a   22. c   23. d   24. c   25. a   26. c   27. b   28. d   29. a   30. d   31. a   32. a
33. c   34. b   35. c   36. c   37. a   38. c   39. c   40. d

10

Vision and Visual Perception

Chapter Outline

Learning Objectives

After reading this chapter, you should be able to answer the following questions.

1. What are the characteristics of electromagnetic energy, particularly for the portion of the spectrum that is visible to humans?

2. What are the functions of the components of the eye? How does light affect cells in the retina?

3. What is the pathway for visual information beyond the retina?

4. What is the significance of retinal disparity?

5. How do the trichromatic and opponent process theories differ in their explanations for color vision?

6. How does the visual system produce the experience of color?

7. What are the characteristics of color blindness?

8. In what way is the visual cortex a retinotopic map?

9. What is lateral inhibition, and how does it explain contrast enhancement and edge detection?

10. What are the functions of simple and complex visual cells?

11. How does spatial frequency theory account for form perception?

12. What are the functions of the magnocellular and parvocellular systems?

13. What are the functions of the ventral and dorsal streams?

14. What are some disorders of visual perception, and what do they reveal about the functions of different brain areas?

15. What are the possible solutions to the problem of final integration?

Light and the Visual Apparatus

Summary and Guided Review

After studying this section in the text, fill in the blanks of the following summary.

The adequate stimulus for the visual system is visible light, which makes up a very small portion of the

_____ (1) spectrum. Other forms of electromagnetic energy that humans cannot detect without special devices are X-rays, _____ (2) energy (which some animal species use to detect prey at night), and radio and television waves. Light is measured not in terms of frequency like sounds, but in terms of_____ (3), the distance oscillating energy travels before reversing directions; the portion of the electromagnetic spectrum humans are capable of detecting is _____-_____ (4) nanometers. (A nanometer is 1 _____ (5) of a meter.) Within this range, light rays of different wavelengths are perceived as different _____ (6).

The eye is filled with fluid, and with the exception of the transparent _____ (7), its outer covering, or sclera, is opaque. Behind the cornea, the flexible _____ (8) allows us to focus on objects at different distances. The circular _____ (9) is a muscle that partially covers the lens, and the opening in its center is the _____ (10), which changes its size to accommodate different levels of light. The visual receptors are located in the _____ (11) at the back of the eye; these cells contain light-sensitive _____ (12). The different types of receptors, _____ (13) and _____ (14), are specialized for different aspects of vision, due to the fact that they contain different types of photopigments and have different neural connections. Rods, which are more numerous, contain _____ (15), which is highly sensitive to light; this accounts for our ability to see under low light conditions. Cones, which contain _____ (16), function best in bright light. There are different types of this photopigment, each responding most to different ranges of wavelengths; this is what allows us to see color. In the retina, cones are concentrated in the _____ (17) in the center, whereas rods are more numerous in the periphery. Foveal cones show less convergence on the ganglion cells than cones outside the fovea, which accounts for better visual _____ (18) for images falling on the fovea. Many rods converge on a single ganglion cell, which contributes to _____ (19) to light but not acuity. The _____ (20) fields of foveal cells are smaller than those in the periphery. In the dark, photoreceptors release _____ (21), which inhibits bipolar cells. When stimulated by light, sodium and _____ (22) channels close, thus disinhibiting the bipolar cells, and increasing the firing rate in the ganglion cells they are connected to. Horizontal and _____ (23) cells interconnect the receptor cells and ganglion cells, and respectively, producing a complex web of information processing.

The ganglion cells' _____ (24) form the optic nerve and exit the retina at the

_____ _____ (25); the optic nerves join for a short distance at the

_____ _____ (26), where axons from the nasal side of the eyes cross

over to the opposite side of the brain. Neurons from the _____ (27) side of the eyes project

to the same side of the brain. Nerves next project to the _____ _____

(28) nuclei of the thalamus and then to the cortex. The partial crossover of information is organized such that,

for example, stimuli detected by the right half of each retina, which receives light from the

_____ (29) visual field, are projected to the _____ (30) hemisphere.

We are able to perceive objects in three-dimensional space due in part to _____

_____ (31), in which each eye receives a slightly different version of a visual scene. The

degree of disparity triggers activity in different cells in the cortex. The ViewMaster, 3-D movies such as *Avatar*,

and stereograms all capitalize on retinal disparity to produce an illusion of three dimensions. Three principles

are helpful in understanding how the visual system works: _____ (32), which allows for

more detailed information processing than excitation alone; _____

_____ _____ (33), which means that more basic elements of visual

stimuli are processed in lower areas of the nervous system, and this information is then analyzed by higher areas

of the cortex; and _____ (34), which reflects the fact that much of visual processing is

segregated in different brain locations.

Short Answer and Essay Questions

Answer the following questions.

1. Briefly describe the "adequate stimulus" for vision.

2. How are the receptive fields of ganglion cells that receive input from cones in the fovea different from those receiving input from rods? How do these differences contribute to the visual specializations of each system?

3. What is the blind spot? Why do we not notice it (most of the time)?

4. How are researchers able to present a visual image to only one hemisphere in people whose brains are intact?

5. How are ViewMaster slides able to produce such convincing three-dimensional effects?

Color Vision

Summary and Guided Review

After studying this section in the text, fill in the blanks of the following summary.

Just as _____ (35) refers to our perceptual experience of the frequency of a sound,

color refers to our perceptual experience of the _____ (36) of light, but does not

correspond perfectly with it. Thus, color is not a property of an object, but an experience produced by the brain.

The _____ (37) theory of color vision, proposed separately by Young and

_____ (38), explained that our ability to see color is due to three different color processes

that are sensitive to red, green, and _____ (39) light. All colors are the result of mixing

different combinations of these colors of light; this principle is used in the design of televisions and computer

displays. The competing _____ _____ (40) theory, proposed by

Hering, explained color vision as the result of receptors whose _____ (41) are broken down

by one type of light and regenerated by another. This theory is based on the observation of complementary

colors, that is, colors that when mixed in equal amounts produce _____

_____ (42) or white. Also, overstimulating the eye with one color of light increases

sensitivity to its complement. This theory explains complementary colors as well as the phenomenon of

_____ _____ (43) aftereffect: When you stare at a green object and

then look at a blank piece of paper, you will experience the same image in _____ (44). It is

important to remember that mixing lights is _____ (45), whereas mixing pigments is

subtractive. Hering's theory was not well accepted because of the notion that a single photochemical could be

affected in opposite ways by different wavelengths of light.

In 1957, Hurvich and Jameson proposed a theory of color vision that included elements of both the

trichromatic and opponent process theories; this theory suggests that our ability to see color depends on two

different levels of processing in the cells of the _____ (46). The first level of color

processing occurs in the _____ (47), which contain one of three different photopigments, each of which is maximally sensitive to different wavelengths of light. These red-, green-, and blue-sensitive cones are interconnected to _____ (48) cells in such a way as to produce opponent process effects. For example, long-wavelength light stimulates the _____ (49)-sensitive cones and _____ _____ (50) ganglion cells, whereas medium-wavelength light stimulates the green-sensitive cones and _____ (51) the red-green ganglion cells. Short-wavelength light excites blue cones and _____ (52) the yellow-blue ganglion cells, leading to a sensation of blue. Staring at a red stimulus eventually _____ (53) the red-green ganglion cells, resulting in inhibition and the experience of green. This explains the phenomenon of negative _____ (54). Physical evidence for this theory was produced by studies involving shining different wavelengths of light onto the retinas of human eyes and measuring which wavelengths were absorbed. This finding shows that there are _____ (55) distinct color response curves; each receptor has a sensitivity peak but its response range _____ (56) with that of its neighbors. The _____ (57) for photopigments in red and green cones are probably the most recently evolved and may have emerged around the time in primate evolution when visual signals became more important than _____ (58) and pheromones for sexual communication. Color-opponent cells have been located in the _____ (59) and _____ _____ (60) nucleus in monkeys. Like other successful theories, this one was able to demonstrate that it was _____ with the known facts, could _____ those facts, and could _____ (61) new findings.

The study of color blindness can also reveal information about how the visual system works. People who are completely color blind lack functional cones and are limited to vision from _____ (62). This is a rare condition. There are two more common types of color blindness. A person who is red-green color blind sees both colors but is unable to _____ (63) between them. People in the second color blind group do not perceive _____ (64) so they see their world in variations of red and green. Many people who are partially color blind are not even _____ (65) that they see the world differently from other people.

Short Answer and Essay Questions

Answer the following questions.

6. How does Figure 10.6 demonstrate that our perception of color does not perfectly correspond to the wavelength of light we sense?

7. Why is it that when yellow and blue paints are mixed, green is produced, whereas when yellow and blue lights are mixed, they produce gray?

8. How does the opponent-process theory explain the negative afterimage effect?

9. Explain the three ways in which Hurvich and Jameson's combined theory has demonstrated that it is successful as a theory; include a specific example for each.

10. What can we conclude about the color receptors in a person who cannot distinguish between red and green but is especially sensitive to green light?

Form Vision

Summary and Guided Review

After studying this section in the text, fill in the blanks of the following summary.

The visual cortex contains a _____ (66) map, which means that the spatial relationships among visual stimuli are conserved from retina to cortex. Form vision allows us to detect the boundaries of objects and is the first step in _____ (67) perception.

In order to perceive a form or object, we must first be able to detect its boundaries. The visual system is designed to respond to boundaries so that they stand out from the rest of the visual field. This fact is demonstrated by the _____ _____ (68) illusion, in which contrast between bands that differ in brightness appears greater at their edges. This illusion, and the visual system's ability to detect contrast in general, is explained by _____ _____ (69) of activity in ganglion cells. In mammals, the ganglion cells have concentric circular receptive fields. _____-_____ (70) cells respond by increasing the rate of firing when light stimulates the receptors in the central portion of the receptive field and _____ (71) their rate of firing when light stimulates the surround portion. Other ganglion cells have an *off-center* and an *on-surround*. Cells with opposed centers and surrounds are particularly responsive to the _____ (72) of objects because edges typically have a high contrast in lighting

While cells in the lateral geniculate nucleus also have _____ (73) receptive fields, those in the cortex respond quite differently, as discovered by Nobel laureates _____ and _____ (74). They identified different types of cells in the cortex that respond to different aspects of these stimuli. _____ (75) cells respond to a line or edge at a specific orientation in a specific portion of the visual field. A simple cell receives input from several _____ (76) cells with adjacent receptive fields arranged in line. _____ (77) cells receive input from several simple cells with adjacent fields; these complex cells are responsive to lines in a particular orientation over a larger area of the retina; some complex cells can also detect _____ (78).

Hubel and Wiesel's theory accounts for the detection of edges, but it cannot account for other surface details by which we identify objects. Edges represent _____ _____ (79) changes in brightness, whereas subtle shading represents low-frequency changes; according to De Valois, complex cells are responsive to low-frequency as well as high-frequency changes. His _____ _____ (80) theory suggests that sensitivity to a range of spatial frequencies accounts for our ability to make out the varied details of a visual stimulus. In other words, visual cortical cells perform a _____ (81) frequency analysis of luminosity variations in a scene.

Short Answer and Essay Questions

Answer the following questions.

11. What is lateral inhibition, and how does it explain the Mach band illusion?

12. What will happen to an on-center, off-surround ganglion cell when light stimulates the entire receptive field? Only the surround? The center and only part of the surround?

13. Compare the receptive fields of simple and complex cells. Explain their differences in function and how this comes about.

14. What would our vision be like if we were able to detect only high-frequency visual information, such as from edges?

The Perception of Objects, Color, and Movement

Summary and Guided Review

After studying this section in the text, fill in the blanks of the following summary.

The text takes the position that visual processing of objects, color, and movement is both modular and

_____ (82), while acknowledging that the representation of some functions in multiple

areas means that the modularity is tempered somewhat by _____ (83) processing.

Beginning in the _____ (84), visual information processing is divided to some extent

between two systems. The _____ (85) system includes ganglion cells located in the fovea

whose circular receptive fields are small and color opponent. These cells are sensitive to the

_____ (86) and fine detail of objects. The _____ (87) system includes

cells whose receptive fields are large, circular, and brightness opponent. This system is involved in our

perception of movement and _____ (88) contrast. Under poor lighting conditions, the

_____ (89) system is most active, and we are particularly sensitive to movement in our

_____ (90) visual field. Reading and determining the color of objects, functions of the

_____ (91) system, become difficult or impossible.

The first cortical area for vision is the primary visual cortex, also known as _____

(92). In the cortex, the parvocellular system makes up the majority of the _____ (93)

stream of information that projects to the _____ (94) lobes; along this route, color

perception and object recognition occur. The magnocellular system forms the majority of the

_____ (95) stream that projects to the _____ (96) lobes; along this

route, spatial information about visual stimuli is processed. Movement perception involves the areas V5/MT and

_____ (97); these areas are active even when viewing still photos implying action. Activity

of cells in these areas is _____ (98) during eye movements, so that stationary objects do

not appear to move. The dorsal and ventral streams converge on the _____

_____ (99), where the information is used, for example, in planning movement. The

ventral/dorsal distinction can be observed in the effects of brain damage in the different pathways. People with

damage to the _____ (100) stream can identify objects, but have trouble orienting and

reaching toward them accurately. People with damage to the _____ (101) stream have

trouble visually identifying objects, but they can move toward and reach for them accurately.

Damage to one or more areas of the cortex involved in vision can lead to a specific type of

_____ (102), which is an impairment of some type of visual perception. For example, people with object agnosia have difficulty recognizing objects; object agnosia usually involves difficulty recognizing faces of familiar people, or _____ (103), which can occasionally occur alone. However, evidence that prosopagnosics respond to familiar faces emotionally suggests that there are separate pathways for recognition and _____ (104) in the brain. An interesting example of this distinction is _____ (105), a condition in which cortically blind individuals respond to visual stimuli that they cannot see. The brain region implicated in object agnosia and prosopagnosia is the _____ _____ (106) cortex, which contains individual cells that respond to specific types of objects, including geometric forms, animals, and faces. In addition, there is evidence that the _____ _____ (107) area in the inferior temporal cortex is especially important for recognition of faces; cells in this area are more active when presented with familiar faces. A nearby area of the inferior temporal cortex is called the _____ (108); it responds to written words as a whole, that is, as objects. Although reduced activity in this area occurs in dyslexia, it does not mean that it is the cause of the disorder.

Another impairment is color agnosia, as characterized by the description of Jonathan I. in the introduction to the chapter. Our experience of color depends in part on _____ _____ (109), the perceptual process that allows us to perceive the color of an object in the same way despite different lighting conditions. This ability seems to depend on cells in area _____ (110). Cortical color blindness, or _____ (111) occurs when people have damage in the occipital-temporal area.

Movement _____ (112) is the impaired ability to detect movement; damage to the MST and parietal cortex may produce an inability to detect _____ (113) movement, which informs us about movement of objects toward or away from us. Individuals with damage to the posterior parietal cortex often display characteristics of _____ (114), such as failing to notice or attend to objects or parts of the body opposite the damage. This is not due to a defect in visual processing, but involves a deficit in _____ (115).

How are we able to make sense of all of the visual information we take in? So far, there is no evidence that a single _____ (116) area exists for incorporating visual information into conscious experience. The most likely answer is that our awareness of visual stimuli is the result of _____ (117) activity throughout the brain. The _____

_____ (118) is the question of how the brain combines information from different areas into a unitary whole. One way to approach this problem is to study a condition called

_____ (119), in which stimulation in one sense triggers an experience in another sense or a concept evokes an unrelated sensory experience (for example, emotions might have colors). People with this condition seem to "overbind" sensory information, either due to excess connectivity between the brain areas involved or inadequate inhibition in otherwise normal pathways. This is yet another example of how anomalies in brain functioning can help us understand the normal function of the brain.

Short Answer and Essay Questions

Answer the following questions.

15. What aspects of vision are the parvocellular and magnocellular systems specialized for? Give an example of each.

16. How does the modular nature of the visual system account for specific agnosias (such as object or movement agnosia)?

17. What is blindsight? What is the possible anatomical basis for it?

18. Describe the procedure used in the "greeble" study. What do the results of this study suggest about the function of the fusiform face area?

Posttest

Use these multiple-choice questions to check your understanding of the chapter.

1. Electromagnetic energy includes

   a. visible light rays.

   b. gamma rays.

   c. infrared rays.

   d. All of the above

2. The range of visible light for humans is

   a. 40–80 nm.

b. 4,000–8,000 nm.

c. 400–800 nm.

d. 40,000–80,000 nm.

3. The ____ is a flexible tissue that allows us to focus on objects at different distances.

   a. cornea

   b. lens

   c. pupil

   d. iris

4. The ____ is actually muscle tissue that responds to different levels of light.

   a. cornea

   b. lens

   c. pupil

   d. iris

5. The conversion of light energy into energy the brain can use begins in the

   a. receptors.

   b. bipolar cells.

   c. ganglion cells.

   d. a and b

6. Photoreceptors

   a. contain photopigments that increase in quantity when stimulated by light.

   b. connect directly with ganglion cells.

   c. are found at the back of the eye.

   d. All of the above

7. Which of the following statements is NOT true?

   a. Iodopsin is the cone photopigment.

   b. Rods function better in dim light.

   c. Cones are responsive to light, but cannot distinguish between wavelengths of different colors.

   d. Rhodopsin is the rod photopigment.

8. All of the following types of cells are found in the retina EXCEPT ____ cells.

a. bipolar

b. horizontal

c. amacrine

d. complex

9. The ganglion cells with the smallest receptive fields receive input from:

a. rods in the periphery of the retina

b. rods 20 degrees from the fovea

c. cones in the fovea

d. cones outside the fovea

10. When light reaches the photoreceptors

a. they release more glutamate.

b. sodium channels open.

c. calcium channels open.

d. None of the above

11. The blind spot contains

a. rods only.

b. cones only.

c. both rods and cones.

d. neither rods nor cones.

12. Visual information from the ___ side of each retina crosses to the other hemisphere at the ___ .

a. right; optic chiasm.

b. nasal; optic chiasm

c. right; lateral geniculate nucleus

d. nasal; lateral geniculate nucleus

13. An object's image falls on slightly different parts of the two retinas, depending on the distance of the object. This is called

a. hierarchical processing

b. modularity

c. neural inhibition

d. retinal disparity

14. Light with a wavelength on the lower end of the spectrum (e.g., 450 nm) is normally perceived as

    a. blue.

    b. green.

    c. yellow.

    d. red.

15. Color televisions produce color in accordance with the principles of

    a. the opponent process theory of color vision.

    b. the trichromatic theory of color vision.

    c. the combined theory of color vision.

    d. None of the above

16. If you stare at a yellow image for a long time and then look at a piece of white paper, you will see the image in

    a. blue.

    b. green.

    c. red.

    d. yellow.

17. Which of the following is NOT true of Hering's original opponent process theory?

    a. It is consistent with principles of mixing light.

    b. It is consistent with the negative color aftereffect.

    c. It proposed four types of color receptors.

    d. It proposed four primary colors.

18. With respect to the cones, yellow light produces

    a. more response in the red than the green cones.

    b. more response in the green than the red cones.

    c. about the same response in the red and green cones.

    d. more response in the blue cones and little response in the green and red cones.

19. With respect to the evolution and genetic basis of color vision

    a. genes for short-wavelength cones evolved relatively recently from a common precursor gene.

    b. red and green genes are adjacent to one another on the Y chromosome.

    c. the development of trichromacy and the use of visual signals in sexual attraction occurred at the same time.

    d. All of the above

20. Which of the following statements regarding people who lack cones is NOT true?

    a. They have poor visual acuity.

    b. They can distinguish only very bright colors.

    c. They are very sensitive to light.

    d. They are more rare than people with red-green color blindness.

21. People with red-green color blindness

    a. are usually aware of their unusual condition.

    b. can see neither red nor green.

    c. may have red photopigment in their green cones.

    d. are less common than those with complete color blindness.

22. Which of the following is NOT a part of form vision?

    a. formation of tonotopic maps

    b. edge detection

    c. contrast enhancement

    d. detection of orientation

23. The Mach band illusion is a result of

    a. object recognition.

    b. lateral inhibition.

    c. retinal disparity.

    d. modular processing.

24. Light in the ___ of an off-center receptive field will result in ___.

    a. center; excitation

    b. surround; excitation

239

c. surround; inhibition

d. center and entire surround; inhibition

25. Which of the following types of cells have bar-shaped receptive fields?

    a. retinal ganglion cells

    b. lateral geniculate cells

    c. simple cells

    d. b and c

26. Which of the following cells has the largest receptive field?

    a. retinal ganglion cells

    b. lateral geniculate cells

    c. simple cells

    d. complex cells

27. Movement is detected by

    a. simple cells.

    b. complex cells.

    c. both simple and complex cells.

    d. neither simple nor complex cells.

28. Hubel and Wiesel's theory accounts for the ability to detect

    a. texture.

    b. edges.

    c. movement.

    d. b and c

29. According to spatial frequency theory,

    a. low-frequency contrast in objects is detected by different cells than high-frequency contrast.

    b. the visual system is capable of detecting only medium- to high-frequency contrast.

    c. the visual system is capable of detecting only low- to medium-frequency contrast.

    d. the brightness of an object is irrelevant.

30. The BEST description of visual processing is that it is

    a. modular.

b. distributed.

c. both modular and distributed.

d. neither modular nor distributed.

31. Which of the following is a characteristic of cells in the parvocellular system?

    a. They have small receptive fields.

    b. They are brightness opponent.

    c. They are responsive to movement.

    d. Their input comes mainly from rods.

32. The magnocellular system dominates the ___ stream, which flows into the ___ lobes.

    a. ventral; temporal

    b. ventral; parietal

    c. dorsal; temporal

    d. dorsal; parietal

33. Magnocellular cells in area V1 are responsive to all of the following EXCEPT

    a. orientation.

    b. movement.

    c. retinal disparity.

    d. color.

34. Movement perception is a function of area

    a. V2.

    b. V4.

    c. V5.

    d. V8.

35. The ventral and dorsal streams converge on the ___ cortex.

    a. posterior parietal

    b. prefrontal

    c. anterior occipital

    d. inferior temporal

36. Object agnosia is often a result of damage to the ___ cortex.

a. inferior temporal

b. prefrontal

c. posterior parietal

d. posterior occipital

37. People with prosopagnosia

    a. fail to recognize familiar faces.

    b. fail to recognize familiar voices.

    c. fail to respond emotionally to familiar faces.

    d. All of the above

38. Specialized face-recognition cells have been located in the

    a. dorsal stream.

    b. fusiform gyrus.

    c. V1 area.

    d. parietal lobe.

39. The ability to perceive that an object is the same color despite different lighting conditions is known as

    a. visual constancy.

    b. color agnosia.

    c. retinal disparity.

    d. color constancy.

40. Light wavelength is coded in ___, and color is coded in ____.

    a. V4; V1

    b. V4; V4

    c. V1; V1

    d. V1; V4

41. Someone with damage to the right posterior parietal cortex would probably exhibit

    a. right side neglect.

    b. left side neglect.

    c. movement agnosia.

    d. color agnosia.

42. Neglect probably occurs because of

   a. a lack of attention to the space on one side of the body.

   b. an inability to perceive objects on one side of the body.

   c. both a and b

   d. neither a nor b

43. Which of the following is NOT TRUE about people with synesthesia?

   a. The condition is very rare.

   b. They can experience motion as sounds, for example.

   c. Some are associators and some are projectors

   d. Synesthetes may "overbind" sensory information due to excessive connectivity of brain areas.

44. According to the text, visual awareness is probably due to

   a. master visual cells in the superior temporal gyrus.

   b. master visual cells in the parietal cortex.

   c. processes distributed across the brain.

   d. master cells in some part of the cortex that has not yet been identified.

Answers

Guided Review

1. electromagnetic

2. infrared

3. wavelength

4. 400-800

5. billionth

6. colors

7. cornea

8. lens

9. iris

10. pupil

11. retina

12. photoreceptors

13. rods

14. cones

15. rhodopsin

16. iodopsin

17. fovea

18. acuity

19. sensitivity

20. receptive

21. glutamate

22. calcium

23. amacrine

24. axons

25. blind spot

26. optic chiasm

27. temporal

28. lateral geniculate

29. left

30. right

31. retinal disparity

32. inhibition

33. hierarchical processing

34. modulairity

35. pitch

36. wavelength

37. trichromatic

38. Helmholtz

39. blue

40. opponent process

41. photochemicals

42. neutral gray

43. negative color

44. red

45. additive

46. retina

47. cones

48. ganglion

49. red

50. red-green

51. inhibits

52. inhibits

53. fatigues

54. aftereffects

55. three

56. overlaps

57. genes

58. odors

59. retina

60. lateral geniculate

61. consistent, explain, predict

62. rods

63. distinguish

64. blue

65. aware

66. retinotopic

67. object

68. Mach band

69. lateral inhibition

70. On-center

71. decreasing

72. edges

73. circular

74. Hubel and Wiesel

75. Simple

76. ganglion

77. Complex

78. movement

79. high frequency

80. spatial frequency

81. Fourier

82. hierarchical

83. distributed

84. retina

85. parvocellular

86. color

87. magnocellular

88. brightness

89. magnocellular

90. peripheral

91. parvocellular

92. V1

93. ventral

94. temporal

95. dorsal

96. parietal

97. MST

98. suppressed

99. prefrontal cortex

100. dorsal

101. ventral

102. agnosia

103. propagnosia

104. identification

105. blindsight

106. inferior temporal

107. fusiform face

108. VWFA (visual word form area)

109. color constancy

110. V4

111. achromatopsia

112. agnosia

113. radial

114. neglect

115. attention

116. master

117. distributed

118. binding problem

119. synesthesia

Short Answer and Essay Questions

1. The adequate stimulus for vision is visible light, which makes up a very narrow portion of the electromagnetic spectrum. It is an oscillating form of energy that travels in waves like sound energy, but is described in terms of its wavelength. Visible light ranges from 400 to 800 nanometers. Different wavelengths correspond to different colors of light, though inexactly.

2. Ganglion cells receiving input from foveal cones have smaller receptive fields than those receiving input from rods. Some cones in the fovea have a one-to-one correspondence with ganglion cells (meaning that a ganglion cell receives input from a single cone). This arrangement allows us to make fine discriminations of the details of objects in our visual field. Ganglion cells receiving input from rods have large receptive fields, be-

cause they receive input from several rods. They are highly sensitive to light and movement but are not useful for distinguishing fine details.

3. The blind spot is the portion of the retina where the ganglion cell axons forming the optic nerve exit the retina, and there are no receptors in this area. We do not notice it because when we see with both eyes, the portion of the visual field that falls on the blind spot in the left eye is different from the portion that falls on the blind spot in the right eye. This way, one eye gets the information that the other one misses. In addition, the brain will provide "fill in" information.

4. An object that is presented very briefly to one side of the visual field (left or right) is typically processed only in one hemisphere. This is because the image falls only on the left or right halves of the retinas (and is then processed in the right or left hemisphere, respectively). As a result of the brief presentation, the person does not have time to reorient the eyes toward to object. (Also, the neural activity does not last long enough to transfer across the corpus callosum.)

5. They take advantage of retinal disparity. The slides project a slightly different image to each eye, reproducing what normally happens when we look at a scene with both eyes. The disparity, or difference, between the two images produces the sensation of depth, giving the scene three dimensions rather than two.

6. In this figure, the circles reflect the same wavelengths of light, but the background color of each leads to the perception that the circles are different colors.

7. Yellow and blue paints contain pigments. The principle of color subtracting applies here: Pigments absorb some wavelengths of light and reflect others. Mixing yellow and blue paint produces green because these pigments absorb all of the wavelengths except those that corresponding to green. When yellow and blue lights are mixed, the effect is additive. Gray or white is produce because these two wavelengths cancel each other out (in their effects on the Y-B cells).

8. Opponent process theory states that there are only two color receptors, one for red and green, and one for blue and yellow. This theory attempts to explain color vision in terms of opposing processes. Hering believed that the photochemical in the red-green receptor is broken down by red light and regenerates in green light. A similar process would work in the blue-yellow receptor. If someone stares at a red stimulus for a minute and then looks at a white wall or sheet of paper, the person will see a green version of the original object. This happens because overstimulating the eye with one light (red) will make it more sensitive to its complement (green). This is consistent with opponent process theory, which states that two wavelengths affect the same re-

ceptor in opposed directions

9. The combined theory is consistent with what was previously known about color, including the principles of light mixing as well as complementary colors. The theory also explains these facts, whereas the trichromatic theory could not explain complementary colors or negative color afterimages. Finally, the theory was used to predict the different cone types and the connections among the ganglion cells before there was physical evidence for them, and these predictions have been confirmed.

10. If someone cannot distinguish red from green, but is highly sensitive to green, then she or he probably has the photopigment for green in the red cones.

11. Lateral inhibition is the result of the way in which receptors and ganglion cells are interconnected. A receptor will have an excitatory effect on one ganglion cell while it inhibits activity in adjacent ganglion cells. This produces the Mach band illusion, which is the perception that at areas of contrast, dark edges are darker and light edges are lighter. This occurs because ganglion cells receiving stimulation from the edge of the dark region are receiving more inhibition (from the receptors stimulated by the light edge) than those farther from the border, and ganglion cells receiving stimulation from the light edge receive less inhibition (from the receptors stimulated by the dark edge) than those farther away.

12. In an on-center, off-surround cell, light falling on the entire receptive field will produce no change in the rate of firing, because the effects of light on the two areas cancel each other out. When the surround is illuminated, the cell will be inhibited, whereas when the center and a portion of the surround are illuminated, the net effect will be excitation.

13. A simple cell receives input from several ganglion cells with adjacent receptive fields oriented in a line. It detects an edge of light contrast that is aligned with its receptive field because the edge stimulates all (or almost all) of its ganglion cells. A complex cell receives input from several simple cells with receptive fields that have the same orientation and are adjacent to each other. Thus, as the edge moves across the receptive fields of these simple cells, the complex cell will continue responding, as long as the orientation doesn't change. This means that, compared to simple cells, complex cells have a larger receptive field, that is, they can detect edges over a wider area of the retina.

14. Objects would appear very simple, like line drawings without gradations of shading and texture (as in Figure 10.23b).

15. The parvocellular system is specialized for seeing in color and fine detail; reading is dependent on this system. The magnocellular system is specialized for perceiving movement and depth; detecting movement in the periphery of the visual field is dependent on this system.

16. The different agnosias (object, color, movement) exist because different parts of the brain are responsible for processing these aspects of visual stimuli. When a specific area is damaged, such as the inferior temporal cortex, the person may experience object agnosia and prosopagnosia but will not experience movement agnosia. Because these functions are handled in relatively distinct areas of the brain, they are disrupted only by damage to specific areas.

17. Blindsight is a phenomenon in which people with damage to the primary visual area perform as if they can see objects, even though they have no awareness of them. This may occur because of connections with parts of the cortex not involved in conscious awareness (connections that bypass V1).

18. In the greeble study, people were presented with different novel facial stimuli. After several trials, they could tell them apart. The "experts," those who could recognize individual greebles, showed activity in the fusiform face area, whereas the novices did not. This suggests that this area is used in recognizing familiar people (or members of another species), and that it is affected by our experiences.

Posttest

1. d 2. c 3. b 4. d 5. a 6. c 7. c 8. d 9. c 10. d 11. d 12. b 13. d 14. a 15. b 16. a 17. c
18. c 19. c 20. b 21. c 22. a 23. b 24. b 25. c 26. d 27. b 28. d 29. a 30. c 31. a 32. d
33. d 34. c 35. b 36. a 37. a 38. b 39. d 40. d 41. b 42. a. 43. a 44. c

11

The Body Senses and Movement

Chapter Outline

The Body Senses

Proprioception

The Skin Senses

The Vestibular Sense

The Somatosensory Cortex and Posterior Parietal Cortex

Pain and Its Disorders

IN THE NEWS: GETTING AN ANESTHETIC SHOULDN'T HURT

APPLICATION: TREATING PAIN IN LIMBS THAT AREN'T THERE

Movement

The Muscles

The Spinal Cord

The Brain and Movement

Disorders of Movement

Learning Objectives

After reading this chapter, you should be able to answer the following questions.

1. What are the structures and functions of the vestibular sense?

2. What are the types of skin receptors? To what stimulus does each respond?

3. How do the somatosensory cortex and posterior parietal cortex contribute to body senses and perception?

4. How is information about pain transmitted in the nervous system? What mechanisms control the experience of pain?

5. How do skeletal muscles work to produce movement?

6. What role does the spinal cord play in generating movement (such as reflexes and patterns of movement)?

7. What brain areas are involved in movement? How does each contribute to movement?

8. What are some disorders of movement?

The Body Senses

Summary and Guided Review

After studying this section in the text, fill in the blanks of the following summary.

Unlike vision and _____ (1), which tell us about things and conditions external to ourselves, the body senses convey information about things we are directly in contact with as well as our own internal conditions. Because the body senses provide information about spatial position, posture, and balance, they are intimately tied in with _____ (2), behavior that allows us to interact with the environment.

We get information about the body from the _____ (3) system, and from the vestibular system. _____ (4) refers to our sense of position and bodily movement. These messages originate in the muscles and joints. The commonly accepted skin senses include touch, _____ (5), cold, and _____ (6), and as such they provide information about both internal and external events. An additional sense might be _____ (7), because it appears to have its own pathways. There are several types of encapsulated receptors, each of which is sensitive to different aspects of _____ (8). _____ (9) corpuscles and _____ (10) disks in the superficial layers of skin detect texture and the fine detail of objects, as well as movement. In the deeper levels of skin, _____ (11) corpuscles and _____ (12) endings detect stretching of the skin and contribute to our perception of the shape of objects. Free nerve endings are sensitive to temperature and _____ (13). The free nerve ending receptors for temperature are members of the _____ (14) family of protein

ion channels. Detection of pain also requires several receptors; these sources are characterized as thermal,

_____ (15), and mechanical. Thermal and chemical pain receptors are also members of the

TRP family; the best known is the _____ (16) heat pain receptor, which also responds to

capsaicin.

The _____ (17) sense, whose receptors are located in the vestibular organs, is involved

in maintaining balance as well as providing information about head position and movement. The three

_____ _____ (18), located near the cochlea, are oriented differently in

space, providing sensitivity to acceleration in different planes. When we accelerate, this force displaces the

gelatinous mass or _____ (19), which in turn changes the firing rate of

_____ (20) cells. The utricle and _____ (21) contain a jellylike

substance and hair cells (in horizontal and vertical patches, respectively); they monitor acceleration and head

position and movement. When the head is tilted or acceleration occurs, the jelly moves and bends the hair cells.

Without the vestibular sense, we would have difficulty sensing when we are out of balance. In general,

proprioception and the vestibular sense provide coordinated information about the movement and

_____ (22) of our bodies. The vestibular system sends projections to the

_____ (23), brain stem, and parieto-insular-vestibular cortex.

Each spinal nerve receives sensory information from a different _____ (24); the body

areas served by these nerves overlap, so if a nerve is injured the dermatome retains some sensation. Body

sensory information is carried by spinal and cranial nerves to the _____ (25) and then to

the somatosensory cortex, mostly on the _____ (26) side of the brain. There are many

similarities in the organization and function of the somatosensory systems and the other sensory systems. The

somatosensory cortex contains a map of the body, some cells have center-surround _____

_____ (27), and somatosensory processing is _____ (28), controlled

by two of the subareas of the primary somatosensory cortex. The primary somatosensory cortex sends

information to the _____ _____ (29) cortex, which integrates

information from both sides of the body. It is particularly responsive to stimuli that have acquired meaning, and

it sends information to the _____ (30) area, perhaps determining which stimuli will be

remembered. Another target area is the _____ _____ (31) cortex,

where information from several sensory modalities is integrated, and output allowing for coordinated movements is sent to the _____ (32) areas of the brain.

A unified _____ (33) image is critical to our ability to function and even to our self-concept. Damage to the somatosensory system can produce conditions such as neglect or denial that a particular _____ (34) exists, even going so far as to request amputation. The entire body can be incorporated into an illusion called the _____-of-_____ (35) experience, during which the person sees his or her body from another location.

Painful stimuli such as intense _____ (36) or temperature, damage to tissue, and exposure to various chemicals are detected by free nerve endings. Pain neurons and non-neural cells release a wide array of signalling molecules referred to as the _____ _____ (37). This process produces swelling and redness, and _____ (38) excitability of the pain neurons so much that they respond even to _____ (39). This effect is adaptive because it encourages one to protect the injured area.

Pain information first travels to the spinal cord. The immediate sharp pain sensed following an injury is a result of information traveling via large, myelinated _____ (40) fibers, whereas the more delayed and persistent _____ (41) pain experienced is the result of activity in smaller C fibers. In the spinal cord, pain neurons release _____ (42) and glutamate.

Reduction of pain can be accomplished by using local _____ (43) that block _____ (44) channels in the pain neurons and reduce their ability to fire. General anesthetics may be injected or inhaled, rendering the person _____ (45). The most frequently used drugs for pain are aspirin, _____ (46), and acetaminophen (Tylenol). Some of these drugs work by blocking the synthesis of _____ (47) that are released in response to injury, hence reducing inflammation. However, _____ (48) has a weak effect on the enzymes, so it does not produce ant-inflammatory effects. More powerful drugs are often required, such as _____ (49), the gold standard for pain reduction. Because this drug causes rapid tolerance and addiction, researchers are studying alternatives such as Tanezumab, an antibody for _____ _____ (50) factor. An experimental nasal spray containing _____ (51) may be useful in the future for treating dental pain, migraine, and pain from the _____ (52) nerve itself.

Pain information travels through the thalamus to the _____ (53) cortex, although other areas such as the _____ _____ (54) cortex and insula are involved in processing the emotional aspect of pain. Under some conditions endogenous substances called

_____ (55) are released, and act on _____ (56) receptors in many

parts of the nervous system. Endorphins are released in times of helplessness, physical stress, acupuncture, and

vaginal stimulation, which might play a role in reducing pain during _____ (57) or sexual

intercourse. Pain relief from a placebo may also involve endorphins, as revealed by _____

(58) blockage of opiate receptors.

According to Melzack and Wall's _____ _____ (59) theory,

pressure signals cause the brain to send an _____ (60) message down the spinal cord,

where it closes a neural gate in the pain pathway. This is one of the pathways by which endorphins reduce pain.

Pain causes the release of endorphins in the brain stem structure called the _____

_____ (61); the endorphins inhibit the release of _____ (62) in the

spinal cord. This "closes" the pain gate.

Fortunately, _____ _____ (63) to pain is a rare condition, because

those who are afflicted unknowingly hurt themselves and often engage in risky and dangerous behavior. This

condition may be genetic. A mutation in the *SCN9A* gene renders one type of _____ (64)

channel nonfunctional, disabling pain neurons. A mutation in the gene for nerve growth factor results in

considerable loss of neural fibers.

Chronic pain is defined as pain that persists after _____ (65) has occurred or

would be expected to have occurred. Chronic pain can be either _____ (66), caused by

activation of pain receptors, or _____ (67), caused by damage to or malfunction of the PNS

or CNS. Many changes occur in the nervous system during chronic pain, such as increased sensitivity of pain

pathways and _____ (68) of spinal inhibitory mechanisms. Although many cortical areas

are activated in patients with chronic back pain, there is a loss of _____

_____ (69).

Sensations from _____ (70) limbs are real for amputee and, despite the fact that

signals are no longer being sent to the brain from the amputated limb, about _____-

_____% (71) of amputees report feeling pain in the missing limb. Local anesthesia,

surgery, and drugs typically benefit less than _____% (72) of patients, which is not better

than results from placebo. More successful strategies have involved techniques that reduce

_____ _____ (73), such as using a functional prosthesis or a

257

_____ (74) illusion to replace sensations from the missing limb.

Short Answer and Essay Questions

Answer the following questions.

1. Melanie is driving along the interstate at 55 mph. She crosses into a 70 mph zone, and accelerates up to 70. She can feel the difference in speed as she accelerates, but once she reaches 70 and sets the cruise control, her only sensation of movement is from the passing landscape. How does the activity in the vestibular system explain her sensations?

2. List the different forms of encapsulated nerve endings and the types of touch to which they are sensitive.

3. Describe four similarities that somatosensation shares with other senses such as vision.

4. Anatomically, what are the bases of sharp and dull pain? How is each adaptive?

5. Describe the pathway by which endorphins are thought to control pain.

6. What is the probable anatomical basis of phantom pain?

Movement

Summary and Guided Review

After studying this section in the text, fill in the blanks of the following summary.

Movement involves striated, or _____ (75), muscles. The two other types of muscles are _____ (76) muscles and _____ (77) muscles, found in the internal organs. Striated muscle cells are controlled by motor neurons at the _____ (78) junction via the neurotransmitter _____ (79). A single neuron may control a few or many muscle cells; the ratio of muscle fibers per neuron determines the _____ (80) of movement possible. Each muscle fiber is made up of _____ (81) filaments that "climb" along the _____ (82) filaments to shorten and contract the muscle. _____ (83)

connect muscles to bone, and movement occurs when muscles contract, pulling against the bone. In the limbs, muscles are paired in an _____ (84) way so that they produce opposing movements. Most muscle tension adjustments occur due to _____ (85) reflexes.

An example of a spinal reflex occurs when the _____ (86) tendon is tapped; this stretches the quadriceps muscle, whose _____ (87) receptors send a signal up the sensory nerve into the spinal cord. The sensory neurons form synapses with _____ (88) neurons, and a message is sent back to the quadriceps, causing it to _____ (89). This allows for quick, automatic postural adjustments. Muscle contractions are detected by _____

_____ (90) organs, which respond by inhibiting motor neurons, and limiting the contraction. The spinal cord also contains _____ _____

_____ (91), which are networks that produce a rhythmic pattern of motor activity such as walking. These generators free the brain for more important activities.

There are several cortical and subcortical brain areas involved in movement, organized in a hierarchical manner. The motor cortex consists of the primary motor cortex and two secondary areas, the

_____ (92) motor area and the _____ (93) cortex. The

_____ (94) cortex is an important center in the planning of movement, because it receives, integrates, and briefly stores information about the body and the environment. Studies of brain activity in monkeys during different stages of a delayed _____-to-_____ (95) task indicate that certain cells in the prefrontal cortex become active when a stimulus is presented and continue firing after its removal. Other cells start firing before activity begins in the premotor areas; this indicates that the

_____ (96) cortex selects the target of behavior and the appropriate motor response. The

_____ (97) cortex programs an activity by combining information from the prefrontal cortex and the posterior parietal cortex. Sequences of movement are coordinated by the

_____ _____ (98) area; activity of different cells in this area produces different types of movements.

The _____ _____ (99) cortex receives input from secondary motor areas and is responsible for executing _____ (100) movement. Cells in this area are relatively unspecialized; each cell may contribute to a range of related behaviors. The basal ganglia and

_____ (101) are involved in modulating movement, although they do not directly control it. The basal ganglia include the caudate nucleus, _____ (102), and globus pallidus, which fine-tune movements, making them smooth. They are also involved in learning _____ (103) of movement so the sequence can be performed as a unit. The cerebellum receives input from the motor cortex and _____ (104) system, and it is involved in several functions related to balance and the control of eye movements in compensation for _____ (105) movements. It coordinates the different components of complex movements and provides corrections as movements are being executed. It is also involved in motor and _____ (106) learning as well as attention.

There are several neurologically based movement disorders. Parkinson's disease, which affects about 2% of the population, results from damage to the _____ _____ (107), the source of dopaminergic neurons projecting to the striatum. Symptoms of Parkinson's disease include tremor, rigidity, and problems with balance, coordination, and the initiation of movement. The cause of Parkinson's disease appears to be familial in fewer than _____ % (108) of cases. Some of the genes involved in Parkinson's disease control the production of deviant proteins that are components of _____ _____ (109), which may contribute to cognitive deficits and depression. Brain injury and environmental _____ (110) found in pesticides may be involved in causing Parkinson's disease, and some people may inherit a reduced ability to metabolize these chemicals. The risk of Parkinson's disease is reduced by 80% in _____ (111) drinkers, and 50% in _____ (112). _____ (113) is believed to reduce the effects of toxins by blocking adenosine receptors, which results in increased dopamine and acetylcholine release. Treatment of Parkinson's disease has traditionally involved administration of the dopamine precursor _____ (114). The use of embryonic stem cells has not produced clinically significant improvement, although treatment using _____ (115) stem cells has shown more promise. Other alternatives to drug treatment include _____ (116) areas in the basal ganglia, but this approach can lead to deficits such as weakness. There has been better success with stimulation of the _____ _____ (117) and subthalamic nuclei, which seems to improve motor function and increase metabolism in motor areas.

Huntington's disease occurs as a result of progressive cell loss in the cortex and _____ (118), producing movement impairments that become more pronounced with time, as well as psychological changes. The disease is fatal. Cell death is thought to result from a build-up of the protein _____ (119); the gene responsible for this protein has been located, and a person inheriting a single copy of the defective gene will develop Huntington's disease. A number of drugs have been used to treat symptoms, but only one drug has received FDA approval. It works by reducing excess

_____ (120) that causes the abnormal movements.

Several autoimmune disorders also involve the disruption of movement. Myasthenia gravis occurs as a result of a decrease in the number or sensitivity of _____ (121) receptors, and it is characterized by muscular weakness that, if untreated, may cause death. A study using a snake venom that binds to acetylcholine receptors revealed that people with myasthenia gravis have significantly fewer of these receptors. Myasthenia gravis can be treated with _____ (122) inhibitors, but a more permanent treatment involves removal of the _____ (123) gland, the body's major source of antibody-producing lymphocytes. _____ _____ (124) involves the loss of myelin in CNS cells, producing scarring and reducing or eliminating the functioning of affected cells. Weakness, tremor, and impaired coordination result. Evidence suggests that myelin is destroyed by the

_____ _____ (125), perhaps as a result of exposure to a virus such as measles, mumps, or Epstein-Barr virus. One drug treatment that has just been approved for multiple sclerosis blocks _____ (126) channels and improves motor performance, particularly walking.

Short Answer and Essay Questions

Answer the following questions.

7. In terms of precision of movement, what are the consequences of the fact that a single motor neuron projecting to the biceps muscle serves 100 muscle cells, whereas a single motor neuron projecting to the eye muscles serves only three cells?

8. How might central pattern generators be useful in treating spinal cord injuries?

9. Explain the delayed match-to-sample task. How does activity in the prefrontal cortex correspond with different components of this task?

10. How do researchers know that the primary motor cortex, and not other motor areas, is responsible for the execution of movement?

11. Compare Parkinson's and Huntington's diseases in terms of what is known about the genetic basis of each. For which disease does the environment seem to play a more important role? Why?

12. Why is myasthenia gravis considered to be an autoimmune disease?

Posttest

Use these multiple-choice questions to check your understanding of the chapter.

1. The receptors in the body that convey information about muscle tension and limb position are part of which sensory system?

   a. vestibular sense

   b. somatosensation

   c. proprioception

   d. None of the above

2. Hair cells are found in the

   a. utricle.

   b. saccule.

   c. semicircular canals.

   d. All of the above

3. Which of the following is NOT considered part of the somatosensory system?

   a. proprioception

   b. vestibular sense

   c. skin senses

   d. interoceptive system

4. Pacinian corpuscles are found ___ the surface of the skin and detect ___.

   a. near; touch

   b. far from; touch

   c. near; warmth

   d. far from; warmth

5. Which of the following areas of the body probably contains the FEWEST touch receptors?

   a. tongue

   b. upper arm

   c. thumb

d. foot

6. Which of the following senses is NOT detected by free nerve endings?

   a. warmth

   b. cold

   c. touch

   d. pain

7. The body segment served by a specific spinal nerve is called a(n)

   a. dermatome.

   b. spinal area.

   c. cupula.

   d. Ruffini area.

8. Information about touch from the right side of the body projects

   a. only to the left hemisphere.

   b. only to the right hemisphere.

   c. to the left and right hemispheres equally.

   d. mostly to the left hemisphere.

9. The primary somatosensory cortex is located in the

   a. anterior parietal lobe.

   b. posterior frontal lobe.

   c. central sulcus.

   d. superior temporal lobe.

10. Capsaicin

    a. acts on the TRPV1 receptor.

    b. is an ingredient of chilli peppers.

    c. can alleviate joint pain.

    d. All of the above

11. A-delta fibers are ___ and are responsible for our experience of ___ pain.

    a. myelinated; sharp

    b. myelinated; dull

c. unmyelinated; sharp

d. unmyelinated; dull

12. Mice that lack receptors for substance P appear to experience

    a. no pain.

    b. only mild pain.

    c. only intense pain.

    d. moderate pain all of the time.

13. Which of the following pain medications acts by reducing inflammation in tissues?

    a. Tylenol

    b. morphine.

    c. acetaminophen

    d. ibuprofen

14. Endorphins are LEAST likely to be released in response to which of the following?

    a. physical stress

    b. vaginal stimulation

    c. placebo

    d. escapable shock

15. Pain causes the release of endorphins in the ___, which in turn causes inhibition of the release of substance P in the ___.

    a. PAG; spinal cord

    b. spinal cord; PAG

    c. PAG; amygdala

    d. spinal cord; cingulate cortex

16. Which of the following is NOT true about pain disorders?

    a. Most amputees do not experience phantom limb pain.

    b. Congenital pain insenitivity is a rare disorder, most likely genetic in origin.

    c. Chronic pain can cause loss of gray matter in the brain.

    d. Successful treatment of phantom limb pain reverses cortical reorganization.

17. Movements of the stomach and intestines are produced by

a. smooth muscle.

b. skeletal muscle.

c. striated muscle.

d. cardiac muscle.

18. Which of the following muscles probably has the MOST individual muscles cells controlled by a single motor neuron?

    a. triceps muscle

    b. eye muscle

    c. index finger muscle

    d. tongue muscle

19. Which of the following statements regarding antagonistic muscle pairs is FALSE?

    a. Each muscle has opposing effects on a limb.

    b. Both muscles may be contracted simultaneously.

    c. Maintaining the balance between opposed pairs of muscles requires conscious, voluntary activity.

    d. Coordination of antagonistic muscles is controlled by the spinal cord.

20. Muscle tension (extent of contraction) is detected by

    a. Golgi tendon organs.

    b. muscle spindles.

    c. Lewy bodies.

    d. a and b

21. Central pattern generators

    a. are found in lower animals but not in humans.

    b. are present in young infants, but they atrophy by adulthood.

    c. work even when the spinal cord is severed.

    d. None of the above

22. In producing movement, the last cortical area to be activated is the

    a. premotor area.

    b. association cortex.

    c. supplementary motor cortex.

d. primary motor cortex.

23. The "memory" of a stimulus used in the delayed match-to-sample task seems to be held in the

    a. primary motor cortex.

    b. supplementary motor cortex.

    c. premotor cortex.

    d. prefrontal cortex.

24. Selection of arm movement needed for reaching a specific target seems to occur in the

    a. primary motor cortex.

    b. supplementary motor cortex.

    c. premotor cortex.

    d. prefrontal cortex.

25. Sequences of movements, such as those involved in typing on a computer keyboard, are coordinated

    by cells in the

    a. primary motor cortex.

    b. supplementary motor cortex.

    c. premotor cortex.

    d. prefrontal cortex.

26. The actual execution of a movement is triggered by activity in the

    a. primary motor cortex.

    b. supplementary motor cortex.

    c. premotor cortex.

    d. prefrontal cortex.

27. Which brain areas contribute to the smoothness of movement?

    a. cerebellum and premotor cortex

    b. supplementary motor cortex and basal ganglia

    c. prefrontal cortex and premotor cortex

    d. cerebellum and basal ganglia

28. Which of the following structures is NOT part of the basal ganglia?

    a. caudate nucleus

b. globus pallidus

c. hippocampus

d. putamen

29. The cerebellum is involved in

   a. the order and timing of complex movements.

   b. the learning of motor skills.

   c. judging the speed of objects.

   d. All of the above

30. Parkinson's disease results from a loss of ___ neurons originating in the ___.

   a. dopaminergic; striatum

   b. dopaminergic; substantia nigra

   c. cholinergic; striatum

   d. cholinergic; substantia nigra

31. Currently, which of the following treatments for Parkinson's disease has been shown to have the FEWEST side effects?

   a. brain stimulation

   b. brain lesions

   c. L-dopa

   d. fetal tissue transplant

32. Which of the following statements is (are) TRUE of Huntington's disease?

   a. It is a degenerative disease, becoming progressively worse over time.

   b. Cognitive and emotional deficits always occur.

   c. Researchers know which gene is involved and how it works.

   d. All of the above

33. People with myasthenia gravis have fewer or less sensitive ___ receptors.

   a. dopamine

   b. serotonin

   c. endorphin

   d. acetylcholine

34. Myasthenia gravis is MOST effectively treated by

    a. acetylcholinesterase inhibitors.

    b. thymectomy.

    c. fetal tissue transplant.

    d. brain stimulation.

35. Multiple sclerosis involves

    a. loss of myelin in the central nervous system.

    b. loss of myelin in the peripheral nervous system.

    c. loss of myelin in both the central and peripheral nervous systems.

    d. none of the above.

Answers

Guided Review

1. hearing/audition

2. movement

3. somatosensory

4. Proprioception

5. warmth

6. pain

7. itch

8. touch

9. Meissner's

10. Merkel's

11. Pacinian

12. Ruffini

13. pain

14. TRP (transient receptor potential)

15. chemical

16. TRPV1

17. vestibular

18. semicircular canals

19. cupula

20. hair

21. saccule

22. position or orientation

23. cerebellum

24. dermatome

25. thalamus

26. opposite

27. receptive fields

28. hierarchical

29. secondary somatosensory

30. hippocampal

31. posterior parietal

32. frontal

33. body

34. limb

35. out-of-body

36. pressure

37. chemical soup

38. increased or enhanced

39. touch

40. A-delta

41. dull

42. substance P

43. anesthetics

44. sodium

45. unconscious

46. ibuprofen

47. prostaglandins

48. acetaminophen

49. morphine

50. nerve growth

51. lidocaine

52. trigeminal

53. somatosensory

54. anterior cingulate

55. endorphins

56. opiate

57. childbirth

58. naloxone

59. gate control

60. inhibitory

61. periaqueductal gray

62. substance P

63. congenital insensitivity

64. sodium

65. healing

66. nociceptive

67. neuropathic

68. depression

69. gray matter

70. phantom

71. 80-90

72. 30

73. cortical reorganization

74. mirror

75. skeletal

76. cardiac

77. smooth

78. neuromuscular

79. acetylcholine

80. precision

81. myosin

82. actin

83. Tendons

84. antagonistic

85. spinal

86. patellar

87. stretch

88. motor

89. contract

90. Golgi tendon

91. central pattern generators

92. supplementary

93. premotor

94. prefrontal

95. match-to-sample

96. prefrontal

97. premotor

98. supplementary motor

99. primary motor

100. voluntary

101. cerebellum

102. putamen

103. sequences

104. vestibular

105. head

106. nonmotor

107. substantia nigra

108. 10

109. Lewy bodies

110. toxins

111. coffee

112. smokers

113. Caffeine

114. L-dopa or levodopa

115. adult

116. lesioning

117. globus pallidus

118. striatum

119. huntingtin

120. dopamine

121. acetylcholine

122. acetylcholinesterase

123. thymus

124. Multiple sclerosis

125. immune system

126. potassium

Short Answer and Essay Questions

1. When your body accelerates, the increase in speed displaces the gelatinous masses (cupulas) in the

vestibular organs, causing the hair cells to bend and change the rate of firing in their neurons. Once you reach a stable speed, the cupulas returns to normal, and the hair cells return to their normal rate of firing, so we do not notice movement.

2. Meissner's corpuscles and Merkel's disks are located near the surface of the skin, and they can detect texture, fine detail, and movement of objects across the skin. Pacinian corpuscles and Ruffini endings are located deeper, and because they detect stretching of the skin, they can detect the shape of objects that are grasped.

3. The visual and somatosensory areas are similar in the following ways: They contain a map of their respective receptive fields (the body and the retina, respectively); the receptive fields of some of the cells are arranged with an excitatory center and inhibitory surround; processing is hierarchical, with certain subareas of the somatosensory cortex passing information along to other areas (similar to the sequential processing seen in the visual system); and both systems contain cells that are feature detectors.

4. Information about sharp pain is carried along large-diameter A-delta fibers; as a result, these pain messages travel to the brain quickly. They signal the onset of a painful stimulus trigger an almost immediate withdrawal or avoidance response (such as pulling your hand away from a hot burner). Dull pain is encoded along smaller-diameter C fibers, and this message travels more slowly, but the pain is more persistent. Dull pain probably reminds us that we have been injured; it may prevent further injury and also motivate us to seek treatment.

5. When pain messages are received in the periaqueductal gray, endorphins are released onto neurons that project down the spinal cord; there these neurons inhibit the neurons responsible for releasing substance P, reducing the flow of pain.

6. When a limb is amputated or no longer sends sensory input to the brain because of a spinal cord injury, the area of the somatosensory cortex served by that limb may be "taken over" by neurons from adjacent areas. Activation of these neurons produces a painful sensation that feels as if it is in the amputated limb.

7. When the ratio of motor neurons to muscles cells is low, as in the case of eye muscles, it allows for a great deal more precision of movement than when the ratio is high, as in the biceps muscle.

8. Central pattern generators contain "instructions" for producing rhythmic movements such as walking. When the spinal cord is severed, no cortical control of the pattern generators exists. However, they can be

stimulated electrically to produce rhythmic stepping movements, and researchers are attempting to use them in therapy with spinal cord patients.

9. In this task, the subject is shown a stimulus, and then the stimulus is removed. After a delay, two stimuli are shown, the original and another one, and the subject must select the original in order to receive reinforcement. During the initial presentation and the delay period, some cells in the prefrontal cortex become active and continue to fire throughout the delay, suggesting that they are "holding" the stimulus in memory. When the opportunity to respond occurs, another group of cells becomes active; because this activity precedes activity in the premotor cortex, it suggests that the prefrontal cortex selects the target and the appropriate response.

10. Activity in the prefrontal and premotor cortices occurs prior to the onset of movement, whereas activity in the primary motor cortex corresponds with movement. This suggests that although the prefrontal and premotor areas are involved in planning movements, the primary motor cortex executes the movement.

11. Huntington's disease is due to a single gene; the individual will develop the disease if the gene has more than 37 repetitions of the bases cytosine, adenine, and guanine, with more repetitions correlated with earlier development. The genetic basis of Parkinson's is not well understood. It is familial (inherited) in only a minority of cases. In familial Parkinson's disease, several different genes appear to be involved. Implicated genes are involved in death of dopamine neurons, production of Lewy bodies, and ability to metabolize toxins that may cause Parkinson's. In the latter cases, exposure to the toxins is probably necessary in order for the disease to develop, so both environment and genetics are important.

12. Myasthenia gravis is treatable by removing the thymus gland, the body's major source of the lymphocytes that produce antibodies. Almost 80% of patients treated with thymectomy recover and most of the remainder improve.

Posttest

1. c 2. d 3. b 4. b 5. b 6. c 7. a 8. d 9. a 10. d 11. a 12. b 13. d 14. d 15. a 16. a 17. a 18. a 19. c 20. a 21. c 22. d 23. d 24. c 25. b 26. a 27. d 28. c 29. d 30. b 31. a 32. d 33. d 34. b 35. a

12

Learning and Memory

Chapter Outline

Learning Objectives

After reading this chapter, you should be able to answer the following questions.

1. How do anterograde and retrograde amnesia differ?

2. What brain areas seem to be involved in memory consolidation and retrieval?

3. How do declarative and nondeclarative learning differ?

4. What is working memory?

5. What is the significance of LTP and related phenomena for learning?

6. What synaptic changes occur during LTP?

7. What factors contribute to memory consolidation?

8. What normal brain processes contribute to forgetting?

Learning as the Storage of Memories

Summary and Guided Review

After studying this section in the text, fill in the blanks of the following summary.

In order to be useful for future behavior, experiences or learning must somehow be stored within the nervous system; without _____ (1), we would be capable of only very simple forms of behavior. This point is demonstrated by the case of HM described in the introduction to the chapter. HM, who underwent removal of much of his _____ (2) lobes to reduce his debilitating seizures, suffered from both anterograde and retrograde _____ (3). Consequently, he had great difficulty forming new memories as well as remembering past events (although he could recall some events that occurred before the age of 16). Because of the extent of damage to HM's brain, it is not known exactly which structures were responsible for his amnesia, although the _____ (4) and associated areas were certainly involved. Moderate anterograde amnesia and minimal retrograde amnesia occur following bilateral damage to the hippocampal area known as _____ (5). Damage to the entire hippocampus produces severe _____ (6) amnesia, and severe retrograde amnesia occurs if the hippocampal _____ (7) is damaged as well. HM's story is considered one of the most important cases in the study of learning and memory. Although he died in 2008 at the age of 82, he continues to make a contribution; researchers at the University of California at San Diego have_____ (8) his brain and are making a 3-D digital _____ (9) available online.

Until information stored in memory undergoes _____ (10), which is the process of forming a permanent physical representation, it is subject to disruption. New memories are easily disrupted, and even old memories may be lost as a result of trauma. Evidence from studies using evoked potential measurements suggests that consolidation involves heightened activity in the hippocampus and _____ (11) gyrus. The process by which stored memories are accessed, or _____ (12), also appears to involve the hippocampus. In rats, consolidation can be disrupted by administeringa _____ (13)-blocking drug, which temporarily disables the hippocampus, for 7 days following training;administering the drug during later testing impairs recall, which indicates that the hippocampus is also involved in retrieval.; However, because very old memories are less affected by hippocampal damage, there must be some other mechanism responsible for maintaining and retrieving them. The fact that learning and effortful attempts at retrieval also activate the _____ (14) area suggests that it might also serve these functions.

The hippocampus is not the actual storage site of memories. Researchers believe that _____-_____ (15) memory depends on the hippocampus but that long-term memory depends on an interaction between the hippocampus and the _____ (16). For example, when subjects recalled recent news events, fMRI activity was highest in the _____ (17), but when asked to recall events over the past 30 years, activity increased in several _____ (18) areas. Consolidated memories are stored in the areas of the cortex where specific types of information are processed; for example, memories for pictures are stored in the _____ (19) region, whereas verbal memories are stored in the left _____ (20) lobe. A "map" of a rat's environment is stored in the hippocampus, where specialized_____ (21) cells are located.

The fact that HM displayed some forms of _____ (22) without being consciously aware of his newly acquired skills suggests that the brain forms at least two kinds of memory.

_____ (23) memory refers to information about facts, people, and events that we can verbalize, whereas nondeclarative memory refers to memory for _____ (24) (including skills learning, emotional learning, and stimulus-response conditioning). Put simply, declarative memories involve the "what" in memory whereas nondeclarative memories concern the _____ (25). Studies with rats demonstrate that different brain areas are involved in each form of memory; declarative or relational memory is disrupted by damage to the _____ (26), whereas nondeclarative memory is disrupted by damage to the _____ (27). In humans, this latter form of learning is disrupted in people with _____ (28) and Huntington's diseases. The

_____ (29) is involved in nondeclarative emotional learning. A subject with bilateral amygdala damage responded to a loud sound with a skin conductance response, but could not be conditioned to respond to a colored slide that was paired with the sound. Activity in the amygdala may also enhance

_____ (30) learning about emotional events, through its connections with the hippocampus.

Both new and old information are held temporarily in _____ (31) memory while it is being used; this is somewhat similar to a computer's RAM, although the capacity of working memory is very small and it fades quickly. The neurological basis of working memory can be studied using the delayed

_____-to-_____ (32) task. Following presentation and removal of the stimulus, cells continue firing in the cortical area appropriate for that stimulus; but if this activity is disrupted, the animal still makes a correct choice, so these are not the location of working memory. Working memory apparently is located in the _____ (33) cortex; cells there continue firing during the delay, even in spite of a distracting stimulus, and they respond selectively to the stimulus and task conditions.. The prefrontal cortex seems to be responsible for managing information in working memory by acting as a central

_____ (34) rather than merely serving as a storage facility for memory.

Short Answer and Essay Questions

Answer the following questions.

1. Distinguish between anterograde and retrograde amnesia. Using HM's case, give one example of each form.

2. Riedel and colleagues studied the role of the hippocampus in learning in rats by placing them in a water maze. The rats could escape from the water by learning the location of a submerged platform. How were the researchers able to show that impairment of the hippocampus can disrupt both consolidation and retrieval?

3. Distinguish between declarative and nondeclarative memory.

4. What did Bechara and colleagues discover about the different roles of the hippocampus and the amygdala in learning?

5. What are place cells and why are they unique?

Brain Changes in Learning

Summary and Guided Review

After studying this section in the text, fill in the blanks of the following summary.

Hebb's rule states that if a presynaptic neuron is active while a postsynaptic neuron is

_____ (35). the synapse will increase in strength. as The synaptic changes are the result of

_____-_____ _____ (36); they are similar to the

neural plasticity exhibited by neurons early in development as synapses are being formed. Long-term

potentiation (LTP) has been observed in the _____ (37) as well as in the visual, auditory,

and motor cortices. In the laboratory, LTP is usually induced by applying pulses of _____-

_____ (38) stimulation to presynaptic neurons. This change may last briefly or for several

months. _____-_____ _____ (39) weakens a

synapse; it occurs when stimulation of presynaptic neurons is insufficient to activate postsynaptic neurons. LTD

may be an important mechanism for modifying memories and _____ (40) old memories to

free synapses for new information. Presynaptic stimulation also influences the sensitivity of nearby synapses; if

a weak synapse and strong synapse on the same postsynaptic neuron are active simultaneously, the weak

synapse will be _____ (41), or strengthened. This effect is called

_____ (42) long-term potentiation. Researchers believe that this type of potentiation is the

basis for _____ (43) conditioning. These three phenomena, LTP, LTD, and associative LTP

all illustrate the expression "cells that fire together _____ (44) together. EEG activity in the

4 to 7 Hz range, called the_____ _____ (45), occurs in the

_____ (46) when an animal encounters novel stimuli. Hippocampal stimulation coinciding

with the peaks of theta waves can induce LTP in just 5 pulses. This rhythm may emphasize important stimuli for the brain and facilitate _____ (47) and _____ (48).

LTP induction involves a cascade of events at the synapse involving the neurotransmitter _____ (49), which has several different types of receptors. Initially glutamate activates _____ (50) receptors but not _____ (51) receptors, because they are blocked by _____ (52) ions. Partial depolarization of the membrane causes displacement of these ions, which then allows the _____ (53) receptors to be activated. This results in an influx of sodium and _____ (54) ions, which further depolarizes the neuron and activates _____ (55), an enzyme that is necessary for LTP.

LTP induction is followed by changes in _____ (56) activity and synthesis of _____ (57), resulting in changes at the synapse and growth of newconnections. Once the postsynaptic neuron is activated it releases _____ _____ (58), a retrograde messenger that causes the presynaptic neuron to release more neurotransmitter. Within 30 minutes after LTP, structural changes occur at the synapse. These include increased numbers of _____ (59) on dendrites that make the neuron more sensitive. Other changes include transport of _____ (60) receptors from the dendrites into the spines. The neurotransmitter _____ (61) unmasks previously silent synapses and initiates the growth of new ones. Furthermore, the birth of new neurons, or _____ (62), occurs in the hippocampus. Over the course of a lifetime these new cells may make up _____ % (63) of the total population of cells. These changes are long term, and they may explain why London cabbies who memorize the layout of the city show an increase in the size of the posterior part of the hippocampus, which is known to be involved in spatial _____ (64).

There is ample evidence that the formation of long-term declarative memories depends on a stage in the _____ _____ (65) lobe, followed by a transition to a more permanent form in the _____ (66). The enzyme _____ (67) appears to be involved in this transfer process. Mice that are homozygous for a mutant gene for this enzyme show no _____ LTP (68). Mice that are heterozygous produce some enzyme, and show hippocampal, but not _____ (69), LTP. Another enzyme, protein kinase M zeta, seems to be necessary for the _____ (70) of LTP during long-term memory; injection of this substance into the inusla 25 days after training eliminates a learned taste aversion. There is evidence that some transfer of information from the hippocampus to the cortex occurs during _____ (71). During this "offline" period, the replay of neural firing that occurred while learning a task provides the cortex the opportunity to undergo _____ (72) at the more leisurely pace that it requires. During sleep more than 100 genes increase their activity and many have been implicated in protein synthesis, synaptic changes, and memory consolidation.

Finally, it is important to understand that although memories may be long lasting, the brain has mechanisms for eliminating or changing information. _____ (73) is a process in which a learned association *appears* to be eliminated; the memory is actually still available, but has been replaced by new learning, which involves the activation of NMDA receptors. The enzyme protein phosphatase 1 and the gene *Drac1(V12)* apparently mediate _____ (74). This gene's protein product _____ (75) causes memory to decay after learning. In rats, it has been shown that _____ (76), which normally occurs after a memory has been retrieved, is a very vulnerable period during which memories can be disrupted by _____ (77) shock or by a drug that interferes with protein synthesis. Finally, retrieved memories may be _____ (78), for example, by being blended with other memories; Loftus and colleagues have shown that _____ (79) memories may be implanted by suggestion. There are a few cases of individuals who seem to remember almost everything! This in not always adaptive, and in one case was the individual was tormented by negative memories. The three cases that have been studied have two other things in common: they have slightly enlarged prefrontal areas and they all show signs of _____ (80) behavior.

Short Answer and Essay Questions

Answer the following questions.

6. How does LTP resemble the developmental mechanism for establishing synapses? What is associative long-term potentiation?

7. What is LTD? Why is it thought to be important for learning?

8. What roles do glutamate and nitric oxide play in LTP?

9. Name three different processes that show that memories are malleable or not "fixed in stone".

10. It is 7:00 p.m. on Tuesday, and your roommate has an exam in her first class tomorrow at 8:00 a.m. She

is not sure if it would be better to spend the next 3 hours studying for the exam and go to bed around 10:30 p.m., or not study tonight, go to bed at 9:00 p.m., and then get up around 5:00 a.m. to study. Based on what the book says about the role of sleep in learning, what advice would you offer your roommate?

11. Winona witnessed a bank robbery by two men, but was able to provide little more than general information in her description. Over the two years since the robbery and following repeated questioning, she has recalled several details. On the witness stand, the defense attorney questions the accuracy of these memories, but Winona insists her memories are vivid and accurate. Based on information in the text, what problems do you see with her testimony?

Learning Deficiencies and Disorders

Summary and Guided Review

After studying this section in the text, fill in the blanks of the following summary.

Until recently, it was believed that loss of memory and cognitive skills was a natural consequence of _____ (81); however, studies indicate that these losses are not inevitable (though it is unclear whether successful aging is due to choosing an active lifestyle or is an inherent characteristic of the individual. Another misconception is that when memory loss does occur, it results from cell loss, particularly in the cortex and the _____ (82). What does seem to happen is that, the hippocampus loses synapses and _____ (83) receptors, which which is the likely cause of diminished LTP and learning. In addition, reduced activity in the _____ (84) cortex, which is linked to the hippocampus, and loss of _____ (85) are also thought to be involved. Cell loss in the _____ _____ (86) region may contribute to memory deficits in both Alzheimer's disease and normal aging, and _____ (87) lobe deficits may be present in many elderly as well.

_____ (88) refers to the loss of memory and cognitive abilities in the elderly. Alzheimer's disease, in which the brain progressively deteriorates, is a form of dementia. In the early stages, _____ (89) memory is impaired, a symptom that becomes worse over time. Alzheimer's disease is strongly associated with aging; _____% (90) of people over 65 are affected, and nearly half of those over _____ (91) are afflicted.

The brains of people with Alzheimer's contain _____ (92) plaques, which interfere with neuron functioning, and _____ (93) tangles; both are associated with cell death. Over time, deficits in brain tissue and functioning can be observed in most of the brain, especially the frontal lobes and the temporal lobes, where they effectively isolate the _____ (94). Another possible reason for memory loss is the accumulation of _____ (95), a soluble form of amyloid that impairs LTP in the hippocampus.

Because plaques and tangles are also a characteristic of _____ (96) syndrome, Alzheimer's researchers looked for genes on chromosome 21, where they found the _____ (97) gene; mice engineered with a mutation of this gene that increases plaques also had deficits in LTP and learning. After examining the results of hundreds of studies, Harvard researchers came up with a list of _____ (98) possible genes. Other studies have found that some genes are downregulated whereas others are _____ (99) in the amygdala and cingulate gyrus of people with Alzheimer's disease.

There are several different forms of drugs that are used to treat Alzheimer's disease, although none of them provides a cure. Alzheimer's patients have a significant loss of neurons that release _____ (100), a neurotransmitter that is important for learning and memory. Three drugs that prevent the breakdown of acetylcholine are currently used to relieve cognitive and behavioral symptoms in mild cases of Alzheimer's. Moderate to severe cases may be treated with _____ (101), which reduces neurons' sensitivity to excessive glutamate, which overexcites and kills neurons. Another approach has been to inject amyloid in order to create an _____ (102) response that would clear plaques from the brain. Another exciting therapy involves implanting genes for _____ _____ _____ (103), which protects cells from dying as well as stimulating cell growth and activity. Implantation of this gene in humans has produced striking increases in brain _____ (104) and slowed the loss of cognitive abilities compared to untreated individuals.

Diagnosing Alzheimer's disease involves a battery of tests, but one of the most important steps is to rule out other causes of _____ (105). One strategy involves using PET scanning and tracers that specifically target _____ (106). This technique might help predict the disease and follow its course over time. Because PET scans are not widely available, a more practical approach might be to test for

_____ (107) for the disease found in skin, blood, and cerebrospinal fluid. A study of

Catholic nuns found that the disease might start long before the diagnosis actually occurs, and that individuals

who did not develop Alzheimer's disease had larger cells in the CA1 area of the_____

(108). However, it is difficult to determine whether these cells were present early in life and provided protection

or were a later adaptation to brain lesions.

_____ _____ (109) is associated with thiamine deficiency, which

is usually related to _____ (110) abuse. This degenerative disorder results in anterograde

and retrograde amnesia due to damage to the _____ (111) bodies, medial thalamic area,

and _____ (112) lobes. In the early stages, _____ (113) can relieve

the symptoms but not reverse the damage. Korsakoff's patients often exhibit _____ (114),

or the fabrication of stories, probably as an attempt to fill in information they can no longer recall. This

characteristic seems to be related to damage to a specific area of the _____ (115) lobe,

rendering patients unable to distinguish current reality and memories of prior events.

Short Answer and Essay Questions

Answer the following questions.

12. Why is memory loss in the elderly no longer considered to be an inevitable consequence of the aging
    process?

13. Briefly describe five possible reasons for age-related memory loss (not including Alzheimer's).

14. In their search for a genetic basis for Alzheimer's disease, why did researchers focus on chromosome
    21?

15. What treatments for Alzheimer's disease are most commonly used? What treatments may be available
    in the future?

16. What is confabulation? Give an example.

Posttest

Use these multiple-choice questions to check your understanding of the chapter.

1. Which of the following was NOT a result of HM's surgery?

   a. lowered IQ

   b. anterograde amnesia

   c. retrograde amnesia

   d. relief from seizures

2. Which of the following deficits is an example of anterograde amnesia?

   a. being unable to recall events occurring just prior to brain injury

   b. being unable to recall events occurring after brain injury

   c. being unable to recall events occurring many years prior to brain injury

   d. none of the above

3. Bilateral brain damage that is limited to hippocampal area CA1 results in

   a. moderate anterograde amnesia and profound retrograde amnesia.

   b. moderate anterograde amnesia and minimal retrograde amnesia.

   c. profound anterograde amnesia and profound retrograde amnesia.

   d. profound anterograde amnesia and minimal retrograde amnesia.

4. Consolidation is the process of

   a. accessing stored information.

   b. altering memories during retrieval.

   c. fabricating information missing from memory.

   d. making memories long lasting or permanent.

5. The hippocampus plays a role in

   a. consolidation.

   b. retrieval.

   c. both consolidation and retrieval.

   d. neither consolidation nor retrieval.

6. Over 25 days of being tested for retention of a spatial discrimination task, researchers found that mice showed

a. increased activity in the hippocampus and increased activity in the cortex.

b. increased activity in the hippocampus and decreased activity in the cortex.

c. decreased activity in the hippocampus and increased activity in the cortex.

d. decreased activity in the hippocampus and decreased activity in the cortex.

7. Effortful attempts at retrieval are associated with increased activity in

a. the prefrontal area.

b. the hippocampus.

c. both the prefrontal area and the hippocampus.

d. neither the prefrontal area nor the hippocampus.

8. Researchers believe that in most cases memories are stored

a. in the hippocampus.

b. in a single storage area of the cortex.

c. evenly throughout the cortex.

d. None of the above

9. Which of the following is NOT a type of declarative memory?

a. episodic memory

b. emotional memory

c. spatial memory

d. autobiographical memory

10. People with damage to the striatum (as in Parkinson's and Huntington's diseases) have difficulty with

a. procedural memory.

b. declarative memory.

c. relational memory.

d. b and c

11. Incorporating emotional information into memory probably depends on the

a. amygdala.

b. cingulate gyrus.

c. basal ganglia.

d. cerebellum.

12. Which of the following statements regarding working memory is FALSE?

   a. It holds information temporarily.

   b. It has an unlimited capacity.

   c. It provides the basis for problem solving and decision making.

   d. It can hold new information as well as memories already stored.

13. The brain area that seems to be MOST important for working memory is the

   a. inferior temporal cortex.

   b. parietal cortex.

   c. prefrontal cortex.

   d. superior frontal cortex.

14. Following stimulation of presynaptic neurons with high-frequency impulses, postsynaptic neurons will

   a. decrease their firing rate.

   b. produce larger EPSPs.

   c. produce smaller EPSPs.

   d. produce larger IPSPs.

15. LTP occurs

   a. only in the hippocampus.

   b. only in the visual cortex.

   c. only in the motor cortex.

   d. None of the above

16. Classical conditioning most likely involves

   a. LTP.

   b. associative LTP.

   c. LTD.

   d. associative LTD.

17. Low-frequency stimulation of presynaptic neurons results in

   a. LTP.

   b. LTD.

   c. more EPSPs.

d. more postsynaptic action potentials.

18. Suppression of ___ rhythms in the ___ inhibits some forms of learning.

    a. theta; hippocampus

    b. theta; cortex

    c. beta; hippocampus

    d. beta; cortex

19. Which of these follows LTP induction?

    a. growth of new dendrites

    b. gene activation

    c. release of dopamine

    d. All of the above

20. In order for NMDA receptors to be activated, ___ must be dislodged.

    a. glutamate

    b. magnesium

    c. sodium

    d. nitric oxide

21. Presynaptic neurons may increase their release of neurotransmitter when the postsynaptic neuron releases

    a. acetylcholine.

    b. magnesium.

    c. sodium.

    d. nitric oxide.

22. Which of the following is TRUE about neurogenesis?

    a. It occurs only in the cortex.

    b. Over the lifespan, it produces less than 5% of cells in a particular area.

    c. It has been most studied in the hippocampus.

    d. b and c

23. A study of the brains of London taxicab drivers revealed that

    a. the entire hippocampus is larger than in other people.

b. all of the spatial areas of the brain are larger than in other people.

c. the posterior portion of the hippocampus was larger than in other people.

d. None of the above

24. The presence of which of the following substances would MOST likely leads to reduced LTP?

a. protein kinase M zeta

b. nitric oxide blockers

c. CaMKII

d. a and b

25. Which of the following statements regarding LTP is MOST likely true?

a. It is only a laboratory (or experimental) phenomenon.

b. Hippocampal LTP is permanent.

c. Cortical LTP is responsible for long-term memory.

d. Only mammals exhibit LTP.

26. Mice heterozygous for a defective CaMKII gene

a. are better learners than normal mice.

b. are incapable of retaining information for more than a few hours.

c. show no LTP.

d. have more CaMKII than mice homozygous for the gene.

27. What is the most accurate statement about sleep and memory?

a. During sleep, neurons in the hippocampus are silent.

b. During sleep, more than 100 genes decrease their activity.

c. "Offline" replay that occurs during sleep helps the cortex undergo LTP.

d. Contrary to what researchers expected, sleep has no measurable effect on memory.

28. Memories seem to be vulnerable to change during

a. reconsolidation.

b. reconstruction.

c. both a and b

d. neither a nor b

29. Which of the following is not TRUE about the process of forgetting?

   a. It has no apparent benefit; it would be better to remember everything, if possible.

   b. It involves the enzyme protein phosphatase 1.

   c. It is a different process from extinction.

   d. It may involve the protein Rac, which causes memory to decay after learning.

30. Regarding memory and aging,

   a. memory failure is an inevitable, normal consequence of aging.

   b. engaging in mental but not physical activity reduces memory loss in older adults.

   c. there is no relationship between aging and memory loss.

   d. remaining mentally active is associated with better cognitive functioning.

31. In older rats,

   a. there are fewer NMDA receptors in the hippocampus.

   b. there are significantly fewer cells in the hippocampus.

   c. there are significantly fewer cells in the cortex.

   d. there is a steady loss of synapses throughout the brain.

32. Loss of cells in the ___ that release acetylcholine is associated with cognitive decline.

   a. hippocampus

   b. basal forebrain region

   c. medial forebrain bundle

   d. entorhinal cortex

33. The MOST common cause of dementia is

   a. Alzheimer's disease.

   b. Korsakoff's syndrome.

   c. stroke.

   d. amnesia.

34. What percentage of people over the age of 65 have Alzheimer's disease?

   a. 50%

   b. 35%

c. 20%

d. 10%

35. In Alzheimer's patients, plaques and tangles found in the ___ lobes disrupt connections between the hippocampus and other structures.

a. frontal

b. parietal

c. temporal

d. occipital

36. Which of the following statements regarding Alzheimer's disease is FALSE?

a. There are at least four different genes that cause it.

b. People with Down syndrome will develop it if they live past 50.

c. The amyloid precursor protein gene is found on chromosome 21.

d. Symptoms of Alzheimer's disease do not appear before the age of 60.

37. Which of the following is the most common treatment for Alzheimer's disease?

a. gene therapy

b. cholinesterase inhibitors

c. injection of amyloid to trigger an immune response

d. memantine

38. Which of the following statements regarding genes and Alzheimer's is TRUE?

a. Researchers have implanted genes for nerve growth factor in aged monkeys.

b. Gene implantation studies in humans haven't yet produced positive results.

c. An individual with the APP gene will develop Alzheimer's disease only after age 65.

d. All of the above

39. Which of the following structures is NOT damaged in Korsakoff's syndrome?

a. hippocampus

b. mammillary bodies

c. medial thalamic area

d. frontal lobes

40. Korsakoff's patients are believed to engage in confabulation because

a. their sense of right and wrong has deteriorated, and they do not care if they lie to others.

b. they have difficulty distinguishing between current reality and their memories of the past.

c. they are completely out of touch with reality.

d. None of the above

Answers

Guided Review

1. memory

2. temporal

3. amnesia

4. hippocampus

5. CA1

6. anterograde

7. formation

8. dissected

9. reconstruction

10. consolidation

11. parahippocampal

12. Retrieval

13. glutamate

14. prefrontal

15. short-term

16. cortex

17. hippocampus

18. cortical

19. occipital

20. frontal

21. place

22. learning

23. Declarative

24. behaviors

25. "how"

26. hippocampus

27. striatum

28. Parkinson's

29. amygdala

30. declarative

31. working

32. match-to-sample

33. prefrontal

34. executive

35. firing

36. long-term potentiation (LTP)

37. hippocampus

38. high-frequency

39. Long-term depression (LTD)

40. clearing

41. potentiated

42. associative

43. classical

44. wire

45. theta rhythm

46. hippocampus

47. LTP

48. LTD

49. glutamate

50. AMPA

51. NMDA

52. magnesium

53. NMDA

54. calcium

55. CaMKII

56. gene

57. protein

58. nitric oxide

59. spines

60. AMPA

61. dopamine

62. neurogenesis

63. 10-20

64. navigation

65. medial temporal

66. cortex

67. CaMKII

68. hippocampal

69. cortical

70. maintenance

71. sleep

72. LTP

73. Extinction

74. forgetting

75. Rac

76. reconsolidation

77. electroconvulsive

78. reconstructed

79. false

80. compulsive

81. aging

82. hippocampus

83. NMDA

84. entorhinal

85. myelin

86. basal forebrain

87. frontal

88. Dementia

89. declarative

90. 10

91. 85

92. amyloid

93. neurofibrillary

94. hippocampus

95. ADDL

96. Down

97. *APP*

98. 13

99. upregulated

100. acetylcholine

101. memantine or Namenda

102. immune

103. nerve growth factor

104. metabolism

105. dementia

106. plaques

107. biomarkers

108. hippocampus

109. Korsakoff's syndrome

110. alcohol

111. mammillary

112. frontal

113. thiamine

114. confabulation

115. frontal

Short Answer and Essay Questions

1. Anterograde amnesia is the failure to form new memories following a brain injury, whereas retrograde amnesia is the failure to retrieve memories for events and information experienced prior to the injury. In the case of HM, there are many examples of anterograde amnesia. For example, he could not find his way home to his parents' new house (they moved after his surgery was done), and he could not recall what type of work he was doing. He also experienced retrograde amnesia; he could not recall several significant events from his late teens and early adult years, such as his high school graduation and the end of World War II.

2. These researchers injected a glutamate blocker bilaterally into the hippocampus of rats. If the drug was given shortly after training, the rats showed poor performance at testing (after the drug had worn off), suggesting that consolidation was impaired. However, trained rats that were given the drug only at the time of testing also failed to perform the task, suggesting that the hippocampus is important in retrieval as well.

3. Declarative memory is memory for information about which we can verbalize, such as memories for events, whereas nondeclarative memory does not require verbalization in order to be used; it includes skills or procedures, emotions, and stimulus-response associations.

4. A patient with bilateral hippocampal damage and one with bilateral amygdala damage underwent a conditioning procedure in which a loud sound was paired with a blue slide. Both patients showed a normal physiological response (SCR) to the sound. The hippocampal patient showed conditioning without being able to verbalize the association. (This patient showed a response to the blue slide but could not state which slide was paired with the sound.) The amygdala patient did know which slide was paired with the sound but did not show an increased SCR to that slide. What this suggests is that the hippocampus is necessary for declarative memory, whereas the amygdala is necessary for emotional learning, a form of nondeclarative learning.

5. Place cells increase their rate of firing when the individual is in a specific location in the environment. These cells are found in the hippocampus whereas other memories are stored in different cortical areas.

6. During early development, synapses are "selected" for survival based on patterns of firing; the syn-

apses that are most likely to survive are those for which pre- and postsynaptic neurons fire together frequently. LTP operates under a similar mechanism, but in the laboratory, it is induced by applying high-frequency stimulation to a group of presynaptic neurons; following LTP, the postsynaptic neurons are more likely to fire when stimulated by the presynaptic neurons. Associative LTP occurs when a weak synapse and a strong synapse on the same neuron are activated simultaneously, which potentiates the weak synapse. Associative LTP may explain the phenomenon of classical conditioning.

7. Long-term depression is the weakening of a synapse as a result of a presynaptic neuron firing when the postsynaptic neuron is not depolarized. It is believed that this is an important mechanism in learning because it prevents LTP from becoming permanent and frees synapses for new associations. LTD may be particularly important for clearing the hippocampal area of old memories so new memories can take their place.

8. In most cases of LTP, glutamate is released and first activates AMPA receptors. The resulting partial depolarization dislodges magnesium ions from the NMDA receptors, which allows them to be activated. Sodium and calcium ions flow in, depolarizing the membrane and activating key enzymes. Nitric oxide is a retrograde messenger released by the postsynaptic neuron; it facilitates the release of neurostransmitter by the presynaptic neuron, which then stimulates the postsynaptic neuron.

9. Extinction, forgetting, and reconsolidation are three such processes.

10. There is some evidence suggesting that sleep facilitates consolidation, so you could advise your roommate to study the night before the exam, and maybe even two nights before, to ensure that sleep-dependent consolidation has a chance to occur.

11. The jury should not consider her current statement to be accurate. Because she did not recall the details until after multiple chances for reconsolidation and reconstruction of the memory, it is likely that her memory for the event has been altered.

12. Not all elderly individuals undergo memory loss or cognitive deficits. For example, the book cites a study in which college professors in their 60s scored about the same as those in their 30s.

13. The hippocampus loses synapses and NMDA receptors, which probably accounts for impaired LTP. There is decreased activity in the entorhinal cortex, which provides connections between the hippocampus and other brain areas. Cells in the brain lose myelin, which interferes with their functioning. The basal forebrain region also undergoes neuron loss; this is an important area because its cells connect to the hippocampus,

amygdala, and cortex. Finally, there are deficits in frontal lobe functioning, which suggests damage there.

14. This chromosome was targeted because of its role in Down syndrome. People with Down have three 21st chromosomes, rather than the usual two, and their brains have plaques and tangles like those of Alzheimer's patients. Researchers thus suspected that one or more genes on this chromosome were responsible for these brain abnormalities.

15. One current type of drug inhibits the breakdown of acetylcholine. Another reduces sensitivity to glutamate (which is overactive in affected neurons). Other potential treatments include anti-inflammatory drugs, amyloid injections to trigger an immune response, and genetic manipulation to introduce nerve growth factor into the brain.

16. Confabulation is the tendency of some amnesiacs, especially people with Korsakoff's syndrome, to make up stories about their lives. Several examples are given in the book about a woman living in a nursing home who at various times seemed confused about where she was; in one instance she complained that she was stranded there and needed to get back to her army post, and another time she explained her circumstances by believing she was a prisoner. In both instances she was confusing current reality with earlier memories from her life, which some believe is characteristic of confabulation.

Posttest

1. a   2. b   3. b   4. d   5. c   6. c   7. a   8. d   9. b   10. a   11. a   12. b   13. c   14. b   15. d   16. b   17. b
18. a   19. d   20. b   21. d   22. c   23. c   24. b   25. c   26. d   27. c   28. a   29. a   30. d   31. a   32. b
33. a   34. d   35. c   36. d   37. b   38. a   39. a   40. b

13

Intelligence and Cognitive Functioning

Chapter Outline

Learning Objectives

After reading this chapter, you should be able to answer the following questions.

1. How is intelligence defined and measured?

2. What are some of the controversies surrounding intelligence testing?

3. In what ways are the brains of more intelligent people different?

4. What brain areas are associated with specific cognitive skills?

5. What evidence supports the argument that heredity is important for intelligence? That environment is important? Can intelligence be enhanced?

6. What are the effects of aging on the brain and on intelligence or cognitive performance?

7. What are some of the causes of intellectual disability?

8. What are the biological bases of autism?

9. What are some brain differences in ADHD? What are some benefits and concerns related to its treatment?

The Nature of Intelligence

Summary and Guided Review

After studying this section in the text, fill in the blanks of the following summary.

_____ (1), defined as the capacity for reasoning, understanding, and benefiting from experience, is challenging to measure. Originally, the intelligence quotient (or IQ) was determined as the ratio a child's mental and _____ (2) age, multiplied by 100. Currently, a person's IQ represents her or his performance compared with that of the general population; the average IQ score is arbitrarily set at _____ (3) for both children and adults, and most scores fall near this number. Only 2% of the population score above 130 or below _____ (4). The first intelligence test, developed by _____ (5), was used to identify children with special needs. IQ scores are positively correlated with school grades, level of education, job performance, and income level; and negatively correlated with _____ (6). Because of the correlation between IQ and academic success/socioeconomic status, critics argue that IQ tests are designed to reflect these forms of success. The _____ _____ _____ (7) test, a culture-free test, is believed by some to provide a measure of "pure" intelligence. Another criticism of IQ tests is that they do not measure cognitive skills that people use in their everyday lives, or _____ (8) intelligence..

_____ (9) asserts that intelligence is actually a cultural invention. If that is true, then finding the biological bases of whatever "intelligence" describes is made more difficult.

There is also controversy over the structure of intelligence. _____ (10) are intelligence theorists who assume that there is a unitary capability underlying intelligence, often referred to as the

_____ _____ (11), or "g". This argument is supported by the fact that different abilities such as math and verbal skills are correlated. _____ (12) argue that mental abilities are distinct from one another; this perspective is supported by the fact that brain damage often impairs one type of skill and not others.

Short Answer and Essay Questions

Answer the following questions.

1. What are two criticisms of intelligence tests?

2. How do lumpers and splitters differ on their positions regarding a general factor of intelligence?

The Origins of Intelligence

Summary and Guided Review

After studying this section in the text, fill in the blanks of the following summary.

The search for an anatomical basis of intelligence has led some researchers to ask whether more intelligent people have bigger brains. However, the brain of the genius _____ _____ (13) was rather small and did not differ from other brains in most respects. One exception is that his

_____ _____ (14) were larger, which are associated with mathematical skills and visual-spatial processing. Other changes included increased number of

_____ (15) cells and other anomalies in the parietal lobes. Scans of brain-damaged individuals support the idea that "g" requires a _____ (16) system, spanning and connecting areas in several lobes of the brain.

If we compare across species, brain size alone is not a good predictor of intelligence. Among humans, who are among the _____ (17) in brain-to-body size ratio, there is some evidence for a relationship between IQ and brain-to-body size ratio, although it is modest. There is a gender difference in the ratio, with males' brains being somewhat _____ (18) in relation to body size than females' brains, although men and women do not differ in intelligence. One possible reason for the gender difference is that women's brains, which have more densely packed neurons and relatively more _____

_____ (19), are more efficient. Another possibility is that the males' advantage in

_____ (20) abilities requires a larger brain. How the brain is organized appears to be more important than overall size. Individuals with "smarter brains" tend to have a _____ (21) cortex and more _____ _____ (22).

The speed at which people process information may be an indication of general intelligence; in fact, IQ and _____ _____ (23) are correlated. An even stronger correlation exists between IQ scores and _____ _____ (24) velocity, which may lead to more efficient processing. _____ (25), which speeds neural impulses and prevents inappropriate communication between adjacent neurons, is also believed to be related to intelligence. People with greater myelination tend to have higher IQs, and the developmental changes of myelination, intelligence, and speed of processing information follow the same curvilinear path across development.

_____-_____ (26) memory, which places a limit on how much information we can handle at one time, is probably influenced by nerve conduction velocity. Because the contents of working memory decays quickly, people whose neurons conduct faster are probably able to transfer information to _____-_____ (27) memory and retain more information than those whose neurons work more slowly. In fact, IQ is more strongly correlated with _____ (28) memory than reaction time, particularly when tasks are complex. Furthermore, people with higher IQs show less _____ _____ (29) while playing Tetris, while people with _____ _____ (30) exhibit more brain activity than above average individuals while performing a mental task. These results suggest that IQ is related to the _____ (31) of neural processing.

Individual components of intelligence may be identified by _____ _____ (32), which involves giving people a variety of tests and then looking for correlations among clusters of related tests. Although performance on all mental tests tends to be correlated, _____ (33), logical-mathematical, and _____ (34) components have emerged as major components of intelligence. One brain-based explanation for these different components is that they evolved separately and consist of different _____ (35) or networks. For example, performing exact calculations depends on activity in _____ (36) language areas, while estimating results involves the visual-spatial association areas of the _____ (37) lobes. Research involving human infants and nonhuman _____ (38) suggests that the brain is "wired" for numbers. There are many examples of "intelligent" behavior from the animal world, including their ability to make and use _____ (39). Ingenuity and planfulness have also been observed in chimps and in some birds, such as crows and _____ (40). In spite of these examples, humans' brains seem to be unique in possessing specialized structures for tool use or the ability to develop them through _____ (41).

Because intelligence is complex, identifying its genetic and environmental components has proven to be extremely difficult. One interesting finding is that while heritability estimates for intelligence are around _____ % (42), the influence of heredity seems to _____ (43) with age. Estimated heritabilities from twin studies show high rates for brain functions, including _____ (44) memory and processing speed, and structural characteristics such as brain _____ (45) and amount of white and gray matter. Locating specific genes involved in intelligence has been frustrating due to lack of _____ (46) of findings. One possibility is the _____ (47) gene, which is related to brain size, and the *PACAP* precursor gene, which is involved in _____ (48) and neural signaling. Over 150 genes have been identified as likely contributorsto some aspect of cognitive ability.

The fact that intelligence is highly heritable does not mean that it cannot be influenced by the _____ (49); rather, genes set a range of potential intelligence levels, and the environment determines where in that range intelligence will fall. Furthermore, it has been necessary to adjust IQ test norms to maintain the average at 100 as people's performance on intelligence tests has steadily _____ (50). Some argue that twin studies are not a fair assessment of the heritability of IQ, because parents and others may treat identical twins as being more similar based on appearance, and hence provide similar learning experiences that could result in more highly correlated IQs (higher concordance rates). However, studies show that parents' belief as to whether their twins are fraternal or identical has no influence on the twins' intellectual similarity, whereas the twins' true _____ (51) relationship does.

The reasons behind racial differences in IQ scores are hotly debated. Some researchers such as Arthur Jensen argue that IQ differences between races are largely _____ (52), while others contend that this is not the case. For example, Scarr showed that there were no differences in performance on cognitive tests among blacks with different degrees of African _____ (53), and the American Psychological Association has concluded that there is little evidence for a genetic explanation of the racial differences.

Environmental contributions to intelligence are also difficult to identify, in part because environmental and genetic factors are _____ (54); because children share both genes and environment with their parents, it is difficult to separate their influences. Also, environmental factors are numerous and individually _____ (55). An exception to this might be the influence of

_____ (56) disease, which some researchers have found to be the best predictor of national differences in intelligence. Some forms of environmental intervention have been successful in improving achievement in at-risk children. Although there are long-term educational and career benefits among children participating in the _____ _____ (57) program, the IQ gains disappear over time. The _____ (58) project seems to produce longer-lasting IQ improvement, possibly because this program starts intervention at the time of _____ (59). Children who are adopted show stronger IQ correlations with their biological than their adopted parents, but African American children from impoverished backgrounds adopted into middle-class homes showed IQ score increases of about

_____ (60) points.

Humans have always been interested in improving their cognitive abilities and intelligence. A poll conducted by the journal *Nature* indicated that _____% (61) of respondents had used drugs to improve their concentration or memory. However, there is no miracle drug yet, although many are being used and abused. Stimulants such as methylphenidate, better known as _____ (62), improve alertness, whereas the _____ (63) receptor agonist guanfacine helps with planning and spatial memory. receptor agonist guanfacine helps with planning and memory. The most advanced drugs in commercial development are _____ (64). Cognitive enhancing drugs provide little help to people who are well rested or who are already high performers; in others, the results are typically minimal and variable. _____ (65) of those polled reported problems, including undesirable side effects and performance impairment.

Short Answer and Essay Questions

Answer the following questions.

3. What are two possible explanations for the gender difference in brain-to-body ratio?

4. Identify several features of brain structure and neural processing that are related to intelligence.

5. Describe how factor analysis is used to identify components of intelligence. What components have consistently emerged?

6. Why is it incorrect to assume that because intelligence is highly heritable, it is influenced very little by the environment?

7. What have adoption studies revealed about the genetic and environmental contributions to intelligence?

Deficiencies and Disorders of Intelligence

Summary and Guided Review

After studying this section in the text, fill in the blanks of the following summary.

As we age, activity decreases in genes that are involved in _____-

_____ _____ (66) and memory storage. Particularly affected are

genes responsible for _____ (67) and _____ (68) recetors. However,

the degree of loss of cognitive functioning has been _____ (69). When older adults are

given tests on material relevant to their lives, they show much less deterioration than on meaningless tasks such

as memorizing lists of words. Also, consistent with the Flynn effect, _____ (70) studies of

the same people as they age reveal less decline than cross-sectional studies of people of differing ages. Speed of

information processing, which is important for _____ (71) memory, does decrease in the

elderly. In normal aging there is a loss of coordination in the _____

_____ (72) network (portions of the frontal parietal, and temporal lobes that are active

when the brain is at rest or focused internally). This loss appears to be related to a decline in

_____ _____ (73) connections between these areas in the brain.

Elderly adults may compensate for less efficient processing by using additional brain areas to complete tasks, or

by increasing _____ (74). Elderly individuals can regain lost skills through practice and

enhancement of _____-_____ (75). Cognitive decline can be lessened

by changing dietary habits, for example, by increasing _____ (76) intake. Drugs that

enhance _____ (77) activity (such as muscimol) may also improve cognitive function. The

sex hormones may also play a role. Older women who take estrogen are at lower risk for

_____ (78) disease. Many neurons contain _____ (79) receptors, and

therefore this hormone may play a role in several cognitive tasks. Men receiving testosterone therapy show

improvement in _____ (80) memory; additional skills are improved by dihydrotestosterone, which is aromatized into _____ (81).

Mental retardation is a term that has negative connotations, causing many practitioners to use the term _____ _____ (82). This term covers disabilities in reasoning, learning, problem solving and adaptive behavior, originating before age _____ (83). A person is considered to have an intellectual disability if th IQ is below _____ (84). Most cases of intellectual impairment fall into the _____ (85) category, which is characterized by less factual knowledge, lack of strategies for learning and problem solving, and slower mental operations. For most individuals in this group, there is no single attributable cause of retardation. About _____% (86) of all cases can be traced to one of the 200-plus physical disorders that cause intellectual impairment, such as meningitis or prenatal exposure to viruses such as _____ (87). Prenatal exposure to _____ (88) is the most common of all causes.

_____ (89) syndrome, which results from an extra 21st chromosome, is the most common *genetic* cause of retardation, occurring in 1 in _____ (90) births. The Ts65Dn mouse strain is a model for Down syndrome; these animals are similar to humans with the disorder in that their _____ (91) cells secrete less of proteins that support cell survival. Another frequent genetic cause of intellectual disability is _____ _____ syndrome (92), due to a mutation of the *FMR1I* gene on the X chromosome. This gene may be important in the pruning or elimination of excess _____ (93). A genetic disorder that interferes with myelination, _____ (94), may not lead to intellectual impairment if the affected individual avoids foods with phenylalanine, as well as the artificial sweetener _____ (95). The buildup of cerebrospinal fluid in _____ (96) may also lead to impairment, but it can be treated if caught early. However, many affected individuals have surprisingly normal IQs.

Autism is a disorder characterized by compulsive, ritualistic behavior, impaired _____ (97), and (usually) intellectual impairment. A similar disorder in the autism spectrum is _____ (98) syndrome, which involves social impairment but more normal cognitive development. There is some controversy over whether the incidence of autism has actually _____ (99) over time. About _____% (100) of autistics are intellectually impaired. Specific cognitive impairments include delayed _____ (101) development, difficulty socializing, and an inability to understand other's states of mind. Autistic children perform more poorly on _____ of _____ (102) tasks than younger normal children and even children with Down syndrome. Researchers have suggested that autistic individuals' difficulty empathizing and learning language through imitation involves with _____ (103) neurons. There is some evidence that people with autism and Asperger's syndrome have insufficient activity in the _____ (104) stream connections that provide input to brain areas associated with imitation (inferior frontal cortex and motor cortex).

Some autistics, referred to as _____ (105), are extremely talented in one area, such as music, drawing, painting, computation, or memorizing. The most likely explanation for these skills is that the autistic lacks _____ (106) or integrative functions within the brain, and this gives the savant access to speedy lower levels of processing. The best-known savant was Kim Peek, who was the basis for the character in the movie *Rain Man*. There are also _____ - _____ (107) autistics such as Temple Grandin, who have normal or above normal intelligence but who still show autistic characteristics such as poorly developed theory of mind.

Although originally thought to be purely psychological in origin, autism is now considered a disorder of the _____ (108). However, because not all autistics show the same pattern of abnormalities, there are probably several ways in which the disorder can develop. Although the brain of an autistic individual is normal or slightly reduced at birth, it undergoes dramatic _____ (109) during the first year, particularly in the _____ (110) and _____ (111) areas. Although the growth ends around 3 to 5 years of age, some structures that were enlarged early in life are undersized in adulthood, indicating a third stage involving _____ (112). Problems attributed to the fusiform face area and the mirror neuron system may actually be due to deficiencies in _____ _____ (113), another term for synchronization within a network.

Several neurotransmitters have been implicated in autism, particularly _____ (114), because some of the medications (for example, fluoxetine) that are used to treat autism increase serotonin activity. The dopamine antagonist _____ (115) reduces repetitive behavior and aggression. Other drugs that block _____ (116) activity reduce symptoms such as withdrawal and hyperactivity. _____ (117), known as the "sociability molecule" is reduced in autistic children. Repetitive behavior decreased when people with autism and Asperger's syndrome were treated with infusions of this substance. Other benefits of oxytocin treatment include improved recognition of _____ _____ (118) of emotion and increased

_____ (119), linked to reducing activity in the amygdala.

Many environmental factors have been associated with autism, including _____ (120), which may affect neural development by inactivating acetylcholinesterase. Autism has also been linked to maternal conditions like rheumatoid arthritis and other _____ (121) diseases that may disrupt brain development in the prenatal period. Autism has also been associated with neurotoxins like mercury, which is also known to be a _____ (122). Even decreased sun exposure, resulting in reduced _____ _____ (123), has been implicated in the disorder.

For over a decade there has been a great deal of controversy over the possibility that autism could be caused by childhood _____ (124) or mercury preservatives in the vaccines; however, reviews of all the studies concluded there is no connection.. Many parents remain convinced of a link between childhood vaccinations and autism, and have brought their claims into the courtroom. Of greater concern is the disturbing _____ (125) in the rate of childhood immunizations in several countries.

Autism has a _____ (126) component, as autistic children have a much higher chance of having an autistic sibling than normal children, and the concordance rate for identical twins is 60%. When analyses consider additional abnormal symptoms found in _____ (127) relatives, the concordance rate for identical twins increases to _____% (128). Autism is more common in _____ (129), and some genes on the X chromosome have been identified as possible autism genes, although the evidence is weak. Genes on other chromosomes may be involved, including those responsible for various neurotransmitters, neural development, and _____ (130) formation.

_____ (131) typically develops during childhood; it includes impulsive and hyperactive behavior as well as problems with attention and learning. The estimates of its incidence vary, from 3–5% up to _____% (132). Those diagnosed with ADHD as children often continue to have problems as adults, including increased rates of criminal behavior, drug abuse, and _____ _____ (133). This link between ADHD and drug use led to concerns about treating children with _____ (134) drugs such as methylphenidate (Ritalin) and amphetamine. However, there is no evidence that these drugs increases the risk of addiction; if anything, they have a _____ (135) effect. Given that stimulant drugs used to treat ADHD also increase _____ (136) activity, it is not surprising that researchers have found _____ (137) activity in pathways for this neurotransmitter, particularly in the _____ (138) cortex. This cortical area is involved in impulse inhibition and reward, which could account for many ADHD symptoms For example, people with ADHD have difficulty foregoing

_____ (139) rewards for better, but delayed, rewards. While stimulant drugs are the drugs most commonly used to treat ADHD, they do not work for everyone. Two other drugs that are used, modafinil and atomoxetine, block the reuptake of _____ (140).

Regarding brain abnormalities in ADHD, one of the most consistent findings is that there is reduced volume in the right hemisphere and right _____ (141) nucleus, as well as changes in the cerebellum. These and other findings indicate a disruption of the _____-

_____ (142) network.

There is strong evidence for a genetic basis to ADHD; the concordance rate for ADHD among identical twins is much higher than among fraternal twins. Heritability averages _____ % (143) across studies. Several genes have been identified as being involved in ADHD, many of them implicated in transporters or _____ (144) for dopamine. Genes for the _____ (145) reuptake transporter have also been found to play a role in ADHD. The _____ (146) gene is important in neural transmission and neuron survival, and variations in the gene predict how well people will respond to ADHD medications.

Environmental factors that play a role in ADHD are often parental in nature, such as maternal

_____ (147) and stress during pregnancy, parental abuse of drugs, and parental mood and

_____ (148) disorders. Other environmental influences include stroke, pregnancy complications, and exposure to toxins such as _____ (149) and pesticides.

Short Answer and Essay Questions

Answer the following questions.

8. Give a reason that the degree of cognitive impairment in the elderly has been overestimated. What impairments are associated with aging? Are they permanent?

9. Identify common causes of intellectual impairment that occur early in life (other than autism and ADHD). Describe one of them in detail in terms of what is known about cause(s), symptoms, and treatment.

10. What does theory of mind mean? Why are autistic individuals thought to have poorly developed theory of mind? Identify some other key symptoms of autism.

11. What are the possible explanations for autistic savants? Which one seems most likely to be correct?

Why?

12. Describe the brain anomalies (structural, developmental, and functional) associated with autism.

13. Why do researchers believe there is a strong genetic component to autism?

14. Describe the controversy about whether there is a link between childhood vaccinations and autism.

15. What evidence points to dopamine as an important factor in ADHD? Address the issue of dopamine's role in treatment.

16. Is there a genetic basis to ADHD? Provide support for your answer. How does the environment play a role in AHDH?

Posttest

Use these multiple-choice questions to check your understanding of the chapter.

1. The intelligence quotient was originally based on

   a. the ratio of intellectual capacity to the population average.

   b. the ratio of mental age to chronological age.

   c. the ratio of chronological age to mental age.

   d. None of the above

2. What percent of the population has an IQ above 130?

   a. 2%

   b. 12%

   c. 20%

   d. 0.2%

3. IQ scores are correlated with which of the following?

   a. grades earned in school

   b. income

   c. job performance

   d. All of the above

4. The Raven Progressive Matrices test is designed to

   a. be culture free.

b. measure nonverbal abilities.

c. measure practical intelligence.

d. a and b

5. Robert Sternberg argues that

a. intelligence tests measure a general, underlying factor of cognitive ability that contributes to specific mental skills.

b. intelligence tests are completely useless.

c. intelligence is how a culture defines people's ability to succeed.

d. tests that measure practical intelligence are better than traditional intelligence tests.

6. An intelligence theorist who proposes that there are seven different components of intelligence would BEST be described as a

a. lumper.

b. splitter.

c. general factor theorist.

d. reaction time theorist.

7. Which of the following is TRUE regarding Albert Einstein's brain?

a. It had fewer glial cells.

b. It was larger (heavier) than the average person's brain.

c. It contained more neurons that the average brain.

d. Its parietal lobes were larger than those of the average brain.

8. PET studies reveal that tasks requiring general intelligence produce higher activity in the ___ areas of the brain.

a. frontal

b. temporal

c. parietal

d. occipital

9. Studies of people with brain damage have shown that general intelligence or "g" requires

a. a distributed network.

b. a system involving the frontal, parietal, and temporal lobes.

c. the ability to integrate different types of processing from several areas of the brain.

d. All of the above

10. Which of the following statements regarding brain size is FALSE?

a. Species with the highest brain-to-body ratio are the most intelligent.

b. There is no correlation between brain size and intelligence in humans.

c. Men's brains are proportionately larger than women's brains.

d. Elephants' brains are larger than humans' brains.

11. Which of the following is more strongly associated with intelligence than brain size?

a. a thicker cortex and larger cortical columns

b. a thicker cortex and many smaller columns

c. larger processing units and greater surface area

d. more layers and larger processing modules

12. Which of the following is probably the BEST predictor of IQ score?

a. brain size

b. reaction time

c. nerve conduction velocity

d. frontal area activity

13. Which of the following statements about myelination is TRUE?

a. People with more gray matter and less white matter tend to have higher IQs.

b. Myelination increases from childhood to maturity.

c. Myelination increases cross-talk between neurons.

d. Myelination is at its peak in the elderly.

14. People with higher IQs tend to

a. have faster nerve conduction velocity.

b. use less energy when processing information.

c. have a high white matter/gray matter ratio.

d. All of the above

15. Which of the following is NOT one of the components of intelligence frequently identified by factor

analysis?

    a. practical intelligence

    b. linguistic intelligence

    c. logical-mathematical intelligence

    d. spatial intelligence

16. Which of the following MOST specifically engages the right parietal lobe?

    a. language functions

    b. mathematical calculations

    c. spatial ability

    d. rote arithmetic tasks, such as using times tables

17. What area(s) of the brain are involved in mathematical abilities such as calculation and estimation?

    a. frontal lobe only

    b. parietal lobe only

    c. both the frontal and parietal lobes

    d. None of the above

18. Which of the following is NOT true with respect to intelligence in animals?

    a. Non-human primates are able to demonstrate language skills but not mathematical abilities.

    b. Chimps show evidence of intelligence by using tools to acquire food.

    c. Crows and owls show planfulness in their methods for obtaining or "luring" food.

    d. Mirror neurons are activated in monkeys when they watch someone retrieve an object with the hand or a tool.

19. The proportion of variability in intelligence due to heredity is HIGHEST in

    a. infancy.

    b. childhood.

    c. adolescence.

    d. adulthood.

20. Which of the following is TRUE with respect to the genetic basis of intelligence?

    a. The heritability of intelligence is about 70%.

    b. The *PACAP* precursor gene is a major determinant of brain size.

c. In a twin study, estimated heritability was highest for brain volume as a structural contributor to intelligence.

d. There are probably 50 candidate genes that have been linked to some aspect of cognitive ability.

21. IQ scoring standards have been adjusted in the last 50 years to reflect the fact that

    a. people are scoring more poorly on the tests than they have in the past.

    b. the average performance on IQ tests has risen.

    c. fewer people are intellectually impaired now.

    d. our genes are making us more intelligent.

22. Studies of identical and fraternal twins reveal that the STRONGREST correlation for IQ scores is between

    a. identical twins, but only if correctly identified by their parents as identical.

    b. fraternal twins, but only if correctly identified by their parents as fraternal.

    c. identical twins, regardless of whether their parents identified them as identical or fraternal.

    d. identical twins incorrectly identified by their parents as fraternal.

23. Scarr's study of IQ scores among African Americans revealed that

    a. there was no relationship between degree of African ancestry and IQ.

    b. those with more African ancestors had lower IQs than those with fewer African ancestors.

    c. there were no differences between African Americans and whites.

    d. none of the above.

24. Which of the following statements regarding environmental contributions to intelligence is FALSE?

    a. Environmental factors may be confounded with genetic factors.

    b. The results from the Abecedarian project suggest that the environment is not as important as genes when it comes to intelligence.

    c. Many environmental factors may contribute weakly to intelligence.

    d. Illness is an important factor is explaining worldwide differences in IQ.

25. Which of the following statements regarding Head Start is FALSE?

    a. There are long-term benefits in IQ scores.

    b. There are long-term benefits in career accomplishments.

    c. There are long-term benefits in mathematics.

d. There are long-term benefits in educational attainment.

26. Adoption studies reveal that adopted children's IQ scores are

    a. relatively unaffected by the adoptive home.

    b. most strongly correlated with their biological parents' scores in childhood and adulthood.

    c. most strongly correlated with their adopted parents' scores in childhood and adulthood.

    d. initially more similar to their biological parents' scores but become more similar to their adopted parents' scores in adulthood.

27. With respect to aging and intelligence,

    a. the declines are significant and irreversible.

    b. loss occurs, but it has been overestimated.

    c. much of the decline has been attributed to loss of glutamate.

    d. performance speed is not affected as much as verbal memory.

28. Which of the following is FALSE about the default mode network?

    a. It is involved in a person's preparedness for action.

    b. The elderly show loss of coordination in this network.

    c. The network primarily involves gray matter.

    d. It involves activity and communication between the frontal, temporal, and parietal lobes.

29. The elderly could compensate for loss of cognitive function by

    a. eating more fish.

    b. practicing skills.

    c. taking drugs that increase GABA.

    d. All of the above

30. Which of the following is TRUE concerning hormones and cognitive function in the elderly?

    a. Testosterone works better than dihydrotestosterone at improving cognitive abilities.

    b. Estrogen is plays a role in increasing cognitive function in females but not males.

    c. Estrogen most likely exerts the majority of its beneficial effects in the parietal lobes of the brain.

    d. Estrogen lowers the risk of Alzheimer's disease in menopausal women.

31. Which of the following has been identified as a possible "smart drug"?

    a. ampakines

b. modafinil

c. guanfacine

d. All of the above

32. What percentage of the population falls in the IQ range for intellectual impairment?

a. 0.02%

b. 0.2%

c. 2%

d. 5%

33. Most individuals with mild intellectual impairment

a. come from families of lower socioeconomic status.

b. are incapable of caring for themselves.

c. are more likely to have a genetic than environmental cause that explains their disability.

d. have an IQ below 50.

34. The leading *genetic* cause of intellectual impairment is

a. prenatal exposure to cigarette smoke.

b. prenatal exposure to alcohol.

c. Down syndrome.

d. hydrocephalus.

35. Down syndrome

a. is caused by the *FMR1* gene, according to new studies.

b. can be studied in a mouse model that has been engineered to produce more norepinephrine.

c. may be caused by more than just the genes on the 21st chromosome.

d. cannot be identified until the baby is born.

36. PKU

a. is typically diagnosed by amniocentesis.

b. can be controlled by diet.

c. is caused by a lack of phenylalanine.

d. if untreated, can lead to mild mental impairment.

37. Which of the following statements regarding hydrocephalus is (are) TRUE?

a. It is treatable.

b. If untreated, it usually causes intellectual disability, but not in all cases.

c. It results from a buildup of cerebrospinal fluid.

d. All of the above

38. Autism

   a. is caused by poor parenting.

   b. has increased from 1% in the sixties and seventies to 5% currently.

   c. is one disorder in the autism spectrum that includes Asperger's syndrome.

   d. involves the least intellectual impairment in the spectrum.

39. Which of the following is NOT a common characteristic of autism?

   a. locked in a world of fantasy

   b. delayed language development

   c. repetitive behaviors

   d. limited interactions with others

40. Theory of mind

   a. is lacking in autistic individuals

   b. may involve activity in mirror neurons.

   c. has been explained by both the "theory theory" and "simulation theory".

   d. All of the above

41. Which of the following statements regarding savants is TRUE?

   a. Their skills usually result from a great deal of concentrated practice.

   b. Their skills typically generalize to other related tasks.

   c. Their skills may involve speedy access to lower levels of cognitive processing.

   d. All savants are autistic.

42. Which of the following is NOT true of Temple Grandin, the high-functioning autistic described in the textbook?

   a. She has a PhD in animal science.

   b. She gives lectures about her condition.

   c. She had normal language development as a child, which explains her high-functioning adult state.

d. She exhibits a poorly developed theory of mind.

43. Which of following brain areas was NOT listed in the textbook as being implicated in autism?

    a. occipital lobe

    b. temporal lobe

    c. brain stem

    d. cerebellum

44. What characterizes early brain development in autism?

    a. an initial stage of degeneration, followed by some recovery

    b. a rapid growth in size during the first year

    c. overgrowth in parietal and occipital areas

    d. very small brains that develop to adult size by adolescence

45. Although research has been inconsistent, which of the following has/have been studied as playing a role in autism?

    a. fusiform face area

    b. mirror neurons

    c. functional connectivity in the default network

    d. All of the above

46. With respect to the genetic basis of autism

    a. the fraternal twin concordance rate for autistic individuals is 92%.

    b. the identical twin concordance rate for autistic individuals is at least 60%.

    c. relatives of autistic individuals have a concordance rate of 10%.

    d. the heritability rate is probably overestimated because parents stop having children.

47. The impairment of sociability in autistics has been linked to

    a. oxytocin.

    b. dopamine.

    c. GABA.

    d. a and b

48. What is the most accurate statement about vaccines and autism?

    a. There is strong evidence that childhood vaccinations cause autism.

b. There is a causal link between autism and the mercury preservative in autism, but not to the vaccines.

c. The initial study supporting the link between the MMR vaccine and autism has been criticized as being methodologically flawed.

d. Because most parents of autistic individuals agree that there is no link between immunizations and autism, there has been a world-wide increase in childhood vaccinations.

49. Which of the following is NOT a symptom of ADHD?

a. attentional problems

b. impulsiveness

c. lack of theory of mind

d. hyperactivity

50. When children with ADHD grow up,

a. they are usually normal.

b. they are normal only if they were medicated as children.

c. they are more likely to exhibit personality disorders.

d. they are unlikely to have children who are subsequently diagnosed with ADHD.

51. Children with ADHD who are treated with stimulant drugs

a. are more likely to become addicted to drugs like amphetamine or cocaine.

b. may be protected from drug abuse.

c. are more likely to smoke marijuana, because stimulant drugs act as gateway drugs.

d. are more likely to become addicted to alcohol, but not other drugs.

52. In people with ADHD, dopamine activity is typically

a. low.

b. higher than normal.

c. normal.

d. lower than normal when the person takes Ritalin.

53. Which of the following show(s) that the prefrontal lobes play a key role in ADHD?

a. People with ADHD tend to be impulsive.

b. People with ADHD prefer immediate rewards over delayed rewards.

c. There is reduced dopamine activity in the area in people with ADHD.

d. All of the above

54. Studies of people with ADHD have shown reduced brain volume in all of the following areas EXCEPT for the:

a. thalamus

b. prefrontal areas

c. caudate nucleus

d. cerebellum

55. Which of the following drugs has NOT been used to treat ADHD?

a. methylphenidate

b. modafinil

c. atomoxetine

d. risperidone

56. Which of the following genes has been implicated in ADHD?

a. a serotonin receptor gene

b. a gene for the serotonin transporter

c. the *LPHN3* gene

d. All of the above

57. All of the following have been considered as environmental contributors to ADHD except:

a. thimerosal

b. lead

c. parental drug abuse

d. pesticides

Answers

Guided Review

1. Intelligence

2. chronological

324

3. 100

4. 70

5. Binet

6. juvenile delinquency

7. Raven Progressive Matrices

8. practical

9. Sternberg

10. Lumpers

11. general factor

12. splitters

13. Albert Einstein

14. parietal lobes

15. glial

16. distributed

17. highest

18. larger

19. gray matter

20. spatial

21. thicker

22. processing units (cortical columns)

23. reaction time

24. nerve conduction

25. Myelin

26. Short-term

27. long-term

28. working

29. glucose metabolism

30. intellectual disabilities

31. efficiency

32. factor analysis

33. linguistic

34. spatial

35. modules

36. frontal

37. parietal

38. primates

39. tools

40. owls

41. experience

42. 50

43. increase

44. working

45. volume

46. replication

47. *ASPM*

48. neurogenesis

49. environment

50. increased

51. genetic

52. inherited or genetic

53. ancestry

54. confounded

55. weak

56. infectious

57. Head Start

58. Abecedarian

59. birth

60. 15

61. 20

62. Ritalin

63. norepinephrine

64. ampakines

65. Half

66. long-term potentiation

67. glutamate

68. GABA

69. overestimated

70. longitudinal

71. working

72. default mode

73. white matter

74. metabolism

75. self-esteem

76. fish

77. GABA

78. Alzheimer's

79. estrogen

80. spatial

81. estrogen

82. intellectual disability

83. 18

84. 70

85. mild

86. 25

87. rubella (German measles)

88. alcohol

89. Down

90. 700

91. glial

92. Fragile X

93. synapses

94. phenyketonuria or PKU

95. aspartame

96. hydrocephalus

97. sociability

98. Asperger's

99. increased

100. 80

101. language

102. theory of mind

103. mirror

104. dorsal

105. savants

106. executive

107. high-functioning

108. brain

109. growth

110. frontal

111. temporal

112. degeneration

113. functional connectivity

114. serotonin

115. risperidone

116. glutamate

117. Oxytocin

118. facial expressions

119. trust

120. pesticides

121. autoimmune

122. mutagen

123. vitamin D

124. vaccinations

125. decrease

126. genetic

127. nonautistic

128. 92

129. males

130. synaptic

131. ADHD

132. 10

133. antisocial personality

134. stimulant

135. protective

136. dopamine

137. reduced

138. prefrontal

139. immediate

140. norepinephrine

141. caudate

142. attention-inhibition

143. 75

144. receptors

145. serotonin

146. *LPHN3*

147. smoking

148. anxiety

149. lead

Short Answer and Essay Questions

1. One criticism of intelligence tests is that they are designed to measure academic and socioeconomic success and thus do not measure important things like practical intelligence. Another criticism is that people who are highly successful sometimes score in the mediocre range on these tests, suggesting that the content of the tests is too narrow. Another is that performance on most intelligence tests is too dependent on familiarity with the culture and language the test was designed for.

2. Lumpers argue that because scores on different tasks such as math and verbal skills are highly correlated, intelligence is a unitary capacity that we apply to many different tasks; a single IQ score is sufficient to represent a person's intelligence. Splitters argue that it is necessary to look at people's scores on different types of tests to get an accurate picture of intelligence, because many people have strengths in some areas and weaknesses in others. Splitters believe that there are actually several types of intelligence.

3. One possibility is that women's brains are more efficient, and another is that men's superiority on spatial tasks requires a larger brain.

4. People with higher intelligence typically have a larger brain and a thicker cortex, and they may have more columns; functionally, they have better short-term memory, shorter reaction times and higher nerve conduction velocity (possibly related to greater myelination). As a result, people with greater intelligence might be better at transferring short-term memory to long-term memory, and use less energy to do so. In other words, their brains are more efficient at accomplishing cognitive tasks.

5. Factor analysis involves giving people several tests measuring different intellectual abilities and then looking for clusters of abilities that are more strongly correlated with one another than with other abilities. Such clusters are assumed to represent approximately the same types of skills. Separate abilities that have been identified repeatedly are linguistic, logical-mathematical, and spatial skills.

6. If a particular trait is highly heritable, the environment can still have profound influence over it. For example, people's IQ scores have been steadily increasing over the past few generations, most likely as a result

of improved environment. In addition, studies have found large IQ increases following adoption into a richer environment. A better way of thinking about how genes influence intelligence is that they provide a range of possibilities, and whatever environment a person is exposed to will then determine where within that range his or her intelligence will fall.

7. Adoption studies have shown that children's IQs are more strongly correlated with their biological parents' IQs than with their adoptive parents' IQs. However, they have also shown that disadvantaged children's IQs can be dramatically improved in an adoptive home.

8. One reason is that the tasks given to elderly research participants may not be interesting or relevant to them. They perform much better on tasks involving meaningful material than on simple word memorization tasks. Another reason is that some studies compare people of different ages, rather than following the same individuals for several years, and the older participants may have had less enriching experiences. Impairments that are noted with aging mostly include speed decreases: perceptual speed, performance speed, and processing speed, the latter of which also accounts for almost all of the loss in working memory. There is also a loss of coordination in the default mode network, due to a decline in white matter connections among areas. Some reversibility of aging effects have resulted from skills training, increased self esteem, and dietary improvement. In addition, improved GABA functioning and treatment with testosterone and estrogen are promising.

9. Conditions that cause intellectual impairment early in life are Down syndrome, phenylketoneuria (PKU), hydrocephalus, and fragile X syndrome. Down syndrome is caused by an additional 21st chromosome individuals typically have IQs in the range of 40-55. There is currently no treatment although research with animal models is being conducted, but some individuals with Down syndrome can function quite well with support. PKU involves an inability to metabolize the amino acid phenylalanine, which accumulates and destroys myelin, leading to profound intellectual disability. These serious effects can be prevented by limiting the amount of phenylalanine in the diet. Hydrocephalus is a condition is which cerebrospinal fluid builds up in the ventricles of the brain and compresses brain tissue against the skull, producing brain damage that leads to intellectual impairment. This condition can be treated by using a shunt to drain the fluid out of the ventricles. Fragile X syndrome is due to a mutation is the *FMR1* gene, resulting in IQs below 75. This gene may play a role in synaptic pruning during development. Males are more likely to have this condition.

10. Theory of mind refers to the ability to infer the mental state of others. Autistic children perform more poorly on theory of mind tasks that normal children and even children with Down syndrome with a lower

mental age. Also, many autistics have difficulty "reading" other people, or making inferences about what other people know. Other symptoms of autism include impaired language development, lack of social interaction and communication, repetitive behaviors, and, typically, intellectual impairment.

11. One possibility is that they acquire skills through extensive, focused practice; however, often their skills appear without any apparent practice. Another possibility is that they have more brain area devoted to a particular skill, although no evidence is given for this in the text. A third possibility, one that is more likely to be correct, is that because they lack central executive functions; as a result, they have atypical access to speedy lower levels of processing, but perform poorly on similar tasks that require higher order processing. This hypothesis is supported by the case of a man with dementia who began composing classical music n spite of limited musical training

12. Brain changes in autism include a rapid period of growth in the first year of life, particularly in the frontal and temporal lobes, followed by some degeneration. Activity deficiencies have been reported in the fusiform face area and mirror neuron system, but this may be due to deficits in synchronization in the default mode network. This lack of functional connectivity is correlated with deficits in social, communication and task performance in autistic individuals.

13. A genetic basis is confirmed for autism: identical twin concordance rates are about 60%, and when the comparison groups include nonautistic relatives who show symptoms, concordance is 92% for identical twins and 10% for fraternal pairs. Because autism occurs more frequently in males, scientists have examined the X-chromosome for candidate genes and a few have been found, but their effects are small. Other genes that have been implicated in autism are involved in neurotransmitter activity, neuron development and migration, and synapse formation.

14. A 1998 study by Wakefield and colleagues suggested that autism was linked to MMR vaccinations or mercury-based preservative. This study was later criticized as being methodologically flawed and was retracted by the journal that published it. Two reviews of all the available literature have found no credible association. However, many parents remain convinced that the link is "real" and causal, and some are refusing to immunize their children against these serious childhood disease.

15. Dopamine activity is lower in people with ADHD, particularly in the striatum and prefrontal cortex; deficits in these areas may contribute to the associated impulsive behavior and learning difficulties. The mechanism may be excess transporters, which remove dopamine from the synapse before it has time to work.

Stimulant drugs used to treat ADHD, such as methylphenidate (Ritalin) and amphetamine, increase dopamine levels; drugs that affect norepinephrine (such as atomoxetine) are more effective is some individuals.

16. ADHD clearly "runs in families", with a heritability of 75% across studies. Several of the genes that have been implicated in ADHD are involved with dopamine receptors and transporters. The *LPHN3* gene, which plays an important role in neural transmission and neuron survival, predicts how well people with ADHD will respond to stimulant medications. Genes that affect serotonin receptors and the serotonin transporter have also been identified as playing a role in the disorder. Parental factors correlated with ADHD that may be environmental or genetic include maternal smoking and stress, parental abuse of alcohol and other drugs, and parental mood and anxiety disorders.Definite environmental contributors include brain injury, stroke, birth/pregnancy complications, and neurotoxins such as lead and pesticides. Chemicals called phthalates found in shampoo and perfumes are now being studied as well.

Posttest

1. b   2. a   3. d   4. d   5. c   6. b   7. d   8. a   9. d   10. b   11. b   12. c   13. b   14. d   15. a   16. c   17. c

18. a   19. d   20. c   21. b   22. c   23. a   24. b   25. a   26. b   27. b   28. c   29. d   30. d   31. d   32. c

33. a   34. c   35. c   36. b   37. d   38. c   39. a   40. d   41. c   42. c   43. a   44. b   45. d   46. b   47. a

48. c   49. c   50. c   51. b   52. a   53. d   54. a   55. d   56. d   57. a

14

Psychological Disorders

Chapter Outline

Learning Objectives

After reading this chapter, you should be able to answer the following questions.

1. What are the characteristics of schizophrenia?

2. How are genes thought to be involved in schizophrenia?

3. How do positive and negative symptoms of schizophrenia differ?

4. What is the dopamine hypothesis of schizophrenia? Why is this hypothesis insufficient to fully explain schizophrenia?

5. What brain deficits are associated with schizophrenia?

6. What are the characteristics of affective disorders?

7. What are some of the possible genetic bases for depression? Bipolar disorder?

8. What is the monoamine hypothesis of depression? What evidence supports it?

9. Why is ECT sometimes used as a treatment for depression? How is it believed to work?

10. What is SAD? How is it typically treated?

11. How is bipolar disorder treated?

12. What brain areas seem to be involved in affective disorders?

13. What are some possible biological explanations for suicide?

14. What are the characteristics of anxiety disorders?

15. What are some biological causes of anxiety disorders?

16. What are the symptoms and possible treatments for posttraumatic stress disorder?

17. Why is obsessive-complusive disorder considered to be an anxiety disorder?

Schizophrenia

Summary and Guided Review

After studying this section in the text, fill in the blanks of the following summary.

According to recent estimates, one out of every _____ (1) people in the United States suffers from a diagnosable mental disorder. Schizophrenia is a mental disorder marked by a number of perceptual, emotional, and _____ (2) deficits along with a loss of contact with _____ (3) and an inability to function in life. Schizophrenia is a _____ (4), meaning that there are severe disturbances in reality, orientation, and thinking. It affects about _____% (5) of the population regardless of gender or socioeconomic status, and about 20% of people hospitalized for psychiatric care suffer from it.

Schizophrenia literally means "split mind" and reflects a distortion of _____ (6) and _____ (7), which are not based in reality. Symptoms include hallucinations, false beliefs called _____ (8), and paranoia. The use of diagnostic categories based on predominant symptoms, such as paranoia, will most likely change in the future because patients often have _____ (9) symptoms and multiple diagnoses. People exhibiting _____ (10) symptoms generally respond to treatment better than those who suffer from chronic symptoms. Many schizophrenics show some degree of recovery, and 22% show full recovery _____ (11) years after the symptoms first appear. Although in the early 20th century schizophrenia was believed to have a _____ (12) basis, the technology for determining this did not become available until the 1960s; in the meantime, social explanations held sway for decades.

Twin and adoption studies suggest a strong genetic component to schizophrenia; heritability has been estimated at _____ to _____% (13). Furthermore, being _____ (14) out of a family with a history of schizophrenia provides little or no protection from the disorder's development. Among identical twins _____ (15) for schizophrenia, children of the "normal" twins were as likely to become schizophrenic as children of the schizophrenic twin. Twin studies may be difficult to interpret however, because of the inconsistency of including _____ (16) disorders in the diagnosis of schizophrenia. For example, when identical twins are discordant for schizophrenia, over half of the _____ (17) twins have spectrum disorders. Another problem is that schizophrenia most likely results from the cumulative effects of multiple

_____ (18), each of which contributes a small effect.

There is a long list of _____ (19) genes, but few have been supported by subsequent

research or the associations are weak. An analysis of a large database has identified 16 possible genes affecting

neurotransmitters, neural development, neurodegeneration, and _____ (20) and

inflammatory responses. Most research has looked for genes common to many patients, but a significant

amount of schizophrenia is due to rare _____ _____ (21) variations. It

is more accurate to think of genes as conferring risk for schizophrenia rather than as the single cause. According

to the _____ (22) model, a person will become schizophrenic if the combined genetic and

environmental causal factors reach or exceed a threshold. Environmental factors might be

_____ (23), such as job difficulties or divorce, or _____ (24), such as

poor nutrition or infection. There is evidence that environmental influences work in part by

_____ (25) means, by altering gene expression.

The symptoms of schizophrenia may be classified as either _____ (26) (including

hallucinations and delusions) or negative (including lack of emotion or motivation). While positive symptoms

tend to have _____ (27) onset and respond to drug treatments, _____

(28) symptoms tend to be chronic and are associated with brain deficits. Crow described Type I schizophrenia as

involving _____ (29) symptoms and increased dopamine _____ (30)

receptors, and Type II schizophrenia as associated with cell loss in the _____ (31) lobes.

The first effective _____ (32) drugs were used in the mid-1950s, although researchers

did not know why these drugs worked. Later, it was discovered that high doses of _____

(33) produce psychotic behavior via increased dopamine activity, suggesting that excess dopaminergic activity

was involved in schizophrenia. This was supported by the fact that drugs that _____ (34)

D_2 dopamine receptors are effective in reducing positive symptoms of schizophrenia.

There are many problems with the dopamine theory of schizophrenia. Not all schizophrenics respond to

dopamine-blocking neuroleptics; some, especially those with chronic symptoms that do not respond to drug

treatment, appear to actually be _____ (35) in dopamine. A significant problem with

dopamine blockers is that they often lead to _____ _____ (36),

producing involuntary tremors and movement because of increased sensitivity of dopamine receptors in the

_____ _____ (37). Newer antipsychotic drugs, referred to as

_____ (38), target D$_2$ receptors to a lesser degree and produce fewer

_____ (39) disturbances. PCP inhibits the _____ (40) receptor, whereas administering _____ (41) activates it. Glycine combined with a typical antipsychotic drug improves cognition and reduces _____ (42) symptoms. These observations indicate the involvement of _____ (43) in schizophrenia. A third transmitter affected by atypical antipsychotics is _____ (44); many of these drugs block 90% of the _____ (45) receptor subtype. It is unwise to focus on a single neurotransmitter in an explanation of schizophrenia if the _____ (46) theory is to survive, it must account for activity in the serotonin and _____ (47) systems and, possibly, others as well.

Enlarged _____ (48), indicating loss of brain tissue, are often associated with schizophrenia and other neurological conditions. Although tissue loss has been found in at least 50 areas, deficits in the _____ (49) and _____ (50) lobes are particularly important.Although activity is decreased in the frontal lobes in general, it is increased in the orbitofrontal cortex, as well as in the _____ (51). The symptoms of schizophrenia have been associated with _____ (52), a condition in which working memory and other functions of the prefrontal cortex are impaired. This may be due to a deficiency of _____ (53) in the prefrontal cortex. The behavioral results of hypofrontality in schizophrenics include flat affect, social withdrawal, and impaired attention.

Schizophrenia may also involve lack of coordination in activity between the _____ (54) formation and the _____ (55) cortex. Different patterns of _____ (56) occur in schizophrenics; enhancement in this activity may be involved in visual and auditory hallucinations. For example, _____ (57) areas are active during auditory hallucinations. In normal people, these areas are activated during "inner speech", but in the schizophrenic this activation might result in misperception of self-generated thoughts. Another effect associated with altered synchrony is the schizophrenic's inability to suppress _____ (58) sounds; this is an impairment of auditory _____ (59). Antipsychotic drugs may improve gating, but _____ (60) actually normalizes it, which helps explain why 70-80% of schizophrenics _____ (61).

Many environmental factors, such as maternal stress and birth complications, have been associated with schizophrenia. Studies suggest that babies born in winter are at greater risk for prenatal exposure to viruses in the second trimester of pregnancy, and infections such as _____ (62) have been linked to schizophrenia. In these cases, the culprit is probably not the virus itself, but the _____ (63) reaction that is triggered. Recent evidence from a study in China suggests that prenatal _____ (64) may also play a role. A non-maternal factor that may contribute to schizophrenia is the _____ (65) of the father at the time of conception.

Some brain deficits, such as failed _____ (66) of neurons in the frontal and temporal lobes, occur during pregnancy. Evidence for early disruption of brain function comes from studies of children who later became schizophrenics; they showed deficits in physical coordination and positive affect (compared to their siblings). By the time a person is diagnosed with schizophrenia, physical changes in the brain have already occurred, probably during _____ (67) and young adulthood. However, some studies of schizophrenic adolescents have found progressive loss of _____ _____ (68) *following* the diagnosis.

Short Answer and Essay Questions

Answer the following questions.

1. In a study described in the text, the offspring of both the schizophrenic and nonschizophrenic members of discordant identical twin pairs were equally likely to become schizophrenic. What does this suggest about the contributions of genes and environmental factors to schizophrenia?

2. What is the vulnerability model of schizophrenia? How does it account for schizophrenia developing in an individual with a low genetic predisposition? How does it account for schizophrenia NOT developing in someone with a high genetic predisposition?

3. Distinguish between Type I and Type II schizophrenia in several ways.

4. How are dopamine, glutamate, and serotonin thought to be involved in schizophrenia? In your answer, consider how antipsychotic medications affect these neurotransmitters.

5. What anatomical and functional brain deficits occur in schizophrenia? Why do some researchers believe that schizophrenia is a disorder of synchrony? When do these deficits develop?

Affective Disorders

Summary and Guided Review

After studying this section in the text, fill in the blanks of the following summary.

Major depression, which is more severe than _____ (69) depression, is characterized by hopelessness, loss of ability to enjoy life, slowed thought, and sleep disturbances. _____ (70) disorder involves cycling between depression and mania, which is characterized by periods of excess energy and confidence and development of grandiose schemes. Unipolar depression is more common in _____ (71), but bipolar disorder is equally common in men and women. The sex difference in depression has made it difficult to identify genes involved in the disorder. In one study men and women shared _____ (72) probable genes, but 7 genes were exclusive to men and 9 genes were exclusive to women. Tthe concordance rate for affective disorders is 69% for _____ (73) twins and 13% for fraternal twins, and adoption has little effect on this rate. Several genes have been implicated in depression. Individuals with one or two copies of the "short" allele of the *5-HTTLPR* _____ _____ (74) gene have an increased vulnerability to depression, along with reduced gray matter in the _____ (75) and part of the cingulate cortex. These changes may also increase susceptibility to _____ (76), which also leads to depression. The effect of this allele may be decreased by another gene, a process called genetic _____ (77); the protective gene in this case is an allele of the gene for _____ (78), a protein that encourages neuron growth and survival. Another gene affecting depression is the *hTPH2* mutation, which is 10 times more likely to occur in people with depression; it impacts the synthesis of _____ (79). Bipolar disorder is also _____ (80), even more so than depression, with heritability estimates of at least 85%. Several potential genes have been identified, and these are not related to unipolar depression; some of the genes have, however, also been implicated in _____ (81). Both unipolar and bipolar depression involve _____ (82) rhythm genes, which makes sense given the disruption in the day-night cycle that occurs in both disorders.

Early drugs for depression, like iproniazid, affect the neurotransmitters norepinephrine and _____ (83), which supports the _____ (84) hypothesis of depression. Drugs such as the tricyclic antidepressants and the atypical antidepressant25

Prozac acts by blocking the _____ (85) of serotonin at the synapse.

_____ (86) is involved in mood, activity level, sleep and temperature cycles, eating, sex, and cognition. _____ (87) is related to motivation and responsiveness to the environment. A component of tobacco smoke serves as a _____ _____

_____ (88), which may explain why so many depressed people smoke, and why they have so much difficulty quitting. The drug _____ (89), which blocks NMDA glutamate receptors, shows some promise as a treatment for depression that is resistant to other drugs.

Electroconvulsive shock therapy is sometimes used to treat depression; this requires applying an electrical current to the brain to produce a brief but strong _____ (90) in the brain, accompanied by convulsive contractions of the muscles, under carefully controlled conditions. Patients are unconscious during the procedure and wake up soon afterwards. ECT is rarely used and only as a last resort after drug treatments have failed. It is more effective than drug treatments, and its effects are experienced more quickly; thus it is likely to be used with patients who do not respond to medications or cannot tolerate their side effects, or who are _____ (91). The benefits of ECT are short term, and its use is often combined with drug treatment over the longer term. ECT affects three _____ (92) transmitters; it also seems to _____ (93) neural firing throughout the brain. ECT and antidepressant drugs may also relieve depression by enhancing _____ (94) in the hippocampus and increasing the release of _____ (95). These new neurons then migrate to their new locations. These new neurons show more _____ (96) than the existing one, but ECT may increase plasticity independently of neurogenesis. The time required for the new neurons to migrate and assume functions coincides with the delay in symptom improvement that occurs with most antidepressant drugs. A different kind of brain stimulation with relatively few side effects is _____ _____

_____ (97); it has been approved by the Federal Drug Administration for use with depression. A more aggressive strategy involves _____ (98) brain stimulation of the anterior cingulate cortex. Stimulation of the _____ (99) nerve may also help by increasing GABA levels in the cortex.

People with depression often suffer from _____ (100) rhythm disturbances, including feeling sleepy early in the evening, waking early in the morning, or spending more time in _____ (101) sleep. Readjusting one's circadian rhythm by altering sleep habits may bring relief, as may reducing REM sleep. In many people, antidepressants _____ (102) REM sleep through their moderating effects on serotonin and norepinephrine activity. People with _____ _____ _____ (103) experience depression, either in the summer or winter, and improve or experience hypomania in the other season. This disorder accounts for 10% of all affective disorders and is much more common in _____ (104). Depression in SAD is usually characterized by excess sleepiness, increased _____ (105) intake, and weight gain. Winer depression is associated with a reduced amount of natural _____ (106); moving to or visiting a more tropical region often brings some relief. Heat is associated with _____ (107) depression; finding ways to stay cool seems to relieve this form of depression. Winter depression is often treated with _____ (108), which involves exposure to intense light for a few hours each day. The light exposure must mimic bright sunlight, and it seems to work by _____ (109) the circadian rhythm. In addition, people suffering from winter depression may self-medicate by eating more carbohydrates, which increases brain _____ (110) levels.

People with _____ (111) disorder exhibit a great deal of variability in their cycling. Stress often triggers _____ (112) phases, although over time the switch tends to occur more spontaneously. Bipolar disorder is most often treated with _____ (113), which stabilizes both manic and depressive episodes; it is believed that this is accomplished through normalization of several neurotransmitter and receptor systems. However, one specific effect of lithium and an alternative drug valproate is the inhibition of _____ (114), a family of enzymes that regulate neural excitability.

Structural abnormalities in affective disorders include larger _____ (115), which is indicative of decreased tissue volume. Frontal areas show decreases as well as the hippocampus, but the _____ (116) is actually larger. Depression is associated with reduced activity in the _____ (117) nucleus and dorsolateral prefrontal cortex and increased activity in the ventral prefrontal cortex, which is connected to the amygdala. Mania is also characterized by increased brain activity; the _____ (118) prefrontal cortex may control cycling, and could be referred to as a "bipolar switch".

People with affective disorders, particularly those with bipolar disorder, are at greater risk for suicide than others in the population. According to the _____-_____ (119) model, the individual has a genetic predisposition for suicide, and the stress of a psychiatric disorder may be the environmental "trigger" for suicide. Suicide, even among nondepressed individuals, is associated with low levels of the serotonin metabolite _____ (120). Low serotonin levels are linked to suicidal behavior, particularly in _____ (121) suicide attempters. Recently, prescriptions for

_____ (122) to teens have decreased over concerns about the drugs' link to suicide; this drop in the prescription rate was followed by an increase in suicide rate among teens in the United States and the Netherlands.

Short Answer and Essay Questions

Answer the following questions.

6. Distinguish between the mechanisms of monoamine oxidase inhibitors, tricyclic antidepressants, and atypical (second generation antidepressants.

7. What are two ways in which depressed individuals may self-medicate to relieve depression?

8. Describe the similarities and differences between unipolar depression and bipolar disorder in terms of symptoms, genetic basis, and treatment.

9. What are the ways of alleviating the symptoms of winter depression?

10. Why does the author of the text suggest that the ventral prefrontal cortex acts as a depression "switch" and the subgenual prefrontal cortex acts as a bipolar switch?

11. Identify the many ways that brain stimulation can be used to treat depression. How might these treatments exert their therapeutic effects on the brain?

12. Why are people with low serotonin levels thought to be the most at risk for suicide?

Anxiety Disorders

Summary and Guided Review

After studying this section in the text, fill in the blanks of the following summary.

Anxiety disorders include generalized anxiety disorder, panic disorder, _____ (123), and obsessive-compulsive disorder. Whereas _____ (124) is an adaptive response to real objects or events in the environment, anxiety involves the anticipation of events and inappropriate reactions to objects and events. Anxiety disorders may be treated with benzodiazepines, which increase sensitivity to

_____ (125). Reduced _____ (126) activity is also implicated in

anxiety disorders, and drugs that increase activity of this transmitter may alleviate anxiety. Anxiety is associated

with heightened activity in the amygdala and _____ _____ (127). In

panic disorder, the entire brain may be overactive, but activity in the left _____ (128) gyrus

is lower.

Posttraumatic stress disorder or PTSD is characterized by recurrent thoughts or images called

_____ (129), lack of concentration, and overreactivity to environmental stimuli. PTSD is

observed in individuals exposed to combat and other traumatic experiences, and is four times more likely to

occur in _____ (130) who are exposed. Not everyone who experiences trauma develops

PTSD; therefore the key must be a person's _____ (131), which has been associated with

smaller _____ (132) volume. PTSD has a _____ (133) of about 30%;

two of the genes are mutations of *FKBP5*. PTSD is not easy to treat with traditional approaches; one alternative

is _____ (134) therapy, which allows confrontation of the anxiety-provoking stimuli under

safe conditions. Another therapeutic technique that capitalizes on reconsolidation is called

_____ _____ (135).

_____-_____ (136) disorder is marked by recurring thoughts

(obsessions) and compulsive actions over which the person has no control. These behaviors are often repetitive

and _____ (137), such as checking locks or appliances or engaging in routines that have no

purpose. OCD runs in families.

OCD is associated with increased activity in the _____ (138) cortex and the caudate

nucleus, which decreases following both successful drug and behavior therapy. OCD occurs with a number of

diseases that involve damage to the _____ _____ (139). Millionaire

Howard Hughes displayed OCD later in his life, after a series of _____(140). His mother's

obsession with germs could be indicative of either environmental or genetic influence on his later disorder.

Serotonin activity is _____ (141) in OCD, and selective serotonin reuptake inhibitors can

reduce the symptoms in some individuals. Other effective drugs include antipsychotics and drugs that decrease

the transmitter _____ (142). One controversial procedure is to sever the connections

between the orbitofrontal cortex and the _____ _____ (143) gyrus.

OCD is related to _____ _____ _____

(144), a disorder in which nonhuman animals overgroom themselves. The human version of this condition is

_____ (145). A behavior found among many people with OCD is

_____ (146); this disorder can result in dangerous and unsanitary living conditions. The

two most famous hoarders were the Collyer brothers who died in a house that was so cluttered that tunnels were

the only way to move about the home. OCD is also related to _____

_____ (147), which is characterized by motor and phonic _____ (148)

that include facial expressions, irrelevant and insulting remarks, and various noises. Although people with this

disorder may be able to control themselves under some circumstances, they cannot do so all the time. The

disorder typically emerges in _____ (149) and becomes more pronounced over time;

_____ (150) are more likely to have this disorder. Heritability for Tourette's is high, and

Tourette's and OCD are thought to have the same _____ (151) basis. Tourette's involves

increased dopamine activity in the _____ _____ (152) of the basal

ganglia, and the _____ (153) blocker haloperidol is the treatment of choice.

Many people with anxiety disorders have other psychiatric problems, especially _____

(154) disorders. The genetic bases for anxiety disorders include mechanisms that influence the activity of the

neurotransmitter _____ (155), but other substances such as adenosine, glutamate, and

dopamine are also involved.

Short Answer and Essay Questions

Answer the following questions.

13. What are the main symptoms of PTSD? Why doesn't everyone exposed to a traumatic event develop

    PTSD? How is it treated?

14. Describe the symptoms and brain changes that occur in OCD. What other disorders are linked to

    OCD? Describe the typical treatment of OCD.

15. How are OCD and Tourette's syndrome similar? Why are they thought to be related?

Posttest

Use these multiple-choice questions to check your understanding of the chapter.

1. How many people in the U.S. are estimated to suffer from a psychological disorder during their lifetimes?

    a. one out of every 3 people

    b. one out of every 4 people

    c. one out of every 5 people

    d. one out of every 10 people

2. Schizophrenia is typically characterized by all of the following EXCEPT

    a. loss of contact with reality.

    b. perceptual, emotional, and intellectual deficits.

    c. periods of intense excitement.

    d. an inability to function in life.

3. Which of the following statements regarding schizophrenia is TRUE?

    a. Researchers do not agree on what subtypes exist.

    b. Researchers universally recognize spectrum disorders.

    c. Schizophrenia is related to multiple personality disorder.

    d. There is little evidence for a genetic basis of schizophrenia.

4. Schizophrenics with ____ symptoms are MORE likely to recover.

    a. chronic

    b. negative

    c. violent

    d. acute

5. Twenty years after first hospitalization, what percentage of schizophrenics seem fully recovered?

    a. 12%

    b. 22%

    c. 35%

    d. 56%

6. In the 1940s, emphasis shifted to ____ causes of schizophrenia.

    a. genetic

    b. physiological

c. hormonal

d. social

7. When spectrum disorders are NOT considered, the concordance rate for schizophrenia among identical twins is

   a. 48%.

   b. 17%.

   c. 89%.

   d. 28%.

8. Jerry and Jason are identical twins. Jerry has schizophrenia, but Jason does not. Which of the following statements is correct?

   a. Jerry's children are more likely to develop schizophrenia than Jason's children.

   b. Jason's children are more likely to develop schizophrenia than Jerry's children.

   c. Jerry and Jason's children are equally likely to develop schizophrenia.

   d. Jerry and Jason's children are no more likely to develop schizophrenia than other members of the population.

9. Which of the following is TRUE about the genetic basic of schizophrenia?

   a. At least 50 genes have been strongly implicated in the disorder.

   b. The genes that have been identified show strong associations to the disorder.

   c. One problem with genetic studies is that they tend to focus on identifying common genes.

   d. Genetic studies have supported the notion that there is a single pathway to schizophrenia.

10. Which of the following genes have been implicated, according to a large database analysis?

    a. genes involved in neurotransmission

    b. genes that affect the immune response

    c. genes that play a role in neural development

    d. All of the above

11. Schizophrenia research indicates that

    a. genes are more important than the environment.

    b. the environment is more important than genes.

    c. most of the genes implicated protect the individual from environmental causes of schizophrenia.

d. environmental factors work in part by epigenetic means.

12. Which of the following is an example of a negative symptom of schizophrenia?

    a. hallucinations

    b. delusions

    c. bizarre behavior

    d. lack of emotion

13. Which of the following symptoms is MOST likely to respond to treatment with antipsychotic medication?

    a. hallucinations

    b. impaired attention

    c. poverty of speech

    d. lack of affect

14. The first effective antipsychotic drugs were

    a. dopamine antagonists.

    b. dopamine agonists.

    c. serotonin antagonists.

    d. serotonin agonists.

15. All of the following support the dopamine hypothesis of schizophrenia EXCEPT:

    a. Amphetamine can produce a psychosis that resembles schizophrenia.

    b. Schizophrenia can be treated by drugs that block NMDA receptors.

    c. Effective drugs block dopamine receptors.

    d. Schizophrenics have higher dopamine activity in the striatum.

16. Tardive dyskinesia results from

    a. blocking of serotonin receptors in the prefrontal cortex.

    b. enhancing dopamine release throughout the brain.

    c. increased sensitivity of dopamine receptors in the basal ganglia.

    d. activating NMDA glutamate receptors.

17. Glycine combined with a typical antipsychotic may be an effective treatment for

    a. acute onset schizophrenia.

b. negative symptoms of schizophrenia.

c. positive symptoms of schizophrenia.

d. All of the above

18. Enlarged ventricles are associated with

    a. schizophrenia.

    b. Alzheimer's disease.

    c. Huntington's chorea.

    d. All of the above

19. Hypofrontality is MOST closely associated with damage to the ___ prefrontal cortex.

    a. dorsolateral

    b. subgenual

    c. ventral

    d. anterior

20. One of the key functions that is disrupted in schizophrenia is

    a. synchrony between the prefrontal lobes and the hippocampus.

    b. coordination of activity between auditory and visual areas.

    c. oscillation synchrony at low frequencies.

    d. None of the above

21. Auditory gating is normalized in schizophrenics by which substance?

    a. traditional antipsychotics

    b. nicotine

    c. anxiolytics

    d. monoamine oxidase inhibitors

22. All of the following are linked to the brain defects associated with schizophrenia EXCEPT

    a. prenatal exposure to influenza.

    b. maternal stress during pregnancy.

    c. birth complications.

    d. prenatal exposure to alcohol.

23. Which of the following statements regarding the development of schizophrenia is TRUE?

a. Gray matter deficits are a result of lack of pruning, which is caused by glutamate excess.

b. Cortical neurons fail to migrate to the appropriate locations in the second trimester of pregnancy.

c. Ventricle enlargement is evident at birth.

d. Brain damage associated with schizophrenia does not begin until adolescence.

24. Which of the following is NOT a symptom of major depression?

a. decreased need for sleep

b. hopelessness

c. loss of energy

d. restlessness

25. Women are MORE likely than men to suffer from

a. unipolar depression.

b. bipolar disorder.

c. both unipolar depression and bipolar disorder.

d. bipolar depression and schizophrenia.

26. The concordance rate for depression among identical twins raised apart

a. is about the same as for those raised together.

b. is much lower than for those raised together.

c. is about the same as for fraternal twins raised together.

d. None of the above

27. Which of the following genes or alleles have been linked to depression?

a. the *VAL66MET* allele for BDNF

b. the "long" allele of the *5-HTTLPR* gene

c. the *hTPH2* mutation, which disrupts dopamine synthesis

d. the "short" allele of the gene for the serotonin transporter

28. The first prescription drug used to treat depression was

a. fluoxetine.

b. iproniazid.

c. chlorpromazine.

d. nicotine.

29. Prozac (fluoxetine) is a

    a. monoamine oxidase inhibitor.

    b. tricyclic antidepressant.

    c. first generation antidepressant.

    d. selective serotonin reuptake inhibitor.

30. Reduced norepinephrine is associated with

    a. sleep.

    b. lack of motivation.

    c. body temperature dysregulation.

    d. sexual activity.

31. A treatment that produces improvement in treatment-resistant depression in less than 2 hours of administration is

    a. glycine.

    b. nicotine.

    c. phototherapy.

    d. ketamine.

32. Which of the following is NOT true of ECT?

    a. It typically involves profound memory loss.

    b. It must result in a brain seizure in order to be effective.

    c. It must be repeated several times.

    d. Its therapeutic effects are as good as or better than those of antidepressant drugs.

33. Which of the following brain changes is (are) associated with ECT?

    a. increased sensitivity to serotonin

    b. decreased sensitivity in norepinephrine autoreceptors

    c. widespread synchrony of neural firing

    d. All of the above

34. All of the following are existing or potential treatments for depression EXCEPT:

    a. deep brain stimulation

    b. ECT administered two to three times a month

c. TMS

d. stimulation of the vagus nerve

35. What mechanism(s) may be responsible for the effectiveness of antidepressant treatments?

a. neurogenesis

b. migration of new cells in the hippocampus

c. greater plasticity in new cells

d. All of the above

36. Depression is associated with

a. a phase-advanced circadian rhythm.

b. REM sleep deficit.

c. a heightened sense of arousal in the evenings.

d. late REM onset.

37. Which of the following statements regarding SAD is TRUE?

a. It is more likely to improve if a person moves away from the equator.

b. It affects people only in the winter.

c. It is more common in men.

d. It can be associated with hypomanic periods.

38. Regarding the role of light in SAD,

a. the length of exposure to light is more important than the amount or intensity of light.

b. the intensity of light is more important than the length of exposure to light.

c. phototherapy works only if it is used early in the morning.

d. phototherapy is more effective than drug therapy because it lowers serotonin levels.

39. People with SAD sometimes self-medicate by

a. eating a lot of carbohydrates.

b. smoking.

c. limiting their intake of junk food.

d. All of the above

40. All of the following are true about bipolar disorder EXCEPT:

a. Lithium is the medication of choice.

b. The manic phase usually lasts longer than the depressive phase.

c. Stress is a common trigger for cycling between depression and mania.

d. Effective drug treatments share the effect of inhibiting the PKC family of enzymes.

41. Which of the following brain areas shows heightened activity during depressive episodes?

    a. caudate nucleus

    b. dorsolateral prefrontal cortex

    c. subgenual prefrontal cortex

    d. ventral prefrontal cortex

42. Which of the following brain areas has been referred to as the bipolar "switch"?

    a. dorsolateral prefrontal cortex

    b. subgenual prefrontal cortex

    c. amygdala

    d. ventral prefrontal cortex

43. Which of the following groups is MOST at risk for suicide?

    a. people with unipolar depression

    b. people with bipolar disorder

    c. people with substance abuse

    d. people with schizophrenia

44. Trevor becomes anxious whenever he gets around water, so he avoids going to lakes, rivers, and other large bodies of water. What type of anxiety disorder does he MOST likely have?

    a. generalized anxiety disorder

    b. phobia

    c. panic disorder

    d. OCD

45. Which of the following relieve(s) anxiety by enhancing GABA activity?

    a. atypical antidepressants

    b. neuroleptic drugs

    c. lithium

    d. benzodiazepines

46. Anxiety is associated with increased activity in the

    a. prefrontal cortex.

    b. locus coeruleus.

    c. hippocampus.

    d. basal ganglia.

47. Which of the following is NOT true about PTSD?

    a. It is characterized by flashbacks and nightmares.

    b. Men are more vulnerable than women.

    c. Its heritability is about 30%.

    d. It has been linked to changes in the hippocampus that might be caused by childhood abuse.

48. Which of the following treatments is NOT particularly effective with PTSD?

    a. psychotherapy

    b. exposure therapy

    c. therapy involving virtual reality

    d. fear erasure

49. Howard Hughes suffered from

    a. generalized anxiety disorder.

    b. phobia.

    c. panic disorder.

    d. OCD.

50. Which of the following brain changes is (are) associated with OCD?

    a. increased activity in the orbitofrontal cortex

    b. a decrease in white matter in the circuit connecting the cingulate gyrus with other brain areas

    c. increased activity in the caudate nucleus

    d. All of the above

51. Which drug is MOST likely to be used in treating OCD?

    a. serotonin reuptake inhibitors

    b. benzodiazepines

    c. haloperidol

d.   monoamine oxidase inhibitor

52. Tourette's syndrome probably results from increased ___ activity in the ___.

a.   dopamine; prefrontal cortex

b.   serotonin; prefrontal cortex

c.   serotonin; basal ganglia

d.   dopamine; basal ganglia

Answers

Guided Review

1. four

2. intellectual

3. reality

4. psychosis

5. 1

6. thought

7. emotions

8. delusions

9. overlapping

10. acute

11. 20

12. physical or biological

13. 60-90

14. adopted

15. discordant

16. spectrum

17. nonschizophrenic

18. genes

19. candidate

20. immune

21. copy number

22. vulnerability

23. external

24. internal

25. epigenetic

26. positive

27. acute

28. negative

29. positive

30. D_2

31. temporal

32. antipsychotic

33. amphetamine

34. blocked

35. deficient

36. tardive dyskinesia

37. basal ganglia

38. atypical or second generation

39. motor or movement

40. NMDA

41. glycine

42. glutamate

43. negative

44. serotonin

45. 5-HT2

46. dopamine

47. glutamate

48. ventricles

49. frontal

50. temporal

51. hippocampus

52. hypofrontality

53. dopamine

54. hippocampal

55. prefrontal

56. synchrony

57. language

58. environmental

59. gating

60. nicotine

61. smoke

62. influenza

63. immune

64. starvation

65. age

66. migration

67. adolescence

68. gray matter

69. reactive

70. Bipolar

71. women

72. 3

73. identical

74. serotonin transporter

75. amygdala

76. stress

77. epistasis

78. BDNF or brain-derived neurotrophic factor

79. serotonin

80. heritable

81. substance abuse

82. circadian

83. serotonin

84. monoamine

85. reuptake

86. Serotonin

87. Norepinephrine

88. monoamine oxidase inhibitor

89. ketamine

90. seizure

91. suicidal

92. monoamine

93. synchronize

94. neurogenesis

95. BDNF

96. plasticity

97. transcranial magnetic stimulation

98. deep

99. vagus

100. circadian

101. REM or rapid eye movement

102. suppress

103. seasonal affective disorder

104. women

105. carbohydrate

106. light

107. summer

108. phototherapy

109. resetting

110. serotonin

111. bipolar

112. manic

113. lithium

114. PKC

115. ventricles

116. amygdala

117. caudate

118. subgenual

119. stress-diathesis

120. 5-HIAA

121. impulsive

122. SSRIs

123. phobias

124. fear

125. GABA

126. serotonin

127. locus coeruleus

128. parahippocampal

129. flashbacks

130. women

131. vulnerability

132. hippocampal

133. heritability

134. exposure

135. fear erasure

136. Obsessive-compulsive

137. ritualistic

138. orbitofrontal

139. basal ganglia

140. accidents

141. high

142. glutamate

143. anterior cingulate

144. acral lick syndrome

145. trichotillomania

146. hoarding

147. Tourette's syndrome

148. tics

149. childhood

150. males

151. genetic

152. caudate nucleus

153. dopamine

154. mood

155. serotonin

Short Answer and Essay Questions

1. Because the children of each twin were equally likely to develop the disorder, genes are clearly involved in the disorder. It is not something one gets exclusively from the environment; otherwise, the children of the normal twin would have a much lower rate of schizophrenia than the offspring of the affected twin. At the

same time, because the "normal" twin possesses the same genes as the schizophrenic twin, the differences in environmental factors between the twins must account for the fact that one of them is more affected than the other.

2. The vulnerability model suggests that schizophrenia develops as a result of the combined influence of genetic and environmental factors that reach or exceed some threshold. According to this model, someone with a low genetic predisposition may become schizophrenic if environmental factors, such as stressors, are strong enough to trigger the disorder. It also explains that someone with a high degree of genetic predisposition may not develop the disorder if he or she is exposed to low levels of environmental challenges.

3. Type I schizophrenia is a type of schizophrenia that has an acute onset; is potentially reversible; is characterized by positive symptoms and a lack of intellectual deficit; and responds well to drugs that block dopamine due to excess D_2 receptors. Type II schizophrenia is characterized by negative symptoms, often including intellectual deficits; responds poorly to antidopaminergic drugs; and possibly involves irreversible brain changes in the temporal lobes.

4. Drugs that block D_2 receptors are effective in some cases of schizophrenia. However, atypical antipsychotics, which increase glutamate levels but block D_2 receptors less, are more effective (work in more cases). Glycine, which increases glutamate release, also produces better results when paired with conventional antipsychotics than these drugs alone. Glutamate increases have been linked to an improvement in negative symptoms. Some atypical antipsychotics also block serotonin receptors. It is likely that these three neurotransmitter systems interact to produce schizophrenia.

5. Anatomical deficits include reductions in brain tissue, particularly in frontal and temporal areas, which may lead to enlarged ventricles. In addition, neurons in the frontal and temporal lobes (including the hippocampus) are disordered and mislocated, indicating errors in migration. Functional deficits include increased dopamine and serotonin activity and decreased glutamate activity; hypofrontality (which apparently contributes to negative symptoms); and disordered connections between prefrontal areas and the hippocampus and between frontal and sensory areas. Some researchers believe schizophrenia is a disorder of synchrony in part because the disordered connections result in lack of synchrony among areas, which is associated with gating problems; in addition, excessive synchrony in sensory areas is associated with hallucinations.

6. Monoamine oxidase inhibitors work by preventing the breakdown of monoamines in the synapse. Tricyclics prevent reuptake of the monoamines. Second-generation antidepressants affect one specific

neurotransmitter, rather than all of the monoamines; for example, fluoxetine (Prozac) prevents the reuptake of serotonin.

7. Many depressed people smoke, and an ingredient in tobacco smoke acts as a MAO inhibitor. Also, people with SAD often eat a lot of carbohydrates, which increases their serotonin levels and may produce some relief from their depression.

8. Unipolar depression and bipolar disorder share the symptom of severe depression, but in bipolar disorder the depression alternates with mania. Depression is more common in women than men, whereas there is no sex difference for bipolar disorder. Both disorders have a genetic basis, but the heritability for bipolar disorder is about 85%, compared to 37% for unipolar depression. While it is well accepted that unipolar depression involves some imbalance in the monoamine transmitter, the biological basis of bipolar disorder is less clear. Unipolar depression is typically treated with drugs that increase serotonin and/or norepinephrine. Bipolar disorder has traditionally been treated with lithium, but newer drugs exist (valproate) or are being tested for effectiveness (PKC inhibitors). Tissue loss is characteristic of depression (with the exception of the amygdala, which is larger), along with reduced brain activity; activity is also decreased during bipolar depression, but increases during mania. Activity in the ventral prefrontal area comes and goes with depression, and the area may be a "depression switch;" the subgenual prefrontal cortex is active during mania, and appears to be a "bipolar swirtch."

9. Winter depression may be alleviated by moving to or visiting a region where there is more natural light (in the direction of the equator). Phototherapy also provides relief if the person is exposed to a few hours of bright light during the day in the winter (when days are short and light levels are less intense than in summer). Consuming carbohydrates may also help, because it increases serotonin levels.

10. The ventral prefrontal cortex is thought to be a depression switch, because it is more active during periods of depression and less active when the person is not experiencing symptoms. The subgenual prefrontal cortex may be a bipolar switch because activity levels within it correspond with the manic and depressive states of the disorder; it is more active during mania and less active during depression. Also, it helps regulate the neurotransmitters involved in affective disorders.

11. All of the following involve some sort of brain stimulation: ECT, which causes seizure activity in the brain; TMS, which increases brain activity by exposing the brain to a magnetic field; deep brain stimulation, which involves stimulation by electrodes placed in areas such as the anterior cingulate cortex; and stimulation of

the vagus nerve. ECT and drugs used for affective disorders may exert their effects on correcting imbalances in transmitters. They may also affect neurogenesis and plasticity in the brain.

12. Low serotonin is a marker for impulsive behavior, regardless of psychiatric disorder. Studies have found lower levels of the metabolite 5-HIAA in suicide attempters and in impulsive suicide attempters compared to nonimpulsive attempters. However, in individuals with two particular gene alleles serotonin reuptake inhibitors can increase suicide risk.

13. PTSD is characterized by flashbacks, nightmares, lack of concentration, and overreactivity to environmental stimuli. The reason some people develop PTSD while others do not has to do with vulnerability, which seems to be linked to reduced hippocampal volume, genetic factors, and childhood abuse. PTSD is difficult to treat with traditional drug and psychotherapy approaches. One alternative is exposure therapy or a newer procedure called fear erasure.

14. The symptoms of OCD are primarily obsessions (recurring thoughts) and compulsions (repetitive and ritualistic acts). Brain changes in OCD occur in a circuit involving the cingulate gyrus's connections to the basal ganglia, thalamus, and cortex. OCD-like behaviors include acral lick syndrome in animals, hair-pulling or trichotilliomania in humans, hoarding, and Tourette's syndrome. Treatments include SSRIs, antipsychotics, glutamate blockers, surgical disconnection of the orbitofrontal cortex from the anterior cingulate cortex, deep brain stimulation, and TMS.

15. OCD and Tourette's syndrome are similar in that the behaviors exhibited are so compulsive. In Tourette's, a person can control the behavior, but only for a while. The reason the two are thought to be related is because they co-occur in families, and both involve increased activity in the basal ganglia. However, they are typically treated using different drugs.

Posttest

1. a   2. c   3. a   4. d   5. b   6. d   7. a   8. c   9. c   10. d   11. d   12. d   13. a   14. a   15. b   16. c   17. b   18. d   19. a   20. a   21. b   22. d   23. b   24. a   25. a   26. a   27. d   28. b   29. d   30. b   31. d   32. a   33. d   34. b   35. d   36. a   37. d   38. b   39. a   40. b   41. d   42. b   43. b   44. b   45. d 46. b   47. b   48. a   49. d   50. d   51. a   52. d

15

Sleep and Consciousness

Chapter Outline

Sleep and Dreaming

Circadian Rhythms

Rhythms During Waking and Sleeping

The Functions of REM and Non-REM Sleep

Sleep and Memory

Brain Structures of Sleep and Waking

Sleep Disorders

IN THE NEWS: IN THE STILL OF THE NIGHT

Sleep as a Form of Consciousness

The Neural Bases of Consciousness

Awareness

Attention

The Sense of Self

Theoretical Explanations of Consciousness

APPLICATION: DETERMINING CONSCIOUSNESS WHEN IT COUNTS

Learning Objectives

After reading this chapter, you should be able to answer the following questions.

1. What are some possible functions of sleep?

2. What controls circadian rhythms?

3. What rhythms of brain activity accompany wakefulness? Sleeping?

4. What are the functions of REM and non-REM sleep?

5. What brain areas control sleep and arousal?

6. What are some sleep disorders?

7. When we sleep, are we unconscious?

8. What are the biological bases of awareness and attention?

9. What brain areas contribute to our sense of self?

10. What are some disorders of the self? What do they tell us about self-awareness?

11. What do we know about the biological bases of consciousness?

Sleep and Dreaming

Summary and Guided Review

After studying this section in the text, fill in the blanks of the following summary.

The study of consciousness within psychology has been controversial. The use of

_____ (1) to study consciousness, popular at the end of 19th century, fell out of favor when

the _____ (2) attempted to rid psychology of subjective methods during the first half of the

20th century. When _____ (3) psychology emerged in the mid-20th century, mental

experiences were once again acceptable to study if they could be examined objectively. However, because of

lack of technology as well as lack of consensus concerning the meaning of consciousness, this topic has

remained controversial. Psychologists who do study it often work with researchers from other disciplines,

including _____ (4), philosophy, and computer science; of the conscious states,

_____ (5) is most commonly studied, because it can be objectively observed and measured.

Although sleep is one of our most basic needs, researchers who study it have been unable to fully explain its

functions. One explanation is that sleep is _____ (6); it allows us to conserve energy and

repair our bodies. Because amount of sleep is correlated with a species' body size, food availability, metabolic

rate, and vulnerability, the _____ (7) hypothesis suggests the amount of sleep is a function of needs for energy conservation and safety. In a study of 39 species, the factors of body size and danger accounted for _____ % (8) of the variability in sleep time. There is considerable evidence that getting adequate sleep at the right time is important. People who are _____ (9) workers experience difficulty getting enough sleep during the day. Rates of vehicle and work-related accidents are higher in the early morning hours than at other times. Also, _____ _____ (10) baseball teams playing games in east coast cities seem to be at a disadvantage if they are not given adequate time to adjust to the time shift. This difficulty in adjustment while travelling across time zones is often referred to as _____ _____ (11).

Our sleep/wake cycle is an example of a _____ (12) rhythm, and the sleep period corresponds with decreases in several physiological measures such as urine production and body temperature. These cycles are controlled by the _____ _____ (13); rats with lesions in this region no longer exhibit circadian cycles of sleep. However, they do sleep, so sleep itself is under the control of other brain areas. When daylight cues are unavailable, people's circadian rhythms tend to increase to _____ (14)-hour cycles. This suggests that natural light is the critical _____ (15) for entraining the SCN to a 24-hour cycle. Furthermore, being exposed to _____ (16) light during wakefulness and darkness during sleep are important for coordinating the different biological rhythms associated with sleep. The fact that we tend toward a 25-hour cycle may explain why it is easier to adjust to _____ (17) times for falling asleep and waking up. Shift workers whose shifts rotate according to phase _____ (18) are able to adjust more easily than those who must accommodate phase advance changes. Although there is evidence to support the existence of a 25-hour cycle, Czeisler points out that the cycle is extended by bright _____ (19) late in the day; thus, he says, the 25-hour cycle is an artifact of allowing subjects in isolation studies to control their room lighting. Light controls the sleep cycle through its influence on the pineal gland's secretion of _____ (20); in totally blind individuals, a failure to produce this substance in response to changing levels of light is associated with _____ (21). Blind individuals with normal melatonin cycling probably rely on signals from the _____ (22) pathway to the SCN. This pathway may be mediated not by rods and cones but by retinal ganglion cells containing the photopigment _____ (23), which is sensitive to short-wavelength light. The internal clock itself consists of two major groups of _____ (24) and their _____ (25) products. The groups alternate in activity as a group's proteins turn those genes off and turn the other group of genes on.

Every day the feedback loop that comprises the circadian clock must be reset by _____ (26). Other clocks in the body are entrained to the day-night cycle by the _____ (27).

Several bodily rhythms in humans follow shorter _____ (28) cycles. Some examples are hormone production, urinary output, and alertness. The basic rest and activity cycle is a rhythm that is about _____ to _____ (29) minutes long. When the person is awake, the EEG is a mixture of _____ (30) waves, associated with arousal and alertness; and _____ (31) waves, characteristic of relaxed wakefulness. _____ (32) waves occur during Stage 1, or light sleep. During Stage 2, we exhibit _____ _____ (33) and K-complexes. Slow-wave sleep (SWS) in stages 3 and 4 is associated with _____ (34) waves; movement, including sleepwalking, often occurs during this time. The EEG activity then indicates a reverse progression through the sleep stages until _____ _____ _____ (35) sleep is achieved. This type of sleep is sometimes called_____ (36) sleep, because it is characterized by eye movements, physiological arousal, dreaming, and brain waves that are similar to a waking state. One unusual characteristic of REM sleep is that in spite of these signs of arousal, the body is in a state of paralysis or _____ (37). The length of REM sleep periods increases over the night as the amount of slow-wave sleep _____ (38).

People deprived of REM sleep will enter it more quickly on subsequent nights and spend more time in this stage of sleep, which implies that the brain or the body has a need for REM sleep. The _____-_____ (39) hypothesis suggests that dreams are the product of spontaneous neural activity during REM sleep and have no function; we merely attempt to make sense of the somewhat random activation. Researchers do not agree on the function(s) of REM sleep. One suggestion is that because REM sleep is more common in infants and children than in adults, it promotes neural _____ (40). Because amount of SWS is associated with _____ (41) in the brain prior to sleep, it has been suggested that SWS is more important for brain than body restoration. It may be involved in cerebral recovery, particularly in the _____ (42) cortex. Individuals given _____ (43) prior to a nap experienced less SW sleep during the nap and had poorer cognitive performance following the nap than those given a placebo, though they reported feeling vigorous and no sleepier than the control group.

Another possibility is that REM sleep is important for learning and _____ (44). In the sleep periods following learning, REM sleep increases in proportion to how well the individual has learned. Learned performance improves following a night of sleep; how much it improves is correlated with the percentage of _____-_____ (45) sleep during the first quarter of the night and with the percentage of REM sleep in the last quarter. However, rats subjected to electrical stimulation of the reticular formation during REM sleep improved on a learning task, but those stimulated during SWS did not. Following learning, there is a replay of electrical activity in the rat's hippocampus during REM sleep, and the hippocampus upregulates genes involved in cortical plasticity. For the first 4–7 days, this replay is synchronized with _____ (46) waves in the hippocampus; afterward the replay shifts to out of phase. Because theta-synchronous stimulation is associated with LTP and asynchronous stimulation is associated with LTD, the results suggest that a period of consolidation is followed by a period of memory erasure; memory deletion is consistent with the _____-_____ (47) hypothesis, which suggests that one function of REM sleep is to streamline our memory-related neural connections by eliminating those that are not needed.

Sleep is a homeostatic mechanism. During wakefulness, adenosine builds up in the _____ _____ (48) area, and eventually this inhibits arousal. Cells in the _____ _____ (49) of the hypothalamus are responsive to temperature; warming them increases slow-wave sleep. This finding supports the idea that one function of slow-wave sleep is to _____ (50) the brain after waking activity. Activity in the _____ _____ (51) nucleus inhibits arousal in several brain areas located in the hypothalamus and pons. Activity in the _____ (52) nucleus of the medulla initiates atonia during REM sleep. Caffeine acts on sleep-related areas in the pons through its effect on _____ (53) receptors.

The brain's arousal system is active during waking and to some extent during _____ (54) sleep. There are two major pathways in the arousal system. In the first pathway, areas in the pons release _____ (55) during waking. Activation of this pathway also shifts from synchronous EEG activity to _____ (56), high frequency, low-amplitude waves by inhibiting nuclei in the _____ (57). This pathway is also active during _____ (58) sleep. A second pathway activates the cortex. It originates from the locus coeruleus, which releases _____ (59) and the raphé, nuclei which release _____ (60). Neurons in the tuberomammillary nucleus arouse the cortex by releasing _____ (61), and those from the basal forebrain area do so by releasing _____ (62). The arousal pathway also includes

neurons in the _____ _____ (63), which send axons to many brain

stem and basal forebrain regions. During waking these neurons release _____ (64), or

hypocretin, to stabilize the sleep and waking system and prevent inappropriate switching into sleep. Sleep

medications that _____ (65) orexin are now being developed, whereas some anesthetics

_____ (66) orexin receptors. During REM sleep, _____ (67) waves

travel from brainstem areas to the thalamus and finally to the cortex. The arousal of the occipital cortex may

account for the imagery that occurs during _____ (68).

_____ (69) is the inability to sleep or to obtain quality sleep. People who get either too

little or too much sleep typically have a shorter lifespan. Body mass index is higher in people who get too

_____ (70) sleep, apparently because several eating-related hormones shift out of balance.

Insomniacs apparently suffer from hyperarousal during sleep; their non-REM sleep contains excess

_____-_____ (71) EEG, and secretion of excess

_____ (72) and adrenocorticotropic hormone indicates disturbance of the hypothalamic-

pituitary-adrenal axis. Many factors contribute to insomnia, but the disorder is often found in people with

_____ (73) disorders. Surprisingly, many _____ (74) medications can

cause insomnia. Another reason for insomnia may be that a person's body temperature cycle is out of sync with

the sleep cycle; going to sleep when body temperature is high results in _____

_____ (75) insomnia, while a phase advance in body temperature results in early waking.

The ideal time to go to sleep is when the body temperature is low. Whether your _____

(76) is synchronized to the 24-hour day depends on both genes and the environment. A counterintuitive

treatment for _____ _____ (77) syndrome involves delaying each

sleep cycle by 3 hours over several consecutive days.

Sleepwalking occurs during _____-_____ (78) sleep, as do

bedwetting and night terrors. There have been cases in which sleepwalkers committed violent acts, including

murder. This condition appears to have a genetic basis; the involvement of one particular gene suggests that in

some cases cells important in sleep regulation have been attacked by the _____ (79)

system. A sleep disorder that usually results in weight gain as well as daytime fatigue is

_____-_____ _____ (80) disorder.

Disorders of REM sleep include _____ (81), in which a person enters REM sleep suddenly and directly from full consciousness. One symptom of this disorder is _____

(82), in which a person becomes suddenly paralyzed but remains conscious. Both of these conditions may stem

from an abnormal form of a gene for the _____ (83) receptor. Extreme physical activity

during REM sleep, such as leaping out of bed, is a symptom of _____

_____ _____ _____ (84). This condition is often

associated with a neurological disorder, such as _____ (85) disease.

Francis Crick suggested that we are in a state of diminished consciousness during REM sleep and

unconscious during non-REM sleep. However, the distinction between consciousness and unconsciousness

during sleep is hardly clear. _____ (86) dreamers report awareness of their dreams as they

happen and also seem to be able to control the content of their dreams. Sleepwalkers and those with REM sleep

behavior disorder carry out complex behaviors while asleep (such as driving a car). Perhaps consciousness

exists on a _____ (87), and different states such as wakefulness, sleep, and dreaming

reflect different levels of awareness.

Short Answer and Essay Questions

Answer the following questions.

1. Why did the study of consciousness fall out of favor among psychologists in the early 20th century?

2. Describe the adaptive explanation for sleep and provide supportive evidence.

3. How may jet lag account for the fact that West Coast baseball teams playing in East Coast cities lose
   more often than East Coast teams playing in West Coast cities?

4. What is the difference between circadian and ultradian rhythms? Where is the clock for the sleep/wake
   cycle located in the brain, and how do we know this? What role does melatonin play?

5. How are blind individuals able to synchronize their circadian cycle if the zeitgeber is light?

6. What underlying brain activity do alpha and beta waves reflect? How are these brain wave patterns
   related to the states of arousal associated with them? How do these brain wave patterns change during
   sleep?

7. According to the reverse learning hypothesis, what is one function of REM sleep? What evidence
   supports this hypothesis? Identify other explanations for REM sleep.

8. Describe the role of the basal forebrain area, hypothalamus, and pons in sleep and arousal.

9. What are possible causes and biological explanations for the sleep disorders insomnia and narcolepsy?

The Neural Bases of Consciousness

Summary and Guided Review

After studying this section in the text, fill in the blanks of the following summary.

Although experts disagree as to a specific definition of consciousness, most would probably concur that being conscious includes awareness, _____ (88), and a sense of self. There is probably no single brain area responsible for consciousness, but rather it arises from the interaction of several different brain areas.

Awareness seems to depend on several brain areas, including the prefrontal cortex; the _____ (89), because of its role in declarative learning; and the parietal lobes. How the brain integrates or binds information from different areas into a unitary whole most likely involves the _____ (90) of neural activity. This type of activity occurs mostly in the _____ (91) frequency range, between 30 and 90 Hz. For example, when researchers presented a light that had been paired with a shock, activity became synchronized between the _____ (92) cortex and the _____ (93) area of the somatosensory cortex. In one study electrodes were implanted in the brains of people who were being evaluated for surgery to treat seizures. When words were presented there was initial localized gamma activity recorded from the _____ (94) area, but if the words were recognized there was synchronized activity in occipital, parietal, and temporal areas. However, awareness is not required for all of our behavior. For example, people with _____ (95) can locate objects that they claim not to see, and considerable learning occurs without awareness.

_____ (96) is the brain's means of allocating its limited resources. The importance of attention is illustrated by data that show the increase in car accidents is the same when drivers are holding their mobile phone as when they are using a speakerphone. Much of the stimuli around us go unnoticed, although highly relevant stimuli such as one's name may be attended to. _____ _____ (97), which occurs when the brain is presented with two different visual stimuli

374

apparently in the same location, results in attention being alternately focused on each object, as demonstrated in the _____ _____ (98) effect. PET scans revealed that when participants were instructed to attend to an object's color, _____ (99) became more active, and when told to attend to the object's shape, the _____ _____ (100) cortex became more active, and when attention was directed toward the object's movement, the activity switched to _____ (101). The shifts were clearly due to _____ (102), because the particular area was active whether the object possessed the feature or not (colored vs. not colored for example). The gateway for sensory information to the cortex is the _____ (103); the cortex can selectively inhibit input from this area to determine which information will reach it. Imaging suggests there are two networks involved in attention. The _____ (104) network operates under goal-directed control whereas the ventral network responds to _____

_____ (105). In addition, the _____ _____ (106) gyrus may play an executive role. This area is active during complex tasks, like the _____ (107) test in which subjects are asked to identify the color of a word that spells out a conflicting color name (for example, saying "red" when the word "green" is presented in a red color).

Our sense of self includes identity and the sense of _____ (108),in which we perceive ourselves as the source of actions or effects. Children over _____ (109) months of age appear to recognize themselves in mirrors, indicating that they have a sense of self. This is true of only a few other animal species: For example, among the primates, chimpanzees and orangutans pass the mirror test, but _____ (110) fail it. Damage to specific brain areas can result in impairment in self-awareness, including failure to recognize one's own reflection. The sense that we are causing an action or event may be due to activity in the _____ _____ (111). However, the sense of self is not represented in a single brain area, but probably results from several distributed functions.

The sense of loss in individuals who have undergone limb _____ (112) and people with body sensory disorders suggests that an intact body image is a part of our sense of self. The majority of amputees experience some manifestation of the _____ _____ (113) phenomenon, such as the sense that the missing limb is stuck in a particular position or that one still has control over it. Even individuals born with missing limbs can experience this phenomenon; therefore this body image does not have to be _____ (114). The most extreme body image illusion, the out-of-body experience, can be caused by damage to the _____ _____ (115) area.

_____-_____ (116) memory is also a source of our sense of identity. People with severe retrograde _____ (117), such as that resulting from Alzheimer's disease or Korsakoff's syndrome, may engage in _____ (118); this is hypothesized to result from a failure to suppress irrelevant information due to damage to the

_____ (119) lobe. Sacks suggests that confabulators are constantly creating both a past and a present, interspersed with fragments of actual experiences.

The ability to empathize with others and understand other's intentions may lie in

_____ (120) neurons; it has even been suggested that malfunction in this system is responsible for some of the symptoms of autism, such the inability to develop a _____ of

_____ (121).

Studies of split-brain patients can tell us something about consciousness and the self. Although most of the time people whose hemispheres have been disconnected perform normally, occasionally they act as if they have two selves. In laboratory studies, when information is presented only to the nonverbal

_____ (122) hemisphere, the person is unable to identify it verbally; and the left hand (controlled by the right hemisphere) must sometimes be restrained to prevent it from helping the right hand perform a _____ (123) task. While some researchers speculate that each hemisphere is capable of a separate consciousness, Gazzaniga argues that the left hemisphere is the brain

_____ (124), which integrates cognitive functions occurring throughout the brain. An alternative perspective is that because the right hemisphere lacks _____ (125) ability, it is simply unable to report on its own contents, and therefore appears to be less conscious or aware than the left hemisphere.

Individuals with multiple personality, or _____ _____ (126) disorder, show shifts in consciousness and behavior that appear to be distinct personalities or selves. Diagnosis of this disorder is controversial. Some experts believe that patients who display it are conforming to their therapists' expectations. However, a few studies have found different physiological profiles (heart rate, immune functioning, EEG activity) when different "personalities" were present, which suggests that there may be a

_____ (127) basis for the disorder. For example, some studies indicate. One explanation is that this disorder represents a case of _____-_____ (128) learning. There are several indications of possible involvement of the brain structures of learning including hippocampal changes during personality switches; frequent backgrounds of childhood abuse (associated with hippocampal damage); association with temporal lobe epilepsy; and temporal lobe differences between personalities.

One effort to understand the brain bases of consciousness focuses on body awareness. While neglect occurs with right parietal damage, the area that appears to be critical for awareness of a paralyzed limb (impaired, for example, in anosognosia) is the _____ (129) area as the source of disruption. While there are other such "islands of consciousness," most researchers believe consciousness requires a widely distributed neuronal network. For example, stimuli outside awareness activate only the sensory area, but when the stimulus enters consciousness activation is more widespread. Many theorists believe network activity is coordinated by gamma oscillations generated by a feedback loop between the _____ (130) and cortex. Some scientists believe that while there is no brain structure that houses consciousness, there must be something that acts as a(an) _____ (131), directing activity in other structures. Candidates for this role have included the thalamus, the _____ _____ (132) cortex, and the _____ (133), but no structure has convincing support. Consciousness researchers are beginning to regard the _____ _____ (134) network as the most important to consciousness; its activity varies with level of consciousness across many conditions. Understanding consciousness is more than academic; determining level of consciousness is crucial in making decisions about care. For example, patients with _____-_____ (135) syndrome are fully conscious, but they are so paralyzed that their ability to communicate is greatly restricted.

Short Answer and Essay Questions

Answer the following questions.

10. Describe a research study that indicates we can learn without being aware of what we have learned.

11. How is binocular rivalry, such as the Cheshire cat effect, achieved? What does this tell us about brain activity underlying attention?

12. How can we test for self-awareness in preverbal children and nonhuman animals?

13. What evidence is there that one does not need to learn body image?

14. Why does Gazzaniga argue that the left hemisphere is more highly conscious than the right hemisphere? What is the significance of the brain interpreter in his argument?

15. What is state-dependent learning? How might state-dependent learning explain the occurrence of

dissociative identity disorder?

16. Most researchers believe that consciousness is distributed across much of the brain; describe their thinking about networks in relation to consciousness.

17. Why is understanding the nature of consciousness more than just an academic exercise? What practical benefits might there be for patients with severe brain damage?

Posttest

Use these multiple-choice questions to check your understanding of the chapter.

1. In the late 19th century, consciousness was studied primarily

   a. by using introspection.

   b. with the EEG.

   c. by examining sleep and dreaming.

   d. by observing others' behavior.

2. Currently, brain researchers

   a. are interested only in studying sleep as a form of consciousness.

   b. agree on a definition of consciousness.

   c. integrate philosophical, biological, and computer science perspectives to study consciousness.

   d. agree that consciousness cannot be studied objectively.

3. Which of the following animal species sleeps the LEAST?

   a. bats

   b. humans

   c. lions

   d. cattle

4. Which of the following statements regarding shift work is TRUE?

   a. Night shift workers perform their jobs as well as day shift workers.

   b. Shift workers sleep less than day workers.

c. Night shift workers generally sleep through the day on their weekends or days off.

d. Job-related accidents are most likely to occur between 10:00 p.m. and midnight.

5. Which of the following baseball teams is LEAST likely to win a game?

   a. the Boston Red Sox playing at the Houston Astros

   b. the Houston Astros playing at the Boston Red Sox

   c. the San Francisco Giants playing at the Atlanta Braves

   d. the Atlanta Braves playing at the San Francisco Giants

6. Circadian rhythms for sleep and waking arise in the

   a. suprachiasmatic nucleus.

   b. hypothalamus

   c. pineal gland.

   d. medulla

7. The MOST significant zeitgeber for the sleep/wake cycles appears to be

   a. moonlight.

   b. sunlight.

   c. clocks.

   d. social contact.

8. Research suggests that in order to increase worker productivity, night shift workers should

   a. sleep in complete darkness.

   b. work in bright light.

   c. take naps every 2 hours while working.

   d. a and b

9. Assuming that the day shift is from 8:00 a.m. to 4:00 p.m., the swing shift is from 4:00 p.m. to midnight, and the night shift is from midnight to 8:00 a.m., which of the following shift-rotation schedules would be MOST beneficial to workers?

   a. day shift to swing shift to night shift

   b. day shift to night shift to swing shift

   c. swing shift to day shift to night shift

   d. night shift to swing shift to day shift

10. How have researchers explained evidence that the internal clock operates on a 25 hour cycle?

    a. The effect is related to the 30 day lunar cycle.

    b. It is just an artifact of allowing people to use alarm clocks to start their day.

    c. Body temperature moves the cycle from 24 to 25 hours.

    d. None of the above

11. ___ is a hormone released by the pineal gland that induces sleepiness.

    a. Melanopsin

    b. Adenosine

    c. Melatonin

    d. Hypocretin

12. All of the following are true EXCEPT:

    a. Mice lacking rods and cones are unable to show normal entrainment and cycling.

    b. Light is able to activate the SCN by way of the retinohypothalamic pathway.

    c. The small percentage of ganglion cells that respond to light directly contain melanopsin.

    d. Melanopsin is most sensitive to light that occurs at dusk and dawn.

13. The circadian clock for sleep and waking

    a. is found in the brain, but it may control clocks in other organs.

    b. involves a feedback loop of two groups of genes and their protein products.

    c. must be reset each day by light.

    d. All of the above

14. Which of the following cycle lengths would be considered an ultradian rhythm?

    a. 24 hour

    b. 12 hour

    c. 48 hour

    d. 36 hour

15. The basic rest and activity cycle

    a. is a circadian rhythm.

    b. is a 60 minute cycle that occurs throughout the day.

    c. shows up in a 90-minute daydreaming cycle.

d. is controlled by temperature.

16. Which of the following statements is NOT true about sleep?

   a. It is an active process.

   b. It is the a cessation of activity due to fatigue.

   c. It involves turning some brain structures on and other structures off.

   d. It includes both active and inactive periods of brain activity.

17. An EEG pattern showing low-amplitude, high-frequency (13–30 Hz) waves characterizes

   a. alertness.

   b. relaxation.

   c. light sleep.

   d. slow-wave sleep.

18. Sleep spindles and K-complexes are MOST likely to be observed in

   a. REM sleep.

   b. Stage 4 sleep.

   c. Stage 2 sleep.

   d. Stage 1 sleep.

19. What type of EEG characterizes Stages 3 and 4 of slow wave sleep?

   a. alpha activity

   b. beta activity

   c. delta activity

   d. theta activity

20. Which of the following is NOT a typical characteristic of REM sleep?

   a. low-amplitude, moderate-frequency EEG

   b. eye movements

   c. arm and leg movements

   d. genital erection

21. Dreams

   a. occur only during REM sleep.

   b. are more vivid in slow-wave sleep.

c. have no personal meaning.

d. probably occur in all people.

22. Someone who is deprived of REM sleep will

    a. spend more time in REM and slow-wave sleep when allowed to sleep without interruptions.

    b. develop temporary narcolepsy or cataplexy.

    c. come to understand the symbolic contents of her dreams.

    d. spend more time in REM sleep when allowed to sleep without interruptions.

23. The activation-synthesis hypothesis of dreaming

    a. states that dreaming is merely a by-product of spontaneous neural activity.

    b. was first proposed by Freud.

    c. involves brain stem areas that generate random activity, but not forebrain areas.

    d. suggests that dream content is not important or significant.

24. Infants spend about ___% of their total sleep time in REM sleep.

    a. 10

    b. 50

    c. 20

    d. 75

25. The developmental hypothesis of REM sleep

    a. states that REM sleep promotes neural development during childhood, especially during infancy.

    b. argues that REM sleep encourages maturation and myelination of higher brain structures.

    c. is supported by the finding that genes involved in neural plasticity are upregulated during REM sleep.

    d. All of the above

26. Slow wave sleep

    a. promotes cerebral recovery, especially in the prefrontal cortex.

    b. occurs in response to low body temperature.

    c. occurs in response to low brain temperature.

    d. in not affected by caffeine, although REM sleep is.

27. Learning and memory

a. decrease REM in the night following the task.

b. involve both REM and non-REM sleep.

c. are related to the circadian cycle of sleep , but not the type of sleep.

d. are linked to REM sleep in animals but not humans.

28. Which of the following structures is most important in neuronal replay that occurs during sleep?

    a. the visual cortex

    b. the hippocampus

    c. the pons

    d. the basal forebrain region

29. Which of the following mammals does not experience REM sleep?

    a. elephant

    b. whale

    c. echidna

    d. feline

30. Which of the following hypotheses suggests that inappropriate neural connections are discarded during REM sleep?

    a. neural development

    b. learning

    c. reverse learning

    d. activation synthesis

31. Slow-wave sleep is LEAST likely to increase if a person

    a. swims 25 laps in a chilly pool.

    b. runs 10 miles on a hot day.

    c. has a fever.

    d. works in an overheated office.

32. Caffeine affects sleep by

    a. facilitating the effects of adenosine in the preoptic area.

    b. stimulating the adenosine receptors in the locus coeruleus.

    c. activating the cells in the basal forebrain region.

d. inhibiting adenosine in the preoptic area.

33. Sleep involves all of the following structures EXCEPT:

   a. the preoptic area of the hypothalamus

   b. the basal forebrain region

   c. the pons

   d. the ventrolateral thalamus

34. Muscular paralysis accompanying REM sleep is moderated by the

   a. magnocellular nucleus of the medulla.

   b. lateral geniculate nucleus of the thalamus.

   c. occipital cortex.

   d. basal forebrain area.

35. Which of the following statements about the arousal systems of the brain is NOT true?

   a. One arousal pathway originates in the pons and produces acetylcholine.

   b. One arousal pathway activates the cortex by the release of norepinephrine from the locus coeruleus.

   c. Cells in the raphe that release dopamine are part of the arousal system.

   d. Histamine from the tuberomammillary nucleus activates the cortex.

36. Neurons in the lateral hypothalamus release ___ to stabilize the sleep and waking system.

   a. serotonin

   b. orexin

   c. histamine

   d. acetylcholine

37. PGO waves

   a. travel from the pons to the thalamus and on to the cortex.

   b. begin about 80 seconds before the start of a REM period.

   c. initiate the desynchrony of REM sleep/

   d. All of the above

38. All of the following are true about insomnia EXCEPT:

   a. It is associated with disorders such as obesity.

   b. It is usually diagnosed in a sleep laboratory.

c. It may involve cortisol release during the night.

d. It is common in people with depression.

39. The best treatment for delayed sleep syndrome is to

   a. take benzodiazepine sleep medications.

   b. stay up later on consecutive days.

   c. increase your body temperature at bedtime.

   d. go to bed three hours earlier for a few days.

40. Sleepwalking

   a. occurs during slow-wave sleep.

   b. may have a genetic basis.

   c. is most common during childhood.

   d. All of the above

41. Narcolepsy is a condition in which a person

   a. suddenly goes from being awake directly into slow-wave sleep.

   b. falls directly into REM sleep from wakefulness.

   c. has too much orexin.

   d. sleeps much more than people without narcolepsy.

42. Someone who literally acts outs dreams is probably experiencing

   a. lucid dreaming.

   b. cataplexy.

   c. REM sleep behavior disorder.

   d. insomnia.

43. All of the following are components that most researchers agree are part of consciousness EXCEPT:

   a. attention

   b. personality

   c. sense of self

   d. awareness

44. Which of the following is evidence of learning without awareness?

   a. recognizing that our unconscious mind is capable of motivating our behavior

b. following a coach's instructions for hitting a ball with a bat

c. using proprioceptive information to sit erect and walk

d. reading instructions for assembling a computer prior to putting it together

45. The Cheshire cat effect is an example of

   a. binocular rivalry.

   b. lucid dreaming.

   c. binocular disparity.

   d. unconscious learning.

46. Attention

   a. is the same as awareness.

   b. is a concept rather a than a physiological process.

   c. is a reflection of changes in brain activity.

   d. All of the above

47. Which of the following is LEAST likely to recognize herself in a mirror?

   a. a 16-month-old human

   b. an adult rhesus monkey

   c. an adult chimpanzee

   d. a 24-month-old human

48. All of the following contribute to the sense of self EXCEPT:

   a. arousal

   b. body image

   c. memory

   d. mirror neurons

49. Phantom limb sensations may be experienced

   a. by amputees.

   b. by people born with missing limbs.

   c. even before an individual has developed a learned body image.

   d. All of the above

50. Which of the following statements regarding confabulation is FALSE?

a. It often includes elements of real memories.

b. It is often consistent and meaningful.

c. It is usually intentional.

d. It is associated with long-term memory loss.

51. Split-brain patients

    a. are unable to perform behaviors requiring coordination both sides of the body.

    b. are able to give verbal descriptions of objects in both visual fields.

    c. clearly demonstrate that the left hemisphere is more highly conscious than the right.

    d. usually perform spatial tasks better with the left hand than the right.

52. Which of the following statements regarding dissociative identity disorder is FALSE?

    a. It is not included in the APA's *Diagnostic and Statistical Manual*.

    b. It was formerly called multiple personality disorder.

    c. It is believed to result from childhood abuse or trauma.

    d. Individuals exhibit different physiological patterns when manifesting different identities.

53. In which of the following conditions is default mode network activity most likely to be normal?

    a. coma

    b. locked-in syndrome

    c. minimally conscious state

    d. vegetative state

54. A single center of consciousness may not exist, but the ___ has been proposed to be an "executive" area that coordinates all of the areas involved in consciousness.

    a. thalamus.

    b. anterior cingulate cortex.

    c. claustrum.

    d. All of the above

Answers

Guided Review

1. introspection

2. behaviorists

3. cognitive

4. biology

5. sleep

6. restorative

7. adaptive

8. 80

9. shift

10. west coast

11. jet lag

12. circadian

13. suprachiasmatic nucleus (SCN)

14. 25

15. zeitgeber

16. bright

17. later

18. delays

19. light

20. melatonin

21. insomnia

22. retinohypothalamic

23. melanopsin

24. genes

25. protein

26. light

27. SCN

28. ultradian

29. 90-100

30. beta

31. alpha

32. Theta

33. sleep spindles

34. delta

35. rapid eye movement

36. paradoxical

37. atonia

38. decreases

39. activation-synthesis

40. development

41. temperature

42. prefrontal

43. caffeine

44. memory

45. slow-wave

46. theta

47. reverse-learning

48. basal forebrain

49. preoptic area

50. cool

51. ventromedial preoptic

52. magnocellular

53. adenosine

54. REM

55. acetylcholine

56. asynchronized

57. thatamus

58. REM

59. norepinephrine

60. serotonin

61. histamine

62. acetylcholine

63. lateral hypothalamus

64. orexin

65. block

66. inhibit

67. PGO

68. dreaming

69. Insomnia

70. little

71. high-frequency

72. cortisol

73. psychological

74. sleep

75. sleep onset

76. chronotype

77. delayed sleep

78. slow-wave

79. immune

80. sleep-related eating

81. narcolepsy

82. cataplexy

83. orexin

84. REM sleep behavior disorder

85. Parkinson's

86. Lucid

87. continuum

88. attention

89. hippocampus

90. synchronization

91. gamma

92. visual

93. finger

94. occipital

95. blindsight

96. Attention

97. Binocular rivalry

98. Chinese Cat

99. V4

100. inferior temporal

101. V5

102. attention

103. thalamus

104. dorsal

105. stimulus demands

106. anterior cingulate

107. Stroop

108. agency

109. 15

110. monkeys

111. anterior insula

112. amputation

113. phantom limb

114. learned

115. inferior parietal

116. Long-term

117. amnesia

118. confabulation

119. frontal

120. mirror

121. theory; mind

122. right

123. spatial

124. interpreter

125. verbal

126. dissociative identity

127. biological

128. state-dependent

129. premotor

130. thalamus

131. executive

132. anterior cingulate

133. claustrum

134. default mode

135. locked-in

Short Answer and Essay Questions

1. The behaviorists, in their attempt to make psychology a completely objective discipline, found fault with studying consciousness, because the primary method was introspection, which was inherently subjective.

2. The adaptive explanation for sleep states that amount of sleep is determined by safety considerations and access to food. Evidence for this hypothesis comes from studying sleep in different animals. For example, vulnerable animals like horses and cattle sleep very little, and those with low vulnerability, like lions, sleep much of the time. Bats and burrowing animals also sleep a lot, because they can find safety by hiding.

3. One possible explanation is that when we travel from west to east, we must adopt a phase advance schedule; this results in sleep loss because we have to try to get to sleep earlier as well as get up earlier than we are used to. Traveling east to west requires a phase delay, or going to sleep and getting up later, which is much easier to accomplish. Baseball players traveling east to play may be at a disadvantage because they are less rested than those traveling west to play.

4. The circadian has a length of a day, whereas ultradian rhythms are shorter than a day. An example of an ultradian rhythm is the basic rest and activity cycle that has a rhythm of about 90-100 minutes. The circadian clock is located in the SCN (suprachiasmatic nucleus). Evidence for this is that when the SCN is lesioned in animals, they do not stop sleeping but they sleep in naps throughout the 24-hour day. The circadian cycle is entrained by cues in the environment such as light; when not synchronized to these zeitgebers the cycle drifts. The SCN controls the pineal gland's secretion of melatonin, a sleep inducing hormone that has been used to treat jet lag and insomnia in shift workers.

5. Apparently some blind individuals are able to entrain to the light-dark cycle because light stimulates the photopigment melanopsin in a small percentage of retinal ganglion cells, which signal the SCN via the retinohypothalamic pathway.

6. Alpha waves are associated with relaxation; these brain waves are of moderate amplitude and lower frequency than beta waves. Beta waves, which have low amplitude and high frequency, are associated with alertness. The beta waves indicate more asynchronous neural activity, whereas alpha waves represent more synchronous activity. In stages 3 and 4 of slow wave sleep the EEG is made up of high amplitude, slow delta waves, whereas in REM sleep the EEG activity looks more like the waking but resting pattern of smaller, faster waves.

7. According to this hypothesis, REM sleep serves to eliminate neural connections that are not useful and to conserve the connections that are useful. This hypothesis is supported by neural net simulations in which reverse learning enhances performance. Such a process may allow smaller brains to be more cognitively sophisticated. Mammals that do not undergo REM sleep have larger brains relative to their body size than

mammals that do undergo REM. REM sleep may also be important for promoting neural development and for learning and memory consolidation, although non–REM sleep is also important.

8. Areas involved in sleep include the basal forebrain and the ventrolateral preoptic area of the hypothalamus. Both regions inhibit arousal-producing neurons in the pons. Adenosine in the preoptic area and the basal forebrain area play a role in sleep; one way that caffeine keeps us awake is by blocking adenosine. There are two main arousal systems. One arises from specific nuclei in the pons that produce acetylcholine. This area shifts the synchronous EEG to a desynchronized pattern, which is observed during both waking and REM sleep. The second pathway activates the cortex by release of norepinephrine from the locus coeruleus and serotonin from the raphe; both of these systems originate in the brain stem. Furthermore, neurons in the lateral hypothalamus send axons to the basal forebrain region and several brain stem areas. These cells release orexin, which seems to stabilize the sleep and waking system.

9. Insomnia is a disorder related to many factors, including stress, psychological disorders such as depression, disruption of the circadian and temperature cycles, and even sleep medications. There is no single biological cause of insomnia, but excess high-frequency activity in slow wave sleep, increased release of cortisol, and genes involved in circadian rhythms have been studied. Narcolepsy is a disorder that occurs when the "stabilization switch" fails, and the person falls asleep during the daytime and experiences REM sleep at inappropriate times. Low levels of orexin are found in people and animals with narcolepsy. Genetic factors affecting the immune system may play a role in the disorder, based on the study of canine narcolepsy.

10. The book describes two studies. In one, participants learned to predict where a target would appear on a screen, although they were unable to verbalize how they were predicting its location. In another study, people formed associations between facial features and personality characteristics but were unaware they had done so.

11. Binocular rivalry occurs when two images are made to appear as if they are in the same location (by presenting one image to one eye and the other to the same retinal location of the other eye). The brain attends alternately to one image and then to the other. While these attention shifts are occurring, activity also shifts between different groups of neurons in the visual cortex, suggesting that attention is "caused" by shifts in neural activation.

12. Self-awareness can be assessed by applying a colored mark to the face and then observing whether the child uses the mirror image to examine or remove the mark. Also, examining one's body using a mirror, rather than examining the mirror image or attacking it, suggests self-awareness.

13. Young children who lose a limb and people born with a missing limb experience phantom limb sensations, which suggests that body image is not necessarily learned.

14. Gazzaniga argues that because the left hemisphere has language and inferential capabilities the right lacks, the right hemisphere's consciousness is more "primitive." In addition, he explains the tendency of the left hemisphere to confabulate reasons for behaviors generated by the right hemisphere (based on stimuli presented to it and not shared with the left) as evidence of a "brain interpreter."

15. State-dependent learning is demonstrated when an individual in a particular state of consciousness (such as under the influence of alcohol, or in a particular emotional state) exhibits better recall for information learned in that state as opposed to some other state. Bower suggests that stress such as abuse (found in the history of 90 to 95% of DID patients) induces an altered state of consciousness, including thoughts and memories, which develops into a distinct personality.

16. According to Tononi, consciousness depends on the brain's ability to integrate information, and some of the results of studies of networks support this idea. For example, when a stimulus enters consciousness, activity spreads beyond the sensory area to other brain areas. Some theorists think awareness requires coordination in networks by gamma-frequency activity, which is generated in a thalamus-cortex loop; damage to the thalamo-cortical system produces unconsciousness. Recent attention has turned to the default mode network; coordination in this network decreases as a result of several conditions of altered consciousness, including sleep, sleep deprivation, anesthesia, unconsciousness, and brain damage that affects level of consciousness.

17. People with brain damage may be in a coma, minimally conscious, in a persistent vegetative state, or in a locked-in state. They are often unable to communicate with caregivers and family due to the nature of the damage. Hence, it is difficult to make informed decisions about appropriate care, prognosis, and whether therapeutic intervention is possible. A rare but informative example is the case of locked-in syndrome, in which a person is fully conscious but with little or no ability to communicate. The ability to assess their level of consciousness is necessary for deciding treatment strategies and goals.

Posttest

1. a 2. c 3. d 4. b 5. c 6. a 7. b 8. d 9. a 10. d 11. c 12. a 13. d 14. b 15. c 16. b 17. a

18. c 19. c 20. c 21. d 22. d 23. a 24. b 25. d 26. a 27. b 28. b 29. c 30. c 31. a 32. d 33. d

34. a 35. c 36. b 37. d 38. b 39. b 40. D 41. b 42. c 43. b 44. c 45. a 46. c 47. b 48. a 49. d

50. c 51. d 52. a 53. b 54. d